TAPESTRY

Listening & Speaking 4

A Revised Edition of
Sound Ideas

· ·

Helen Kalkstein Fragiadakis
Contra Costa Community College

Virginia Maurer
Harvard University

HEINLE & HEINLE
™
THOMSON LEARNING

United States · Australia · Canada · Mexico · Singapore · Spain · United Kingdom

HEINLE & HEINLE

———★———™

THOMSON LEARNING

Developmental Editors: Jennifer Monaghan, Jill Korey O'Sullivan
Sr. Production Coordinator: Maryellen E. Killeen
Market Development Director: Charlotte Sturdy
Sr. Manufacturing Coordinator: Mary Beth Hennebury
Interior Design: Julia Gecha
Illustrations: Pre-Press Company, Inc.
Photo Research: Martha Friedman

Cover Design: Ha Nguyen Design
Cover Images: PhotoDisc®
Composition/Production: Pre-Press Company, Inc.
Freelance Production Editor: Janet McCartney
Copyeditor: Donald Pharr
Printer/Binder: Bawden

For permission to use material from this text, contact us:
web   www.thomsonrights.com
fax   1-800-730-2215
phone   1-800-730-2214

For photo credits, see page 273.

Heinle & Heinle Publishers
20 Park Plaza
Boston, MA 02116

UK/EUROPE/MIDDLE EAST:
Thomson Learning
Berkshire House
168-173 High Holborn
London, WC1V 7AA, United Kingdom

AUSTRALIA/NEW ZEALAND:
Nelson/Thomson Learning
102 Dodds Street
South Melbourne
Victoria 3205 Australia

CANADA:
Nelson/Thomson Learning
1120 Birchmount Road
Scarborough, Ontario
Canada M1K 5G4

LATIN AMERICA:
Thomson Learning
Seneca, 53
Colonia Polanco
11560 México D.F. México

ASIA (excluding Japan):
Thomson Learning
60 Albert Street #15-01
Albert Complex
Singapore 189969

JAPAN:
Thomson Learning
Palaceside Building, 5F
1-1-1 Hitotsubashi, Chiyoda-ku
Tokyo 100 0003, Japan

SPAIN:
Thomson Learning
Calle Magallanes, 25
28015-Madrid
España

Library of Congress Cataloging-in-Publication Data
Fragiadakis, Helen Kalkstein.
  Tapestry listening & speaking 4 / Helen Kalkstein Fragiadakis, Virginia Maurer.
    p. cm.
  ISBN 0-8384-0029-9 (alk. paper)
  1. English language—Textbooks for foreign speakers. 2. English language—Spoken
English—Problems, exercises, etc. 3. Listening—Problems, exercises, etc. I. Title:
Tapestry listening and speaking four. II. Maurer, Virginia. III. Title.

PE1128 .F665 2000
428.3'4—dc21   99-089164

A VERY SPECIAL THANK YOU

The publisher and authors would like to thank the following coordinators and instructors who have offered many helpful insights and suggestions for change throughout the development of the new *Tapestry*.

Alicia Aguirre, *Cañada College*
Fred Allen, *Mission College*
Maya Alvarez-Galvan, *University of Southern California*
Geraldine Arbach, *Collège de l'Outaouais, Canada*
Dolores Avila, *Pasadena City College*
Sarah Bain, *Eastern Washington University*
Kate Baldus, *San Francisco State University*
Fe Baran, *Chabot College*
Gail Barta, *West Valley College*
Karen Bauman, *Biola University*
Liza Becker, *Mt. San Antonio College*
Leslie Biaggi, *Miami-Dade Community College*
Andrzej Bojarczak, *Pasadena City College*
Nancy Boyer, *Golden West College*
Glenda Bro, *Mt. San Antonio College*
Brooke Brummitt, *Palomar College*
Linda Caputo, *California State University, Fresno*
Alyce Campbell, *Mt. San Antonio College*
Barbara Campbell, *State University of New York, Buffalo*
Robin Carlson, *Cañada College*
Ellen Clegg, *Chapman College*
Karin Cintron, *Aspect ILS*
Diane Colvin, *Orange Coast College*
Martha Compton, *University of California, Irvine*
Nora Dawkins, *Miami-Dade Community College*
Beth Erickson, *University of California, Davis*
Charles Estus, *Eastern Michigan University*
Gail Feinstein Forman, *San Diego City College*
Jeffra Flaitz, *University of South Florida*
Kathleen Flynn, *Glendale Community College*
Ann Fontanella, *City College of San Francisco*
Sally Gearhart, *Santa Rosa Junior College*
Alice Gosak, *San José City College*
Kristina Grey, *Northern Virginia Community College*
Tammy Guy, *University of Washington*
Gail Hamilton, *Hunter College*
Patty Heiser, *University of Washington*
Virginia Heringer, *Pasadena City College*

Catherine Hirsch, *Mt. San Antonio College*
Helen Huntley, *West Virginia University*
Nina Ito, *California State University, Long Beach*
Patricia Jody, *University of South Florida*
Diana Jones, *Angloamericano, Mexico*
Loretta Joseph, *Irvine Valley College*
Christine Kawamura, *California State University, Long Beach*
Gregory Keech, *City College of San Francisco*
Kathleen Keesler, *Orange Coast College*
Daryl Kinney, *Los Angeles City College*
Maria Lerma, *Orange Coast College*
Mary March, *San José State University*
Heather McIntosh, *University of British Columbia, Canada*
Myra Medina, *Miami-Dade Community College*
Elizabeth Mejia, *Washington State University*
Cristi Mitchell, *Miami-Dade Community College*
Sylvette Morin, *Orange Coast College*
Blanca Moss, *El Paso Community College*
Karen O'Neill, *San José State University*
Bjarne Nielsen, *Central Piedmont Community College*
Katy Ordon, *Mission College*
Luis Quesada, *Miami-Dade Community College*
Gustavo Ramírez Toledo, *Colegio Cristóbol Colón, Mexico*
Nuha Salibi, *Orange Coast College*
Alice Savage, *North Harris College*
Dawn Schmid, *California State University, San Marcos*
Mary Kay Seales, *University of Washington*
Denise Selleck, *City College of San Francisco*
Gail Slater, *Brooklyn and Staten Island Superintendency*
Susanne Spangler, *East Los Angeles College*
Karen Stanley, *Central Piedmont Community College*
Sara Storm, *Orange Coast College*
Margaret Teske, *ELS Language Centers*
Maria Vargas-O'Neel, *Miami-Dade Community College*
James Wilson, *Mt. San Antonio College and Pasadena City College*
Karen Yoshihara, *Foothill College*

ACKNOWLEDGMENTS

We would like to express our appreciation to the entire Heinle & Heinle *Tapestry* editorial team who guided us as we created this new edition of what was originally called *Sound Ideas*. Erik Gundersen, Jennifer Monaghan, and Maryellen Eschmann-Killeen, thank you for your ideas, time, and patience. To our project manager Margaret Saunders, thank you. We are especially grateful to Becky Stovall of CNN whose research resulted in finding just the right video clips for this book, and to Kirby Wiggins of National Public Radio who patiently helped us locate stimulating listening pieces. We give special thanks to the numerous teachers and students whose suggestions and encouragement inspired us in our work.

Tapestry Listening & Speaking 4: Contents

ACADEMIC POWER STRATEGIES	CNN VIDEO CLIPS	PRONUNCIATION: THE SOUND OF IT	LISTENING OPPORTUNITIES
Learn how to take meaningful and useful notes in English as you listen to a lecture or discussion.	"Larry King Interviews 'Beatle,' Ringo Starr" Larry King uses his expert conversation skills to gain information about this very famous musician's past association with the Beatles.	Stress and intonation	Listening: an authority on communication skills explains how to start, continue, and end conversations
Learn about on-campus computer resources.	"From Morse Code to Satellite Phones" A report on how far we've come in telecommunications—from Morse Code to telephones, to cellular phones, and now to satellite phones.	Pronunciation of numbers	Listening: a radio interview with Miss Manners® about rules of etiquette for communicating by e-mail or with a cell phone
Talk to your instructors outside of class to find out what you need to do to improve your work.	"Dr. Clown" Hospital doctors dressed as clowns try to get their patients to laugh.	Pronouncing -ed at the end of regular past tense verbs	Listening 1: a radio interview with a doctor who explains how laughter strengthens the human immune system Listening 2: a radio interview with a doctor from Bombay who has developed a laughter-based exercise popular in India
Find out about your school's policies on academic dishonesty.	"Cheating in the Navy" A cheating scandal among students at the U.S. Naval Academy in Annapolis, Maryland.	Stressed and unstressed words	Listening: a radio report about the widespread problem of cheating at American universities
Assess and improve your study habits by becoming aware of your learning style.	"Toy Barriers and Thai Food Wars" Examples of two places where American exports don't automatically receive consumer interest and approval.	Thought groups	Listening: a discussion about the global predominance of American popular culture and its effect on other countries

ACADEMIC POWER STRATEGIES	CNN VIDEO CLIPS	PRONUNCIATION: THE SOUND OF IT	LISTENING OPPORTUNITIES
When you must speak on the spot, use a framework that allows you to sound organized and competent.	"Genetics and Privacy Issues" A discussion of some of the privacy issues related to genetic testing for disease.	Intonation patterns in questions	Listening 1: a short talk about the effectiveness of placebo medication and the ethical questions surrounding doctors' prescribing of placebos Listening 2: a discussion about whether it is ever ethical for doctors to lie to their patients
Analyze how you manage your time and whether you have enough time to study.	"Busy Families" A busy couple tries to balance work and family.	Recognizing unstressed words in natural speech	Listening: a discussion about the difficulty of balancing work and family life and the impact this has had on society
Cope with performance anxiety by practicing stress-reducing exercises recommended by experts.	"In-Floor Ads" An example of how advertising now bombards us from under our own feet.	Pronouncing the two /th/ sounds correctly	Listening 1: a short talk about stores that are designed to manipulate consumer response Listening 2: a discussion about how our sense of smell has a significant impact on how we spend money
Take advantage of different kinds of services and opportunities designed to give you added support at your school.	"New Citizens and the Vote" The views of naturalized U.S. citizens on their newly acquired right to vote.	Stress in noun compounds	Listening 1: a Vietnamese immigrant talks about wasteful American habits Listening 2: a Vietnamese immigrant talks about giving up a Vietnamese name to take on an American name
Find ways to improve your listening and speaking skills outside of class.	"Melting Icebergs" A report on the receding glaciers of Antarctica.	Pronouncing -s endings	Listening 1: a linguist explains why half the world's languages are in danger of becoming extinct in the next century Listening 2: a conservationist explains how the destruction of the rainforest is having a negative effect on chocolate production

Welcome to TAPESTRY!

Empower your students with the Tapestry Listening & Speaking series!

Language learning can be seen as an ever-developing tapestry woven with many threads and colors. The elements of the tapestry are related to different language skills such as listening and speaking, reading, and writing; the characteristics of the teachers; the desires, needs, and backgrounds of the students; and the general second language development process. When all of these elements are working together harmoniously, the result is a colorful, continuously growing tapestry of language competence of which the student and the teacher can be proud.

Tapestry is built upon a framework of concepts that helps students become proficient in English and prepared for the academic and social challenges in college and beyond. The following principles underlie the instruction provided in all of the components of the **Tapestry** program:

◈ Empowering students to be responsible for their learning

◈ Using Language Learning Strategies and Academic Power Strategies to enhance one's learning, both in and out of the classroom

◈ Offering motivating activities that recognize a variety of learning styles

◈ Providing authentic and meaningful input to heighten learning and communication

◈ Learning to understand and value different cultures

◈ Integrating language skills to increase communicative competence

◈ Providing goals and ongoing self-assessment to monitor progress

Guide to Tapestry Listening & Speaking

Setting Goals focuses students' attention on the learning they will do in each chapter.

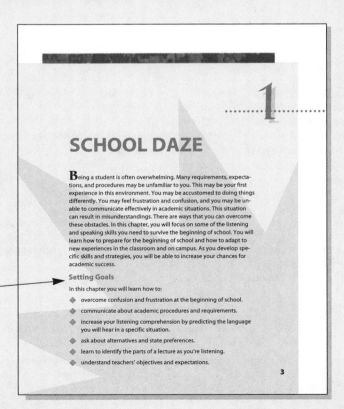

SCHOOL DAZE

Being a student is often overwhelming. Many requirements, expectations, and procedures may be unfamiliar to you. This may be your first experience in this environment. You may be accustomed to doing things differently. You may feel frustration and confusion, and you may be unable to communicate effectively in academic situations. This situation can result in misunderstandings. There are ways that you can overcome these obstacles. In this chapter, you will focus on some of the listening and speaking skills you need to survive the beginning of school. You will learn how to prepare for the beginning of school and how to adapt to new experiences in the classroom and on campus. As you develop specific skills and strategies, you will be able to increase your chances for academic success.

Setting Goals

In this chapter you will learn how to:

◈ overcome confusion and frustration at the beginning of school.

◈ communicate about academic procedures and requirements.

◈ increase your listening comprehension by predicting the language you will hear in a specific situation.

◈ ask about alternatives and state preferences.

◈ learn to identify the parts of a lecture as you're listening.

◈ understand teachers' objectives and expectations.

3

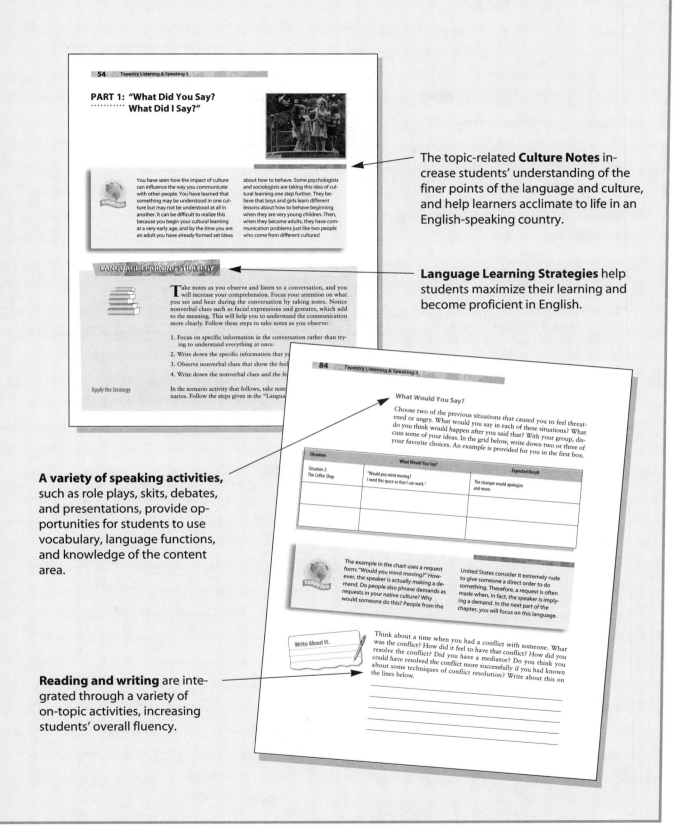

PART 1: "What Did You Say? What Did I Say?"

You have seen how the impact of culture can influence the way you communicate with other people. You have learned that something may be understood in one culture but may not be understood at all in another. It can be difficult to realize this because you begin your cultural learning at a very early age, and by the time you are an adult you have already formed set ideas about how to behave. Some psychologists and sociologists are taking this idea of cultural learning one step further. They believe that boys and girls learn different lessons about how to behave beginning when they are very young children. Then, when they become adults, they have communication problems just like two people who come from different cultures!

LANGUAGE LEARNING STRATEGY

Take notes as you observe and listen to a conversation, and you will increase your comprehension. Focus your attention on what you see and hear during the conversation by taking notes. Notice nonverbal clues such as facial expressions and gestures, which add to the meaning. This will help you to understand the communication more clearly. Follow these steps to take notes as you observe:

1. Focus on specific information in the conversation rather than trying to understand everything at once.
2. Write down the specific information that yo[u]
3. Observe nonverbal clues that show the feel[ings]
4. Write down the nonverbal clues and the fe[elings]

Apply the Strategy

In the scenario activity that follows, take note[s] narios. Follow the steps given in the "Langua[ge]

The topic-related **Culture Notes** increase students' understanding of the finer points of the language and culture, and help learners acclimate to life in an English-speaking country.

Language Learning Strategies help students maximize their learning and become proficient in English.

What Would You Say?

Choose two of the previous situations that caused you to feel threatened or angry. What would you say in each of these situations? What do you think would happen after you said that? With your group, discuss some of your ideas. In the grid below, write down two or three of your favorite choices. An example is provided for you in the first box.

Situation	What Would You Say?		Expected Result
Situation 2: The Coffee Shop	"Would you mind moving? I need this space so that I can work."		The stranger would apologize and move.

The example in the chart uses a request form: "Would you mind moving?" However, the speaker is actually making a demand. Do people also phrase demands as requests in your native culture? Why would someone do this? People from the United States consider it extremely rude to give someone a direct order to do something. Therefore, a request is often made when, in fact, the speaker is implying a demand. In the next part of the chapter, you will focus on this language.

Write About It.

Think about a time when you had a conflict with someone. What was the conflict? How did it feel to have that conflict? How did you resolve the conflict? Did you have a mediator? Do you think you could have resolved the conflict more successfully if you had known about some techniques of conflict resolution? Write about this on the lines below.

A variety of speaking activities, such as role plays, skits, debates, and presentations, provide opportunities for students to use vocabulary, language functions, and knowledge of the content area.

Reading and writing are integrated through a variety of on-topic activities, increasing students' overall fluency.

Tapestry Threads provide students with interesting facts and quotes that jumpstart classroom discussions.

Engaging listening selections provide authentic news broadcasts, interviews, conversations, debates, and stories.

The Sound of It refines listening, speaking, and pronunciation skills, and helps students gain confidence communicating in English.

REAL PEOPLE/REAL VOICES

Getting Ready to Listen

The world is so fast that there are days when the person who says it can't be done is interrupted by the person who is doing it.

—ANONYMOUS

You are going to hear two people talking about the stress in their lives. Andrew is a student who has just finished his first semester at college. Henry is a working man with children. For each of them, make one prediction about what causes them stress. Write down your prediction on the line.

Andrew—college student

I think _____ causes Andrew stress.

Henry—working parent

I think _____ causes Henry stress.

Listen

Listening 1: Andrew's and Henry's Experiences

Write A if the statement is true about Andrew and H if the statement is true about Henry.

1. _____ Worries give him the most stress.
2. _____ He has a frantic schedule.
3. _____ Academic pressure makes him nervous.
4. _____ He worries about his kids.
5. _____ Sport helps him to deal with stress.
6. _____ Solving one problem at a time helps him to deal with stress.

After You Listen

For each of the two speakers you heard on the tape, give a suggestion for how he can deal with his stress.

Andrew: _____

Henry: _____

The Sound of It: "Filler" Sounds and Words

In spoken language, a *filler* is a sound or word that fills in the space and gives the speaker time to think before continuing. In spoken English, "um" is the most common filler. It's important to recognize this sound so that you don't confuse it with part of another word. Listen to the tape again, and count the number of times each speaker uses the filler "um."

Andrew: _____

Henry: _____

Academic Power Strategies give students the knowledge and skills to become successful, independent learners.

Apply the Strategy activities encourage students to take charge of their learning and use their new skills and strategies.

CNN® video clips provide authentic input and further develop listening and speaking skills.

ACADEMIC POWER STRATEGY

Contribute your ideas in group activities. Actively participating in group activities helps you remember your ideas and gives your teacher a chance to see you working hard to succeed in class. There are some easy things you can do to practice speaking in group discussions:

1. Ask questions. Ask your teacher. Ask other students. Show that you are interested and want to learn.
2. Use your notes to help prepare ideas you can share.
3. Paraphrase—repeat in your own words an idea from a lecture, discussion, or activity.
4. If you have something to say but it's not a good time, make a note to yourself and save your good idea to share later in the discussion.

Apply the Strategy

In small groups, discuss your observation of each simulation based on your notes in the grid. Be sure that everyone in the group contributes ideas. Compare your responses to other members of your group. Do you agree or disagree on the problem, the reason, and the perception?

TUNING IN: "The Bilingual Storyteller"

You will see a CNN video clip about a man who tries to help children be proud of their cultural identities. Before you watch the clip, talk with a partner and answer these questions.

Do you think it is easier for children or adults to adapt to a culture that is different from the culture of their families?

Why do you think this?

What are some of the things parents and other adults can do to help children become comfortable in a new culture?

Antonio is a teacher. He tells stories to children. He tells the stories in a mix of English and Spanish. The stories help the children

Test-Taking Tips offer students practical steps for improving their test results.

Check Your Progress helps students monitor their own progress.

Test-Taking Tip

Work with a partner to prepare for speaking-based tests. Practice speaking with your partner about subjects you think you may be asked about on the test. First, one of you can play the part of the "interviewer" while the other takes the role of the "interviewee;" then you can reverse roles. The interviewer should prepare questions to ask before the practice interview begins.

CHECK YOUR PROGRESS

On a scale of 1 to 5, where 1 means "not at all," 2 means "not very well," 3 means "moderately well," 4 means "well," and 5 means "very well," rate how well you have mastered the goals set at the beginning of the chapter:

1 2 3 4 5   overcome confusion and frustration at the beginning of school.

1 2 3 4 5   communicate about academic procedures and requirements.

1 2 3 4 5   increase listening comprehension by predicting the language in a specific situation.

1 2 3 4 5   ask about alternatives and state preferences.

1 2 3 4 5   learn to identify the parts of a lecture while listening.

1 2 3 4 5   understand teachers' objectives and expectations.

If you've given yourself a 3 or lower on any of these goals:

- visit the *Tapestry* web site for additional practice.
- ask your instructor for extra help.
- review the sections of the chapter that you found difficult.
- work with a partner or study group to further your progress.

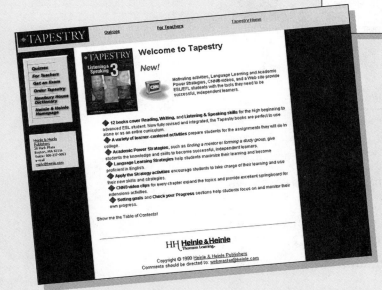

Expand your classroom at Tapestry Online
www.tapestry.heinle.com
- Online Quizzes
- Instructor's Manuals
- Opportunities to use and expand the Academic Power Strategies
- More!

For a well-integrated curriculum, try the **Tapestry Reading** series and the **Tapestry Writing** series, also from Heinle & Heinle.

To learn more about the **Tapestry** principles, read *The Tapestry of Language Learning,* by Rebecca L. Oxford and Robin C. Scarcella, also from Heinle & Heinle Publishers. ISBN 0-8384-2359-0.

Running on Empty

Drawing by Handelsman; © 1991; The New Yorker Magazine, Inc.

With a partner, fill in the empty balloons with what the people might be saying.

- Would you say that the people in the cartoon are having a light or a serious conversation? Why?
- Notice the cartoon caption: "Running on Empty." What do you think that means?
- What do you think is the cartoonist's message?

SMALL TALK—NOT DEEP, BUT IMPORTANT

Many of us have some difficulty knowing what to say when we meet new people or talk with people we don't know well. Fortunately, there are specific strategies that we can use when we want to start, continue, or end a conversation. In this chapter, you will learn some of these tips from a communication skills expert.

Setting Goals

In this chapter you will:

- learn about ways to start, continue, and end conversations.

- learn vocabulary related to making conversation.

- learn how to take meaningful and useful notes in English.

- learn to listen carefully to stress and intonation to help you find out what a speaker feels is important information.

- use expressions to introduce your opinion or your own experience as you participate in small group discussions.

- practice listening in real contexts outside of class and keep a Listening Log to record these experiences.

 **Getting Started**

It is natural to feel nervous about making conversation in situations where you are with people whom you don't know or don't know well. Talk about this with a partner as you write short notes in the chart below. When you are finished, share interesting aspects of your discussion with the rest of your class.

	You	Your Partner
Describe how you felt the last time you were with people whom you didn't know well.		
Where were you?		
Did you start a conversation (in any language)?		
If yes, what did you say?		
If no, did someone start talking to you?		
If you were involved in a conversation, what did you talk about, and how did you keep the conversation going?		
How did you end the conversation?		

LISTENING: HOW TO BE A GOOD CONVERSATIONALIST

Getting Ready to Listen   **Profile of the Speaker**

Read the following biographical information about the speaker that you will listen to.

Known as "America's First Lady of Communication," Dr. Lillian Glass is recognized as one of the world's foremost authorities on communication skills and personal image. She has written nine books on the subjects of communication and relationships, and is also a highly sought-after motivational speaker.

Dr. Glass has successful private practices in New York City and in Beverly Hills, where she trains many top celebrities, heads of corporations, and politicians to improve their personal image through improving the way they speak and communicate.

Dr. Glass has coached many celebrities on their voices, accents, and dialects. She herself is an expert dialectician and can imitate dialects from all over the world. Dr. Glass taught Dustin Hoffman how to perfect his "female" voice for the film *Tootsie,* and Julio Iglesias to improve his accent in his award-winning song, "To All the Girls."

Predicting

In the passage you will listen to, which has been taken from her tape-recorded book called *Say it Right: How to Talk in Any Social Situation,* Dr. Glass explains how to start a conversation, how to keep it going, and how to end it. Before you hear her talk, predict what you think she will say, using the concept map below. A **concept map** is a visual way for you to organize your ideas and take notes. Add as many items around each circle as you wish, and then compare your predictions to those of a partner.

How to Start a Conversation

How to Keep a Conversation Going

How to End a Conversation

Words and Phrases You Will Hear

> A single conversation across the table with a wise man is worth a month's study of books.
>
> —CHINESE PROVERB

Words and Phrases Related to Small Talk

Often, seeing words and phrases before you hear them can help your listening comprehension. Take a look at the following list and briefly discuss any unfamiliar items with your teacher.

make conversation	fight the impulse to interrupt
connect with people	be enthusiastic and upbeat
get a conversation going	show enthusiasm
keep a conversation going	be flexible
elaborate on what they're saying	be open
draw a person out	bring a conversation to a close
go into detail	break eye contact
make good facial contact	recap all that was said
cultivate a wide range of topics	

Vocabulary Building

Try to guess the meanings of the boldface words. Look for the definitions already given in the sentences. Share your guesses with a partner or with your class.

1. Starting a conversation usually means coming up with an opening line, or **ice breaker.**

   An ice breaker is _____.

   In what situations do you need ice breakers?

   _____

2. To keep a conversation going, you keep asking questions based on the last thing a person says. This is called the **elaboration technique.**

   The elaboration technique involves _____.

   When would you use this technique?

   _____

Listen

How to Be a Good Conversationalist

Listen for the Main Idea

Listen to "How to Be a Good Conversationalist." This listening passage has been divided into three parts. Write the main idea of each part in the empty circles in the concept map on the next page. Compare what you have written with a partner or with your class.

How to Be a Good Conversationalist

Part 1.

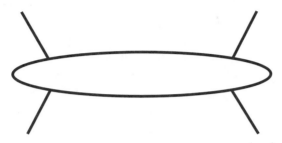

Part 2.

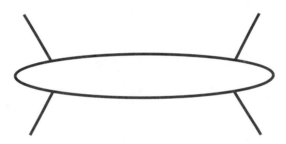

Part 3.

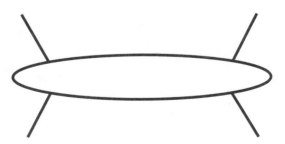

Listen for More Information

Listen again, and add details to the three sections of the concept map. Add as many circles and lines as you wish.

Learn how to take meaningful and useful notes in English as you listen to a lecture or discussion. It is valuable to take notes for a number of reasons:

- As can be seen in the graph below, it is normal to forget, even after a few hours, what we have heard.

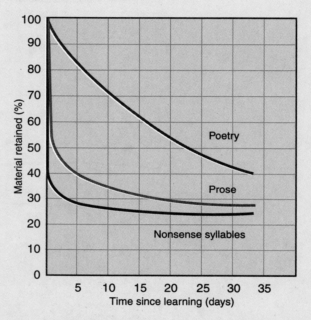

From *Your College Experience,* 3rd edition, by J. N. Gardner and A. J. Jewler. © 1997. Reprinted with permission of Wadsworth Publishing, a division of Thomson Learning. Fax 800-730-2215.

- The act of writing makes the material easier to remember.
- The act of writing forces us to decide what is and what is not important enough to write down.
- Note taking forces us to focus on and identify main ideas and important details.
- We can identify the areas that we do and don't understand.
- Instructors often give assignments and exams based on lectures as well as reading assignments.

Before you take notes, work in groups or with your class to answer the questions below. Then complete the True-False exercise. Discuss your answers.

- What is your experience taking notes in your native language and in English?

- Were you ever taught a system?

- Do you believe that it is a good idea to develop note-taking skills? Why or why not?

Write T (true) or F (false) next to each of the following statements:

_____ 1. If you can't tell what is really important in a lecture, you should write down everything the instructor says.

_____ 2. If an instructor moves through the material very fast, it is better to tape-record the lecture and not worry so much about listening in class.

_____ 3. If the instructor puts an outline on the board or on an overhead projector, you should copy it down immediately.

_____ 4. In a class that is mainly discussion, it is best just to listen and talk rather than to take notes.

Source: True-False exercise from *Learning Success*, Wadsworth, p. 88–89.

You have already taken some notes in a concept map. In the next exercise, you will take "indented notes" as you listen to the same material.

Apply the Strategy

Take notes and indent to show the organization of what you hear. Look at the example notes on the next page about Part I of the listening passage. The main point comes first and starts on the left. Specific information that comes after it is below it and "indented" a little bit to the right. Also, the most important information is in capital letters, and other important information is underlined.

For note-taking tips regarding abbreviations and signals, see Appendix A.

(continued on next page)

Now, listen to Part II of "How to be a Good Conversationalist" and take notes on what you hear, using the indented note-taking technique.

Lecture about Small Talk

Date: _____

Part I: HOW TO START A CONVERSATION

Icebreakers = opening lines

• positive (not complaints)

• examples:

    compliments

    news events

• be sincere, respectful, interested

Part II: HOW TO KEEP A CONVERSATION GOING

Asking Questions

_____

_____

7 Tips

_____

_____

_____

_____

_____

_____

_____

Part III: HOW TO END A CONVERSATION

Signals

_____

_____

_____

_____

After You Listen

1. Compare your notes to your predictions on page 5. Did Dr. Glass give any tips that you expected to hear?

2. Compare your notes with a partner. Decide whether there is anything you want to add or take out. Discuss how you feel about using "indented notes." Listen again and add more details.

3. Using your notes, orally answer the following questions with a partner:

    a. What are two examples of ice breakers?

    b. What is the elaboration technique? Why is it used?

    c. What do each of the seven tips mean?

    d. What are three signals that people give to show that they are ending a conversation?

4. To *reconstruct* means to rebuild. Reconstruct what you heard by giving an "oral reconstruction." Work in a group of three, with one student presenting Part I, another student presenting Part II, and the third student presenting Part III.

    An oral reconstruction is not a summary. A summary is shorter than the original material, and it contains only the main idea and some details. An oral reconstruction can be very detailed:

    • Use only your notes, and speak in your own words. Do not write.

    • Be careful not to add any information that was not on the tape, and don't add your opinion. Your goal here is to present what was said.

    • Show that you are giving another person's opinions and ideas by using "language of attribution." Do this by using some of the following phrases:

    According to Lillian Glass, . . .
    In Dr. Glass's opinion, . . .
    Dr. Glass believes that . . .
    Dr. Glass explains that . . .

    • While one partner is speaking, the others should indicate that they are paying attention by making eye contact and occasionally nodding and smiling.

    • After everyone practices, groups of students might orally reconstruct their notes in front of the class.

A **summary** is an oral or written general explanation of something that you heard, saw, or read. You can summarize a lecture that you heard or a movie that you saw. You can also summarize a newspaper article or a reading from a book. A summary is always shorter than the original.

Using only your notes, write a one-paragraph summary of Dr. Glass's talk. Be sure to use your own words. For specific guidelines on how to **paraphrase** (put someone else's ideas into your own words), refer to Appendix B. For information on summarizing, refer to Appendix C.

State the main idea of the talk in the first sentence. Here are some suggestions for ways to start:

- According to Dr. Lillian Glass, . . .
- In Dr. Lillian Glass's opinion, . . .
- In the listening passage "How to Be a Good Conversationalist," Dr. Lillian Glass discusses/discussed . . .
- The listening passage "How to be a Good Conversationalist" is/was about . . .

Format of your paragraph:

First sentence: Use one of the sentence patterns above.
First or second sentence: Mention the three parts of the tape.
Third and possibly fourth sentence: Give a few details about Part I.
Subsequent sentences: Give a few details about Parts II and III.

Talk About It

In a small group, answer the questions on page 13 related to Lillian Glass's talk. Assign one person to act as discussion leader and another person to act as recorder. The discussion leader will make sure that everyone participates and stays on the subject. The recorder will take notes and later report briefly to the class on the main points of your group's discussion.

Language You Can Use

Expressing Opinion and Giving Experience

As you speak in your group, check off when you use any of the following phrases to express your opinion and/or give your experience:

_____ In my opinion, . . .

_____ I think/believe/feel that . . .

_____ It seems to me that . . .

> **American men's information-focused approach to talk has shaped the American way of doing business. Most Americans think it's best to "get down to brass tacks" as soon as possible, and not "waste time" in small talk or "beating around the bush." But this doesn't work very well in business dealings with Greek, Japanese, or Arab counterparts for whom "small talk" is necessary to establish the social relationship that must provide the foundation for conducting business.**
>
> **—DEBORAH TANNEN**

_____ Not everyone will agree with me, but . . .

_____ For me, . . .

_____ In my case, . . .

_____ From my experience, I have found . . .

1. To you, is the hardest part of a conversation in English (1) starting it, (2) keeping it going, or (3) ending it? What is the hardest part of a conversation in your native language? Be sure to explain your answers.

2. Do you think you are a good conversationalist in English? In your native language? Why or why not?

3. What are some other ice breakers besides giving a compliment or talking about the news?

4. Glass suggests that to keep a conversation going, it helps to ask _who, what, when, where, why,_ and _how_ questions. In your native culture, would doing this be considered acceptable or impolite?

5. Glass tells her listeners to be aware of their "facial language." This means that in addition to looking into each other's eyes, people in a conversation should focus on each other's faces. What do you think? Would this be comfortable for you?

6. Glass also recommends that people not interrupt each other. In your native culture, is interrupting during a conversation considered acceptable, or is it impolite? Explain.

7. To end a conversation, Glass suggests that people break eye contact or say a few transitional words to hint that the conversation is over. Can you suggest any other ways to politely end a conversation?

Every culture has certain "taboo" topics. _Taboo_ means improper and unacceptable. In the United States, the following topics are usually not brought up in general conversation because they are considered very personal and private:

- money (a person's income, the price paid for possessions, monthly rent or mortgage)
- age
- marital status
- religion
- political affiliation

Close friends would probably discuss these topics, but even they might avoid personal questions about money. Would these topics be considered taboo in your native country?

> **Don't knock the weather; nine-tenths of the people couldn't start a conversation if it didn't change once in a while.**
>
> **—KIN HUBBARD, U.S. HUMORIST**

Imagine that your classroom is the scene of a party and that you need to make small talk with people whom you don't know well.

- Using an ice breaker, start a conversation with a person standing near you. You may want to give a compliment or talk about a recent news event.

- Then use the elaboration technique to try to keep the conversation going. As Glass says, "Keep asking questions based on the last thing a person says." You will need to ask *who, what, when, where, why,* and *how* questions. When you are the one to answer questions, try to give details.

- When your teacher claps his or her hands or rings a bell, stay with your partner, but use one of the signals recommended by Glass to end the conversation. You might briefly break eye contact and say something like "Well, I enjoyed talking to you" or "It's been interesting talking with you. Thank you for the information about _____." If you like, you can shake hands and say "Nice meeting you."

- Then walk over to another student and use an ice breaker to start another conversation. Continue this procedure for as long as your class wishes.

Once everyone sits down again, form small groups and explain what was easiest and what was most difficult for you—starting, continuing, or ending the conversations.

The Sound of It: Stress and Intonation

LANGUAGE LEARNING STRATEGY

L isten carefully to stress and intonation to help you find out what a speaker feels is important information. You can improve your use of stress and intonation by becoming aware of how these aspects of pronunciation are used by native speakers. Lillian Glass makes great use of "word stress" (emphasis) and "rising intonation" (pitch) to convey the importance of certain words.

Apply the Strategy

Play the tape again from the beginning. In the second sentence, notice how strongly Dr. Glass says the words *connects* and *important* and how her voice rises:

A great conversationalist is someone who con⌐nects   with people and makes them feel im⌐por⌐tant.

Now listen to the sentences that follow the one above and underline the words given special emphasis by Dr. Glass. More than one word in a sentence may receive this special emphasis.

1. When they talk to you, they make you feel like you're the only person in the room.

2. Becoming a good conversationalist requires knowing three things: first, how to start a conversation; second, how to keep it going; and third, how to end it.

3. Starting a conversation usually means coming up with an opening line or ice breaker.

4. The best kind of ice breaker is one that's positive.

5. The last thing people want to hear from a stranger is how noisy the party is, how awful the food is, or how ugly the people are dressed.

6. A compliment is always a good ice breaker and will usually be appreciated.

Continue listening, and notice where Dr. Glass's voice gives special emphasis and rising intonation. As a speaker, she decides which words are important and then uses stress and intonation to communicate that importance to the listener.

Read the preceding six sentences aloud, giving special attention to the words that you feel should be emphasized.

▷**Read**

Adair Lara is a *San Francisco Chronicle* columnist who is known for writing about everyday matters that readers can easily identify with. Below are excerpts from her column about difficulties in making small talk. The column is titled "So, What's New With You?" Read to find the answers to the following questions:

1. What is the problem?

   _____

2. Which of Lillian Glass's techniques would be a solution?

   _____

> The time to stop talking is when the other person nods his head affirmatively but says nothing.
>
> —ANONYMOUS

So What's New With You?

by Adair Lara

1 I went to a party the other night and spent the evening feeling strained[1] and reserved[2] and silent, perched[3] on the edge of my chair, clutching[4] my wineglass. By the time our hostess had shown us the third of their remodeled bathrooms, I was bored and unhappy and hated myself for feeling that way.

2   And I had, of course, become dull[5] and uninteresting myself, one of those people with folded arms who waits icily for something worthy of her notice to happen. I heard myself uttering such bright remarks as, "This is quite a place, isn't it? I like what they've done with the staircase."

3   . . . I want desperately to make the leap from[6] Small Talk to Big Talk, but I can't figure out how to do it. Instead, I find myself groping for[7] subjects and falling back, more often than not, on "How's work?"

4   . . . I don't know what questions to ask either. I ask a person what it's like to live in Chicago, and what I get is, "Oh, we just love it there."

5   I am intensely interested in other people. I always want to know where they grew up and what choices they've made and how they feel about them. But I don't want to interview them or listen to them: I want an exchange. I want to hear them saying things they've never said before, hear myself doing the same. Yet the closest we come, usually, is to argue with someone over whether "Titanic" was a good movie.

6   . . . My friend Molly says she's learned to ask people, "What struck[8] you about that?" Larry King says a good follow-up is, "Why? Why do you love it in Chicago?"

Source: *San Francisco Chronicle,* June 18, 1998

Towards the end of her column, Adair Lara mentions Larry King. King is the well-known host of an interview program on CNN called *Larry King Live.* King is regarded as an excellent interviewer because he is a good listener and knows what questions to ask to keep a guest talking. He is featured in the following video.

[1]**strained:** tense
[2]**reserved:** quiet
[3]**perched on:** seated on
[4]**clutching:** holding something tightly
[5]**dull:** boring
[6]**make the leap from:** make a big jump from
[7]**groping for:** searching for
[8]**struck:** hit

TUNING IN: "Larry King Interviews 'Beatle,' Ringo Starr"

© CNN

Larry King interviewed former Beatle drummer Ringo Starr. You will watch an excerpt from this interview in which King asks Starr about his past association with the Beatles. Focus on identifying the questions that King asks to keep the conversation going.

Vocabulary in the Video

a hit: a very big success (often a song, a show, or a music group is referred to as a hit).

to fit in: to be comfortable in the group that you are associating with.

Question forms:

- In retrospect, _____? = In hindsight, _____?

  These expressions mean "Now that you can look back at the past, what do you think about _____?"

- You mean _____?

  This is used to ask the speaker if what you understood is correct. After you say "You mean," you restate what the speaker has just said.

Watch the Video

Now watch King interview Starr. Focus on the questions that King asks to keep Starr talking:

- First, just watch and listen.

- Second, listen and try to write down some of the questions that King asks. For longer questions, it will be necessary to pause the tape so that you will have time to write. Use the chart on the following page. For now, leave the spaces on the left blank.

- Third, compare the questions you wrote to those of a partner or group. Add to your list, and then watch the interview again, giving special attention to how King keeps the conversation going.

After you have completed the above three steps, write whether the question is an **information question** (WH) or a **yes-no question** (Y/N) on the left next to each question. Which type of question did King use more often? Is this what Dr. Glass would have predicted when she discussed the elaboration technique?

WH or Y/N	Questions That Larry King Asks Ringo Starr:	
_____ 1.		?
_____ 2.		?
_____ 3.		?
_____ 4.		?
_____ 5.		?
_____ 6.		?
_____ 7.		?
_____ 8.		?
_____ 9.		?

◆ **Using What
You Have Learned**

Take turns being Larry King. Imagine that you are on TV interviewing your partner about an aspect of his or her life. Keep the conversation going by asking some of the types of questions that Larry King uses in the videotape. If you prefer, the person being interviewed can take the role of a famous person. Reverse roles so that both partners have the opportunity to be the interviewer. You might also want to choose two students to come to the front of the room to perform the interview for all to see.

Aspect of your partner's life that you will talk about:

_____

_____

_____

Possible question patterns:

1. Why do you think _____

_____ ?

2. _____ , right?

(Ask this when you want to make sure that you understood what your partner said.)

3. In retrospect, _____

_____ ?

4. You mean _____

_____ ?

Listening Log

LANGUAGE LEARNING STRATEGY

Practice listening in real contexts outside of class at least five times a week (watching CNN, watching sitcoms or news, going to the movies, listening to the radio or tapes, etc.), and keep a Listening Log to record these experiences. This will provide opportunities for you to apply or practice what you have learned and will also provide you with new cultural information.

Apply the Strategy

Create a Listening Log so that you can keep track of what you hear and learn. Your Listening Log will be a collection of your daily listening experiences with English. You can keep your log in a section of your binder or in a separate small notebook. (See Appendix D for examples of and details about Listening Logs.)

Why should you keep a Listening Log? Because doing so will help you:

- practice focused listening—that is, listening for the main idea and details.

- practice note taking, summarizing, and giving personal reactions.

- practice conversational techniques by enabling you to tell your classmates about a radio or TV program and then answering their questions with clarification and details.

- inspire your classmates to watch or listen to certain programs that you found entertaining, newsworthy, or just interesting.

(continued on next page)

You will be asked to report on one of your Listening Log entries in a small group. Your teacher will decide how many log entries will be required each week and how often the logs will be collected.

PUTTING IT ALL TOGETHER

Public Speaking

Demonstration ("How to") Speech

Lillian Glass's talk is basically a demonstration, or "how to" speech, because she tells us *how to* do something. This is the format that she follows. Key words and phrases that help us focus are in bold.

1. Dr. Glass starts with the question "Have you ever wished you were better at **making conversation?**" By starting with a question, she involves her audience and motivates us to find out what tips she has to offer.

2. Glass then gives an overview of what she will talk about. She says, "Becoming a good conversationalist requires knowing **three things:** first, how to start a conversation; second, how to keep it going; and third, how to end it." From this sentence, we know that her talk will have three parts.

3. She mentions the need for ice breakers and then gives us some **specific examples.**

4. She connects the first part of her talk to the second by saying, "**Once you've** got a conversation going, the best way to keep it going is by asking the other person questions. . . ."

5. Glass mentions the elaboration technique, and since she knows that this will be a **new expression** for her audience, she explains what it means.

6. She states that she has **seven tips,** and then goes over them one by one. Once she mentions the number seven, we listen carefully for the specific seven tips. Her tips are in the **imperative form**—e.g., "Be aware. . . .," "Don't gossip."

7. Glass connects the third part of her talk to the earlier parts by saying, "If you started a conversation with another person, and you're having difficulty ending it, there are several **signals** you can send to the other person. . . ." We, the audience, then listen for "signals."

In summary, Glass

- starts with a question that arouses our curiosity and announces her topic.

- gives a general overview of what she will talk about.

- talks about each part separately with examples, definitions when necessary, and key words to tell us what is coming (e.g., *seven tips, signals*).

- connects one part to another with transitional sentences so that her talk is smooth and coherent.

- often uses the imperative form to tell us "how to" make small talk.

Following the model described in this summary, give your own *how-to* speech. You may want to explain how to do something or demonstrate how to do something using objects. If you can provide visual aids, that will be helpful.

Possible topics:

- how to learn a foreign language

- how to prepare a particular kind of food

- how to use and program a cellular phone

- how to use a computer program

- how to _____

Steps:

- Choose a topic.

- Write an outline, and have it approved by your instructor. Indicate which visual aids you will use (handouts, overhead projector, information on the board, objects you bring in, etc.).

- Practice your speech aloud at home, and then practice it in a small group in class.

- Give your speech to your class. After your speech, take questions from the audience.

- Fill out the speech self-evaluation form in Appendix G.

◆ Listening Log Report

Work in a group of three or four students. Each student will report on one Listening Log entry. When you report on your log entry,

- tell your group members what you watched or listened to.

- give a short oral summary followed by your personal reaction. Do not read what you have written.

- check your listeners' comprehension by asking questions such as "Do you understand what I mean?" and "Am I being clear?" If not, rephrase or restate to make your points more clear.

- answer your listeners' questions and ask for their reactions.

As you listen to members of your group report,

- maintain eye contact.

- smile and nod when appropriate.

- ask questions to get information and clarification. In other words, use the elaboration technique.

◆ **Search the Web**

1. At the end of her column "So, What's New With You?" Adair Lara asked her readers to write to her to let her know how they moved from Small Talk to Big Talk. A few weeks later, Lara wrote a follow-up column titled "Good Ways to Talk About Talking" and included many of her readers' suggestions. To find this column, visit the following World Wide Web address and look for Lara's column dated July 14, 1998: **http://www.sfgate. com/columnists/**

2. To learn more about Larry King, check out the following web site: **http://cnn.com/CNN/anchors_reporters/king.larry.html**

Test-Taking Tip

Practice for speaking tests by predicting what subjects you are likely to be asked to speak about. Then, try speaking about each of these topics for at least a minute, without stopping. If you have difficulty doing this, first, on paper, brainstorm or outline a list of information and ideas related to your topic. Then try speaking about the topic again, this time incorporating some of the ideas from your list.

CHECK YOUR PROGRESS

On a scale of 1 to 5, where 1 means "not at all," 2 means "not very well," 3 means "moderately well," 4 means "well," and 5 means "very well," rate how well you have mastered the goals set at the beginning of the chapter:

1 2 3 4 5   learn about ways to start, continue, and end conversations.

1 2 3 4 5   learn vocabulary related to making conversation.

1 2 3 4 5   learn how to take meaningful and useful notes in English.

1 2 3 4 5   learn to listen carefully to stress and intonation to help you find out what a speaker feels is important information.

1 2 3 4 5   use expressions to introduce your opinion or your own experience as you participate in small group discussions.

1 2 3 4 5   practice listening in real contexts outside of class and keep a Listening Log to record these experiences.

If you've given yourself a 3 or lower on any of these goals:

- visit the *Tapestry* web site for additional practice.
- ask your instructor for extra help.
- review the sections of the chapter that you found difficult.
- work with a partner or study group to further your progress.

JEFF STAHLER reprinted by permission of Newspaper Enterprise Association, Inc.

In this cartoon, the maitre d' (host) asks the couple if they would like to sit in the *phoning* or *non-phoning* section.

- What is the question that people are often asked when they enter a restaurant?
- What do you think is the message in this cartoon?

HIGH-TECH COMMUNICATION— A CURSE OR A BLESSING?

The old telephone ring seems to be on its way out. Our world today is filled with electronic rings and beeps, and cellular phones seem to be almost everywhere. While some people see this as progress, others find it intrusive. In this chapter, Miss Manners® will talk about politeness issues related to the use of cellular phones and e-mail.

Setting Goals

In this chapter you will learn:

- about politeness issues associated with the use of cellular phones and e-mail.

- vocabulary associated with high-tech and basic communication.

- to predict what you think you will hear.

- about computer resources at your school.

- how to analyze your participation in a group discussion.

◈ **Getting Started**

What do you think of high-tech communication? Do you love it? Hate it? Are you afraid of it? Does it bother you? It bothers Adair Lara, a columnist who writes for the *San Francisco Chronicle*. Read the following excerpt from her column, titled "It's the Pauses That Refresh."

1 When we got faxes, e-mail at home, and then pagers and cellular phones, we thought, "Hey, cool! A phone I can carry anywhere, so people can call me 24 hours a day! Even at restaurants, movies, ballgames! I can work in my car! I can work all the time!"

2   The world used to be filled with times when you couldn't work. You'd be walking to your job in the sunshine, or driving your car, singing along to the Rolling Stones. Airplanes were for ordering drinks and reading magazines and watching movies, guilt-free. During these times, no one knew exactly where you were or what you were doing, and that was fine with you, and even with them. It was breathing time, daydreaming time, time to listen to '60s tunes[1] on the radio, time to think up schemes,[2] muse, ponder[3]—all those verbs for what the human imagination does when it is not being distracted by the business at hand.[4]

3   Letting machines into our in-between spaces means we lose that precious world of anticipation,[5] that time between leaving and arriving. We lose the empty pockets of time where creativity happens. We lose.

Do you agree or disagree with Adair Lara that "we lose" with the many high-tech inventions? Discuss with a partner or in a group your reaction to what she says.

LISTENING: MISS MANNERS®
ON CELL PHONE AND E-MAIL ETIQUETTE

◈ **Getting Ready to Listen**

You will listen to a radio program called *Fresh Air*. The interviewer, Terry Gross, talks to newspaper columnist and writer Judith Martin, otherwise known as "Miss Manners®," about the rules of etiquette (rules of social behavior) that people should use when communicating long distance. Miss Manners®' book on this subject is called *Basic Training: Communication*.

MISS MANNERS reprinted by permission of United Feature Syndicate, Inc.

[1]**'60s tunes:** rock music from the 1960s
[2]**schemes:** plans that may be secretive
[3]**muse/ponder:** think about something slowly; contemplate
[4]**the business at hand:** things that need to be done
[5]**anticipation:** expectation

The interview is divided into two parts:

- Part I includes the introduction of Miss Manners® and a discussion of the use of cellular (cell) phones.

- Part II is about e-mail (electronic mail).

It is common in the United States to seek professional advice regarding how to behave in certain situations. Popular advice experts who have columns in newspapers include Abigail Van Buren ("Dear Abby"); her sister, Ann Landers; and Judith Martin, more commonly known as "Miss Manners.®" Many people write to Abigail Van Buren and Ann Landers to ask advice about personal problems. People write letters to Miss Manners® asking for advice on proper "etiquette," meaning the rules for acceptable social behavior. Do similar advice columns exist in newspapers in your native country? If so, what kinds of questions do people often ask?

Words and Phrases You Will Hear

Words and Phrases Related to Cell Phones and E-mail

Often, seeing words and phrases before you hear them can help your listening comprehension. Take a look at the following list and briefly discuss any unfamiliar items with your teacher.

About Phones

beepers	a cord
heated (phone) conversations	plugged into

About Computers

cyberspace	a safety catch
high-tech anarchy	the send button
a bulletin board	

On-Line Computer Behavior

to respond to e-mail	to fire off a joke
to acknowledge messages	

◇ Vocabulary Building

Part I

You will hear the following sentences in the interview. Try to guess the meanings of the boldface words and phrases. Use the hints to help you guess.

1. Let's talk about cellular phones, and these **are cropping up** everywhere now.

   Hint: Cellular phones are becoming more numerous everywhere.

   are cropping up = _____

> Fifty-four percent of (married) cellular phone users say that their phone has improved their marriage.
>
> —*HARPER'S MAGAZINE*

2. Telephones **are disturbing** when people scream into them, in which case **the disturbance** is talking too loudly, not being on the telephone.

   Hint: If you were reading quietly and then you heard someone yell into a phone, how would you feel?

   are disturbing = _____

   the disturbance = _____

3. There are two **mistaken notions** about the cellular phone.

   Hint: Some people have the wrong idea about politeness rules related to using cell phones.

   mistaken notions = _____

LANGUAGE LEARNING STRATEGY

Apply the Strategy

Predict what you think you will hear. Making your own prediction and hearing others' predictions will help you before you listen. You will become more motivated to hear what the speaker actually says.

In the listening passage, Miss Manners® says that the etiquette rules for using cellular phones should be the same as the rules for something else. What do you think that "something else" is?

Write your prediction here: _____

_____

_____

Listen (Part I)

Miss Manners® on Cell Phones

Listen for the Main Idea

Listen to Part I to find out what that "something else" is, and then you will have Miss Manners®' main point regarding cellular phone use. Did you predict what she said, or were you surprised?

Listen for More Information

- Read the sentences below.

- Listen to Part I again. Keep the sentences in front of you, but write the answers only after you listen.

- Write T (true) or F (false) in the spaces on the left. Base your answers on what you hear in the passage. If a sentence is false, fix it so that what it says is true.

_____ 1. New ways to communicate long distance can bother people and also decrease their privacy.

_____ 2. Miss Manners® believes that it is not acceptable to talk on a cell phone in a restaurant.

_____ 3. According to Miss Manners®, the rules for using a cellular phone are exactly the same as the rules for using a phone with a cord.

Talk About It

With the increased use of cellular phones, there have been suggestions for restrictions on their use. Specifically, some people have been bothered by the noise pollution created by the ringing and conversations in public places. And it is widely believed that the use of cellular phones while driving increases the risk of traffic accidents.

With a partner or group, discuss these issues as they pertain to the following:

1. What is the point being made in the cartoon on the next page? What would Miss Manners® say about it?

2. While Miss Manners® doesn't seem to mind cellular phones as long as they are used properly, there are others who are extremely angry, or *outraged,* by their noise and the frequent impoliteness of their users. This anger is vividly expressed by writer Ellen Goodman in her *Boston Globe* column "Cell Phones—the New Outrage" (March 25, 1999).

   Goodman complains about noise pollution on commuter trains. She is referring to the noise made by numerous people chatting on phones on their way to work. She mentions that a New York commuter railroad is considering a "no-phone zone," and she points out that in Hong Kong restaurants people are asked to check their phones when they check their coats. Goodman suggests restaurants "with two sections: Phone or no phone." And she asks, "What about a no-phone lane on the highway?"

   What do you think of these suggested and real restrictions on the use of cellular phones? Are you as outraged as Goodman? Explain.

3. Read the following excerpts from a *San Francisco Chronicle* article titled "Safety Concerns Over Drivers Schmoozing on Cell Phones." When you finish, discuss any experiences you have had or heard of regarding cell phone safety. In addition, if any of the information below causes you to have a negative or positive reaction, explain your feelings.

> People with cellular phones in their cars run a 34 percent higher risk of having accidents. The danger increases when drivers use the phone while doing something else, such as lighting a cigarette or drinking coffee.
>
> *—ACCIDENT ANALYSIS AND PREVENTION*

- Maybe this bumper sticker says it best: Hang up and drive!

- Because of concerns about safety, nine nations have banned cell phone use in cars.

- A Cleveland suburb passed an ordinance that forces drivers to keep both hands on the steering wheel.

- "I'll see some weaving," said CHP officer Shawn Chase of San Francisco. "And when I pull them over, I find out they're on the phone."

- "They're [cell phones are] great to have in an emergency," Chase said. "And the majority of people use them wisely."

- People also find it handy to make calls from their car to make excuses for running late to work or appointments.

- The cellular phone industry recognizes the potential danger . . . and officials say they are trying their best to educate the public:

Cell Phone Tips

The Cellular Telecommunications Industry Association offers these safety tips while using your cell phone in the car.

- Get to know your wireless phone's features such as speed dial and redial.
- When available, use a hands-free device, such as an earpiece or a phone cradle.
- Position your cell phone within easy reach.
- Do not take notes or look up phone numbers while driving.
- Dial sensibly and assess the traffic. If possible, place calls when you are not moving or before pulling into traffic.
- Dial 911 to report serious emergencies only. It is a free call from all cell phones.

Source: *San Francisco Chronicle,* April 5, 1999.

◆ **Vocabulary Building**

Part II

You will hear the following sentences in the interview. Try to guess the meanings of the boldface words and phrases. Use the hints to help you guess.

"Netiquette" is a combination of the words *network* and *etiquette*. Netiquette is a set of rules for behaving properly while communicating online. An example: Don't write in capital letters because it looks like you are shouting.

1. E-mail is a fascinating situation in connection with etiquette because for the first time, we have a community that has none of the **safeguards** . . . that ordinary community life has.

   Hint: Safeguards keep you safe.

   safeguards = _____

2. They (people who communicate in cyberspace) are very **etiquette-aware** and always writing etiquette rules because the activities that they enjoy in cyberspace can be totally ruined by bad manners.

   Hint: These people are careful not to be rude when writing e-mail.

   etiquette-aware = _____

3. The Maryland state government had a bulletin board for citizens to make their comments and people were putting **obscene comments** on it, and they had to **shut it down.**

   Hint: A bulletin board in a school or office is hung on a wall and is used as a place to put up signs and other information. A bulletin board in cyberspace is a place where people can send comments for others to see. Unfortunately, the Maryland state government had to close this bulletin board because people were writing comments that were not polite for the public.

   obscene comments = _____

   shut it down = _____

4. The activity is not possible if people are going to be blatantly rude on it, not only obscenity, but **hogging** all the time. . . .

   Hint: *In sports, if someone "hogs" the ball, he or she takes the ball away from other people too much.*

   hogging = _____

5. Do you write a **salutation,** "Dear So and So," and **a close,** you know, "Fondly," "Sincerely," "Thanks"?

   Hint: *The sentence above contains examples of these aspects of letter-writing.*

   a salutation = _____

   a close = _____

6. . . . I have a rule there, that the more emotional the message, the more **cumbersome** the method by which you have to send it.

   Hint: *It is cumbersome to carry a big, heavy package.*

   cumbersome = _____

Listen (Part II)

Miss Manners® on E-mail Etiquette

Listen for the Main Idea

This interview focuses on three aspects of e-mail. As you listen, see if you can identify these three parts:

1. _____

2. _____

3. _____

Listen for More Information

Read the following questions and possible answers before you listen to the interview again. Circle the letters of the answers that you already know. Then listen to find the answers to the questions that you are still unsure of.

1. According to Miss Manners®, normal everyday safeguards that we can't have with e-mail include:

   a. being able to read body language, knowing people's real names, and knowing some of the same people that others know.

   b. use of the many rules of etiquette.

2. Which people think etiquette is old-fashioned?

   a. People who communicate in cyberspace.

   b. People who don't communicate in cyberspace.

3. What was the problem with the Maryland state electronic bulletin board?

   a. People who used it sold things illegally.

   b. People who used it wrote impolite comments.

4. What point does Miss Manners® make with the Maryland bulletin board example?

   a. That rules for what is considered acceptable behavior have changed.

   b. That even cyberspace activities work better when people are polite.

5. How does Miss Manners® characterize e-mail?

   a. It is closer to a letter than to a telephone call.

   b. It is more like a postcard because it is not private.

6. What does Miss Manners® believe about using salutations in e-mail messages?

   a. Using salutations is important.

   b. Using salutations is optional.

7. What does Miss Manners® consider the most important line in e-mail?

   a. The line with the first sentence.

   b. The subject line below the address.

8. How does Miss Manners® believe that people should communicate when they are emotional?

   a. By letter, because it requires more time for thought.

   b. By telephone, because the human interaction is important.

Listen and Take Notes

Now you will have the chance to try a new way to take notes as you listen again to the same material.

In Chapter 1 you learned about indenting. You put the main points on the left and then indented to the right when you added details related to the main points. You will do the same now, but these notes will go on the right two-thirds of your notebook page. On the left, you will have a special column for any questions or ideas that come to your mind about the material that you hear. By having the Question/Ideas column, you can write your thoughts while they are fresh, so you won't forget them. Of course, you will write in this column *after* you finish listening to the passage.

What is described above is called the "split-page format." To "split" is to divide, and you will divide your page as in the example on the next page that uses the subject of small talk from Chapter 1.

Directions

Take out a piece of paper and copy what is written on the sample page (see page 37 for notes on e-mail etiquette). The underlined headings are included to help you take notes. Copy them before you listen to the interview again, being sure to leave plenty of space after each heading so that you will have room to write details.

As you listen, write *only* in the Notes column. As in Chapter 1, indent your notes to show the organization of what you hear. Main points should start farthest to the left. Specific information that relates to each main point should appear below this and indented a little bit to the right. You can also use capital letters and underlining to indicate the most important points.

For note-taking tips regarding abbreviations and signals, see Appendix A.

◆ After You Listen

1. Reread your notes. Then, in the column on the left, write down the following:

   - questions you have about what you heard. Put the questions next to the parts of your notes that you are referring to.

   - ideas that you want to remember. For example, maybe you just thought of a problem that someone you know had with e-mail. Write it down before you forget. Or maybe you thought of a point that you would like to talk about later in a group discussion.

2. Compare notes with a partner.

3. Using your notes, orally answer the following questions with your partner.

   a. Miss Manners® explains that people who use e-mail are usually very aware of etiquette rules "because the activities they

Example of the use of the split-page format:

QUESTIONS/IDEAS	NOTES: SMALL TALK—LILLIAN GLASS
	HOW TO START A CONVERSATION

What about complimenting someone of the opposite sex? It can be misunderstood.	<u>Ice Breakers</u> = opening lines
	• positive (not complaints)
	• ex:
	    compliments
	    news events
	• be sincere, respectful, interested

	HOW TO KEEP A CONVERSATION GOING
I need to try this.	<u>Asking Questions—</u> who, what, when, etc.
I have trouble keeping eye contact. But what if I don't understand?	<u>Tips</u> • be aware of body and facial lang. • don't gossip • devel. wide range of topics to talk about • have sense of humor • don't interrupt • be enthusiastic • be flex.
	HOW TO END A CONVERSATION
Hard for me.	<u>Signals:</u> • break eye contact • use trans. wds (well, at any rate, anyway) • recap (sum up) what was said • give handshake

QUESTIONS/IDEAS	NOTES: MISS MANNERS/E-MAIL ETIQUETTE
	<u>No Safeguards</u>
	<u>Maryland Example</u>
	<u>Comparison—E-Mail/Letter</u>
[On your paper, leave more space between sections than you see in this example.]	<u>Problem—No Safety Catch</u>

enjoy in cyberspace can be totally ruined by bad manners." She gives an example of what happened in Maryland with the state government bulletin board for citizens. What happened?

   b. According to Miss Manners®, how is using e-mail different from writing letters?

   c. From Miss Manners®' point of view, why is it dangerous to send e-mail if you are in an emotional state?

4. Using only your notes, orally reconstruct the interview about e-mail with a partner. Each of you should reconstruct half of the interview. (For details on how to give an oral reconstruction, see Chapter 1, page 11.)

Write a one-paragraph summary of Miss Manners®' views. Refer only to your notes. Be sure to use your own words. Refer to Appendix B for guidelines on paraphrasing and Appendix C for guidelines on summarizing.

Format of your summary paragraph:

First sentence should include the following key words: Miss Manners/ rules of etiquette/modern methods of communication.

Subsequent sentences: Include the main points that you think are important. Add a few details when it is necessary to clarify a main point.

In your summary, it will be necessary to show that you are giving Miss Manners® opinions. You will need to use "language of attribution." Here are some examples:

According to Miss Manners, . . .

From Miss Manners' point of view, . . .

Miss Manners claims that . . .

In Miss Manners' opinion, . . .

She believes/feels/thinks that . . .

Talk About It

1. In the interview, Miss Manners® talks about the lack of safeguards when using e-mail. This lack of safeguards exists partly because we cannot see or hear who we are writing to. A person reading e-mail cannot hear the sender's "tone of voice" to know how she or he is feeling. With this in mind, look at the cartoon below and discuss why Clara is improving e-mail.

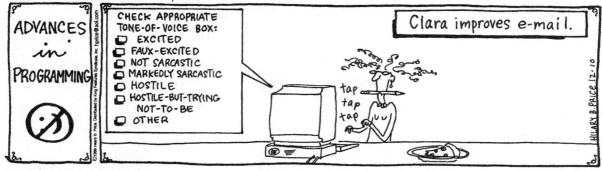

Hillary B. Price, 12/10/98

2. *Emoticons,* also known as "smileys," are often used in e-mail to indicate happiness, sadness, and other emotions. Smileys are combinations of punctuation marks and letters that form expressions. In the West, for example, happy is written :-). You have to tilt your head sideways to see this smiling face.

   Japanese smileys, on the other hand, are right side up, so you don't have to tilt your head to see them. According to the *New York Times* article "Happy in the East (^_^) or Smiling in the West" (8/12/96), people who use the Internet in Japan have adapted Western smileys to their own language and culture. For example, a girl's smile (^.^) is written with a dot for the mouth "because it is still considered impolite for women to bare their teeth in a grin, to the extent that some women still cover their mouths with their hand when they laugh. The 'banzai' smiley, written \(^_^)/ or sometimes \(^o^)/, shows a character with arms raised in a traditional cheer."

Look at the chart below. Which smileys would you be more likely to use in e-mail? Why? If you know other smileys, explain them to your classmates.

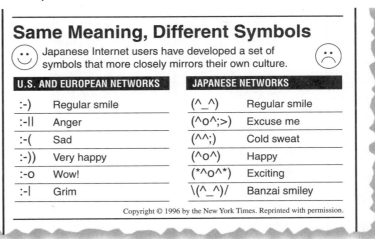

Same Meaning, Different Symbols

Japanese Internet users have developed a set of symbols that more closely mirrors their own culture.

U.S. AND EUROPEAN NETWORKS		JAPANESE NETWORKS	
:-)	Regular smile	(^_^)	Regular smile
:-||	Anger	(^o^;>)	Excuse me
:-(	Sad	(^^;)	Cold sweat
:-))	Very happy	(^o^)	Happy
:-o	Wow!	(*^o^*)	Exciting
:-|	Grim	\(^_^)/	Banzai smiley

Copyright © 1996 by the New York Times. Reprinted with permission.

3. You have listened to information about cellular phones and e-mail. Now it is time to find out what you and your classmates think of these sometimes controversial technological inventions. Complete the chart on page 40 with your own and three of your classmates' opinions. You will need to get up and out of your seat to interview different students about their views. Take very short notes; don't try to write full sentences.

In your conversations, try to use some of the language below. When you find that you are using one of the phrases or expressions, put a check mark on the line at the left.

Language You Can Use

Expressing Your Opinion

_____ It seems to me that . . .

_____ (Un)Like Miss Manners, I believe . . .

_____ I have had experience with _____, and I think it is . . .

_____ I haven't had any experience with _____, so . . .

_____ While it may be true that _____, I still think it is . . .

_____ I absolutely believe that . . .

_____ Without a doubt, _____ is . . .

Before you interview your classmates, think about and then write down your own feelings about cellular phones and e-mail.

Name	Cellular Phones	E-Mail
You		
Classmate #1:		
Classmate #2:		
Classmate #3:		

ACADEMIC POWER STRATEGY

Apply the Strategy

L earn about on-campus computer resources. Being "computer literate" in the twenty-first century is extremely important. If you don't already know how to use computers for Internet research, e-mail, typing of reports, and language practice, find out about gaining access to your school's or college's computers. You can probably also find some ways to receive training at your school or in your community.

Divide into groups to research the various computer resources at your school, on your campus, or in your community. You might get information about facilities in computer labs, departments, and libraries. Find out about:

- the kinds of computers that are available.

- what types of software you can use (and whether any of the software is designed to help students learn English).

- Internet and e-mail access.
- computer training for students.
- training in keyboarding (typing).
- the days and hours these facilities are open.

Create an information flyer for your classmates, presenting in a short announcement the information that you obtained.

TUNING IN: "From Morse Code to Satellite Phones"

You will watch a CNN video clip that includes information on the history of devices used for communication, from the Morse Code used with telegraph lines to satellite telephones that can be used anywhere in the world.

© CNN

Vocabulary in the Video

Before you watch the video, work with your classmates and teacher to understand the vocabulary listed below.

Words and Expressions with Positive Connotations	Words and Expressions with Negative Connotations
Wireless phones offer **mobility.**	Some people have never received an **unsolicited call.**
Telecommunications satellites connect us with the world.	The deluge of unwanted calls and faxes is the **junk mail** of the telephone age.
Wireless telephones, cellular and satellite, offer developing countries an immediate **leap** into the telephone age.	The problem is how to **get rid of** all the information that is coming at us.
	Most people in the world are not **drowning in** information.

Watch the Video

Watch the video at least two times. The first time, just watch. The second time, write down some notes in each category below. From this information, you and your group will create two comprehension questions and two discussion questions to ask other groups.

> That's an amazing invention [the telephone], but who would ever want to use one of them?
>
> —RUTHERFORD B. HAYES,
> 19TH U.S. PRESIDENT

Growth of Telecommunications
Growth of telephone calls in the U.S. and around the world
History
Wireless phones
Satellite telephone
Telecommunications satellites
Problems
Developing countries

The Sound of It: Pronunciation of Numbers

Many numbers are used in this video clip. Watch the tape again and try to write the numbers that you hear in the spaces below. When you are finished, practice reading the sentences aloud, giving special attention to the pronunciation of the numbers.

1. There are nearly _____ people in the world.
2. Nearly _____ of them have never made a telephone call.

3. That's nearly _____ people who have never gotten a busy signal.

4. The number has doubled in only _____ years.

5. It was a little more than _____ years ago that Samuel Morse sent his code of dots and dashes along a telegraph line.

6. _____ years later in _____, Alexander Graham Bell sent the human voice over a wire.

7. In China and in India, there are only _____ phone lines for every _____ people. In the United States, there are _____.

LANGUAGE LEARNING STRATEGY

A nalyze your participation in a group discussion. By doing this regularly, you will gain insight into how you communicate in a group and, as a result, make more conscious efforts to improve your interactive communication skills. Analyze whether in a discussion you:

- made an effort to check that others understood what you said.
- gave explanations, definitions, and examples when necessary.
- asked for clarification when you didn't understand.
- paraphrased what others said to find out if you understood correctly.
- encouraged others to speak.

Apply the Strategy

After you finish the discussion in the "Talk About It" activity that follows, fill out this questionnaire to evaluate your group conversation skills.

(continued on next page)

CONVERSATION SKILLS QUESTIONNAIRE			
While talking to classmates:	**Often**	**Sometimes**	**Never**
1. I checked to make sure that everyone understood what I said by asking questions such as "Do you know what I mean?" and "Are you following me?"			
2. I gave explanations, definitions, and specific examples when I saw that members of my group weren't following me. I used sentences such as "Let me explain that" and "To help you understand, I'll give you an example."			
3. I asked specific questions such as "What do you mean by _____?" and "Could you give an example of _____?" and "Could you explain the part about _____?" when I needed clarification.			
4. I paraphrased what others said to make sure that I understood. I used sentences such as "In other words, you mean _____" and "You're saying, then, that _____."			
5. I encouraged others to speak by making such remarks as "I'd like to know what _____ thinks about that" and "What do you think about _____?"			

Source: Adapted from *The Tapestry of Language Learning,* 1992, by Robin C. Scarcella and Rebecca L. Oxford. Boston: Heinle & Heinle, p. 158.

◁ Talk About It

With your group and using your notes, create four questions related to the video clip. Two should be comprehension questions that check for understanding of specific information in the tape, and two should ask for students' opinions about the new technology. Write the four questions on one sheet of paper. Exchange your questions for those of another group.

Sample comprehension question:

What is the newest kind of telephone?

Sample discussion question:

What do you think of satellite telephones?

Then follow these steps:

- Have a discussion as you and the members of your group answer the other group's questions orally. Choose one student to write short notes on the paper along with the questions.

- Combine the two groups. Tell the other group what your group said in answer to their questions. Refer to the notes if necessary.

- When you finish your discussion, fill out the Conversation Skills Questionnaire to evaluate your participation.

PUTTING IT ALL TOGETHER

 **Guest Speaker**

Invite a guest speaker to talk about your school's computer resources and ways to effectively use the Internet and e-mail. Follow the steps for inviting a guest speaker in Appendix E.

Public Speaking

Reporting Survey Results

Survey

Make a chart like the one you used to interview three classmates on page 40, and use it as you interview at least five native speakers of English about their opinions of cellular phones and e-mail or other types of modern technology. If you prefer, conduct these interviews with a partner from your class. Then present your results to your class. Evaluate your presentation by filling out the speech self-evaluation form in Appendix G.

Guidelines on Conducting a Survey

1. Find out where you can find people to interview. You do not have to approach complete strangers on the street. It will be easier if you interview people whom you already know. For example, you might want to interview your neighbors, friends, relatives of people you already know, or people you encounter regularly but don't know well.

2. Explain to each person you interview what you are doing and why, and give him or her an idea of about how long it will take to answer your questions. You might want to start by saying something like this: "Excuse me, I am conducting a survey for a class assignment, and I wonder if you would mind answering a few questions. It would be for just a few minutes." Many people will be happy to answer your questions if they know you are doing it for a class assignment.

3. Even when you have prepared specific questions, you may need to ask for more information on a particular point. Ask follow-up questions when necessary.

4. If you do not hear or do not understand part or all of what a person says, ask for repetition or clarification.

In your presentation,

- summarize the results of your survey.

- explain what you find interesting, revealing, or surprising about the results.

- elicit questions from members of the audience to find out their reactions to the results of the survey.

Visual Aids

Since it is helpful to use a visual aid when you make a presentation, do one of the following:

- put your completed chart on a transparency and use an overhead projector to show your notes. Speak to your class, using the notes just as guides to remember your conversations.

- make copies of your completed chart and hand these out to your classmates.

Language You Can Use

One of the people I talked to believes/thinks/feels that . . .

According to two people we interviewed, . . .

The librarian strongly believes that . . .

In my writing teacher's opinion, . . .

Two out of the three people dislike . . .

Listening Log Report

Bring your Listening Log to class and report on one entry in a group.

Search the Web

Learn more about high-tech communication by searching the Web. Possible key words: cellular phones, e-mail, netiquette, smileys, satellites, satellite telephones, telecommunications.

Test-Taking Tip

Go into the test with a positive attitude. Focus on what you know rather than on what you do not know. Your attitude can have a large effect on how well you do on tests. Keep your mind on your strengths, rather than your weaknesses. Remind yourself that you are well prepared and that you are going to do well. Think of the test as an opportunity to show how much you have studied.

CHECK YOUR PROGRESS

On a scale of 1 to 5, rate how well you have mastered the goals set at the beginning of the chapter:

1 2 3 4 5   learn about politeness issues associated with the use of cellular phones and e-mail.

1 2 3 4 5   learn vocabulary associated with high-tech and basic communication.

1 2 3 4 5   learn to predict what you think you will hear.

1 2 3 4 5   learn about computer resources at your school.

1 2 3 4 5   learn how to analyze your participation in a group discussion.

If you've given yourself a 3 or lower on any of these goals:

- visit the *Tapestry* web site for additional practice.
- ask your instructor for extra help.
- review the sections of the chapter that you found difficult.
- work with a partner or study group to further your progress.

- Do you ever laugh really hard?

- What kinds of things make you laugh?

- Do you think laughing can be beneficial to your health? How?

HUMOR—CAN LAUGHTER BE THE BEST MEDICINE?

3

M ost people think of laughter as an emotional experience. But did you know that it is also a physical experience that can produce many benefits for your health? In this chapter, we will explore some of the findings that doctors and researchers have made about how humor can promote healing and keep us healthy.

Setting Goals

In this chapter you will learn:

- information on ways that laughter can promote health.

- vocabulary related to the topics of laughter and the immune system.

- how to analyze your strengths and weaknesses as a language learner.

- how to develop an organized, systematic approach to learning vocabulary.

- how to use personal experience in developing a conversation.

- how to pronounce *ed* at the end of regular past-tense verbs.

- to talk to your instructors outside of class to find out what you need to do to improve your work.

◆ **Getting Started**

1. How would you define humor? How would you define laughter? What is the relationship between the two?

2. Researchers now believe that laughter has a physical effect on the body. Do you believe this? Do you feel any different physically when you laugh?

◆ **Getting Ready to Listen**

Humor comes from the Latin word *umor*, which means "to be like water and flow; to be fluid and flexible." It is the opposite of being tight, inflexible, and in control.

The following article on humor was originally published in *Laugh It Up*, a publication of the American Association for Therapeutic Humor. Read the three questions and then read the article. When you finish, check your comprehension by answering the questions orally with a partner.

1. What is "wit," and why is it important?

2. What is "mirth," and why is it important?

3. How is laughter a physiological experience? Why is it important?

Exploring the Land of Mirth and Funny: A Voyage Through the Interrelationships of Wit, Mirth and Laughter

1   It has been said that humor consists of wit (a thought-oriented experience), mirth (an emotionally-oriented experience), and laughter (a physiologically-oriented experience). And while each can be experienced independently of the others, when experienced together they synergistically[1] create the witty/mirthful/laughful experience we refer to simply as humor.

Wit as a thought-oriented experience

2   Wit changes how we cognitively[2] process, appreciate, or "think" about life's events and situations. Jokes are a classic example of how wit changes thinking. In a joke we are guided down one path, only to be tracked over onto an alternative path. It is the discrepancy[3] and even trickery of the alternative path (the punch line)[4] that we experience as humorous. Such discrepancy and trickery teaches us to seek alternative explanations for events, which is one process of healthy thinking and creative problem

[1] **synergistically:** from *synergy,* which refers to the interaction of two or more forces in such a way that the combined effect is greater than the sum of their individual effects
[2] **cognitively:** using the mind consciously
[3] **discrepancy:** disagreement; lack of agreement (between stories, amounts, etc.)
[4] **the punch line:** the last few words of a joke or story that give meaning to the whole and cause amusement or surprise

Norman Cousins, writer and humanitarian, was probably best known as the editor of *The Saturday Review* and author and editor of over 20 books. In one book, *Anatomy of an Illness*, he tells his story of battling disease with vitamins and laughter.

solving. Norman Cousins once called this process "train wrecks of the mind" meaning that wit causes us to track over to other thinking patterns and perspectives. Alternative thinking processes provide perspective, and can reduce negative thinking common during depression, anxiety, and anger.

Mirth as an emotional experience

3 Humor changes how we feel emotionally by helping us to experience mirth. While labeling it humor, Mark Twain once described the mirthful experience in the following way:

> Humor [mirth] is the great thing, the saving thing, after all. The minute it crops up, all our hardnesses yield, all our irritations and resentments slip away, and a sunny spirit takes their place.

4 Mirth can be a powerful experience for eliminating unhealthy feelings. We have all experienced the joy (mirth) of a humorous experience, and know the pleasure of that feeling. As we experience the emotional sensation of mirth, other feelings such as depression, anxiety, and anger are, at least temporarily, eliminated.

5 That is, one cannot experience mirth and at the same time experience such powerful emotions as irritation, resentment, or upset. In fact, the experience of mirth not only eliminates these emotions, but as Twain so astutely[5] realized, mirth replaces these emotions or gives "mirth" to a "sunny spirit" such as the lighter experience of joy, pleasure, happiness, etc.

Laughter as a physiological experience

6 Laughter changes how we feel physically and it affects our biochemistry. We are all familiar with the feeling of lightness that follows deep belly laughter. Norman Cousins reported that 10–20 minutes of deep belly laughter gave him hours free from the pain of his debilitating disease.[6] Laughter has been described as a "jogging[7] of the internal organs." The physiological benefits of laughter—such as an increase in certain antibodies,[8] decrease in levels of stress hormones,[9] and a decrease in heart rate of "heavy laughers"—have

[5]**astutely:** cleverly

[6]**debilitating disease:** a disease that makes a person's health weak

[7]**jogging:** shaking, causing an up and down movement

[8]**antibodies:** substances produced in the body to fight against disease

[9]**hormones:** any of several substances directed from organs of the body into the bloodstream so as to influence growth, development, etc.

been presented in numerous research studies. Laughter is also believed to stimulate the muscular and skeletal systems. Laughter serves as the physiological/biochemical element of humor.

7   The "humor experience" is a synergistic interrelationship of the effects of humor as it changes cognition,[10] emotion, and physiology. People experience humor in different ways. For example, some people are more likely to "appreciate" wit (cognitive) without experiencing mirth or laughter. These people are likely to say they understand the joke and like the joke but do not laugh or experience the mirth.

8   Others are more likely to experience mirth (emotional) without a cognitive or physiological reaction. Children, in much of what adults view as "silly behavior," are experiencing mirth while they may not be appreciating wit, and they may not even be laughing (although they frequently are).

9   We also know that we can experience laughter that is independent of wit or mirth. Spontaneous[11] laughter or laughter contagion[12] are examples. Even laughter that is triggered during anxiety may be an example of laughter stimulated without wit or mirth. The fullest and, most powerful humor experience, however, is one that is experienced with all three components simultaneously.

10   While each of us probably has a "primary humor receptor" (cognitive, emotional, or physiological)—or primary way of processing humor (e.g. cognitively, emotionally, physiologically)—we are likely to use all three avenues in varying amounts at varying times. The more that we can train ourselves to appreciate (cognitive), feel (mirth) and physically experience (laugh), the more potent[13] and healthful the humorous experience will become.

Source: Steven M. Sultanoff, Ph.D, originally published in *Laugh It Up*, Publication of the American Association for Therapeutic Humor, July/August 1994, p. 3. Reprinted with permission.

LISTENING 1:
LAUGHTER MAKES YOU HEALTHIER

• •

 **Vocabulary Building**   You will hear the following sentences in the interview. Try to guess the meanings of the boldface words and phrases. Use the hints to help you guess.

[10]**cognition:** the act or action of knowing, including consciousness of things and judgment about them
[11]**spontaneous:** quick and unplanned
[12]**contagion:** the act of spreading easily from person to person
[13]**potent:** powerful

1. There has been much **anecdotal evidence** in recent years that laughter is indeed good medicine.

   Hint: An anecdote is a short, interesting story about a particular person or event.

   anecdotal evidence = _____

2. Doctors have begun **to quantify** that perception, exchanging actual studies that show **the human immune system** strengthens as we laugh.

   Hint: A quantity is a measurable amount or number.

   to quantify = _____

   Hint: A person who is immune to a certain disease will not get it.

   the human immune system = _____

3. This is probably **one of the most startling things** we didn't expect to find.

   Hint: The second half of the sentence gives an important clue: ". . . we didn't expect to find."

   one of the most startling things = _____

4. Natural killer cells are a special type of cell that **go after virally infected cells**.

   Hint: If you want something really badly, you go after it.

   Hint: A virus is a microscopic living thing that causes infectious diseases like the common cold.

   go after virally infected cells = _____

5. For a number of the components that we measured . . . we saw their increases that would stay all the way from the day of the experiment . . . and we did numerous experiments up through the next morning. So there is quite **a residual effect**.

   Hint: If you don't wash dishes carefully, there may still be some residue sticking to some of the plates. Sometimes after you drink a cup of coffee, there is some residue remaining in the bottom of the cup.

   a residual effect = _____

6. A lot of us first became aware of this . . . reading the works of Norman Cousins, **the late editor and writer,** who had lymphoma and was convinced that laughter **forestalled his death.**

   Hint: The word late *has several meanings, including "existing in the recent past, but existing no longer" as in "the late government."*

   the late editor and writer = _____

   Hint: I had planned to meet my friend at the airport, but he forestalled me by catching an earlier flight and taking a taxi to my house.

   forestalled his death = _____

7. It's more than **a diversion.**

   Hint: Our family went to New York City for vacation because it offers lots of diversions for people of all ages and we knew we would have a good time.

   a diversion = _____

Words and Phrases You Will Hear

Often, seeing words and phrases before you hear them can help your listening comprehension. Take a look at the following list and briefly discuss any unfamiliar items with your teacher.

Words and Phrases Related to Health

a type of immune cell called natural killer cells

to cure one of cancer

tumor cells

one of the hormones of the immune system

immunoglobulens (antibodies)

lymphoma

physiological changes

alternative medicine

positive emotional states

Funny Television Programs (see Culture Note)

The Honeymooners
Candid Camera

Idioms

it blew us out of the water
to turn on
to kick into gear

The interview contains references to two television comedy programs that were popular in the United States in the 1950s and 1960s. *Candid Camera* was an unusual television program in which ordinary people in some public place were unknowingly set up to encounter a strange or puzzling situation. Often their reactions to the situations in which they found themselves were quite funny. These people had no idea that they were being filmed and after a few minutes of being filmed secretly, they were told, "Surprise! You're on *Candid Camera!*" With the permission of the people filmed, these short film clips were the basis of each week's program. *The Honeymooners* was one of the first sitcoms (situation comedies) on television and starred Jackie Gleason, a well-known comedian of the time.

Many people in the United States still enjoy watching old reruns of classic TV comedy programs like these or of classic comedy films such as those of Charlie Chaplin or the Marx Brothers. What about you? What are some of your favorite television movie comedies? Do you prefer reruns of old comedy programs or new programs?

 Listen

Listening 1: Laughter Makes You Healthier

Listen for the Main Idea

Listen to the interview. Then write one sentence that summarizes the main idea.

_____

_____

_____

Listen for More Information

Read the following questions and possible answers before you listen to the interview again. Circle the letters of the answers that you already know. Then listen again to find the answers that you are still unsure of.

1. Who is being interviewed?

    a. a science writer

    b. a medical researcher

    c. a biochemistry professor

2. What do natural killer cells do?

    a. attack antibodies

    b. infect immune cells

    c. destroy tumor cells

3. What is a cytokine?

    a. a type of tumor cell

    b. a type of virus

    c. a type of hormone

4. What does a cytokine do?

    a. It increases the activity of natural killer cells.

    b. It decreases the number of antibodies.

    c. It infects healthy cells.

5. What did researchers discover from their experiments about the increase of antibodies?

    a. The increase lasted for as much as one day.

    b. The increase happened in the morning.

    c. The increase varied from experiment to experiment.

6. How did many people first become aware of the relationship between laughter and healing?

    a. by reading the works of Norman Cousins

    b. by watching videos recommended by Norman Cousins

    c. by hearing about the scientific studies of Norman Cousins

7. Why did Norman Cousins watch funny videos?

   a. They provided a distraction from his illness.

   b. They made him tired and sleepy.

   c. They lessened his pain for short periods of time.

8. What did Norman Cousins believe?

   a. Humor was more effective than seeing a doctor.

   b. Laughter caused a physical change in his body.

   c. Alternative medicine helped relieve his pain.

Listen and Take Notes

Use the "split page format" described on page 35 in Chapter 2 to take notes as you listen again to the material.

- Take out a piece of paper and copy what is written on the sample page below. The underlined headings are included to help you take notes. Copy them before you listen to the tape, but be sure to leave plenty of space after each heading so that you will have room to write details.

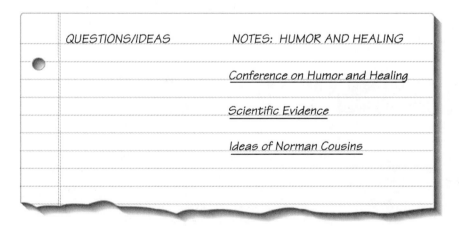

- As you listen, write *only* in the Notes column. Indent your notes to show the organization of what you hear. Main points should start farthest to the left. Specific information that comes after each main point should appear below and be indented a little bit to the right. You can also use capital letters and underlining to indicate the most important points.

For note-taking tips regarding abbreviations and signals, see Appendix A.

After You Listen

1. Reread your notes. Add ideas and questions to the left column.

2. Compare notes with a partner.

3. Using your notes, orally answer the following questions with your partner:

    a. Who is Dr. Lee Berk, and why is he being interviewed?

    b. What is the scientific evidence that laughter can strengthen the immune system?

    c. Why does the interviewer bring up the name of Norman Cousins?

    d. Why did Norman Cousins watch funny videos?

    e. What did Norman Cousins mean when he said "Beliefs are biology"?

4. Using only your notes, orally reconstruct the interview in your own words. Work with a partner and take turns presenting your oral reconstruction.

LANGUAGE LEARNING STRATEGY

Analyze your strengths and weaknesses as a language learner to help you focus on how to improve your language learning. It is not enough to realize that you got an answer right or wrong. Try to understand why you were able to do well or why you didn't succeed.

Apply the Strategy

Compare your notes with the tapescript and answer the following questions:

1. Which important points did you include in your notes?

2. Are there important points or useful details that you missed? If so, what are they?

3. Analyze why you were able to get some important points and details but not others.

Check off the factors that helped or hindered your comprehension as you listened:

_____ familiarity or lack of familiarity with vocabulary

_____ amount of prior knowledge about the topic

_____ knowledge of proper nouns and cultural references

_____ speakers' pronunciation or rate of speaking

_____ trying to write while you listened

_____ other: _____

4. Write here two things that you can do to help yourself understand more of what you hear in the future.

_____

_____

_____

Write About It.

Write a one-paragraph summary of the interview. Refer only to your notes. Be sure to use your own words. Refer to Appendix B for guidelines on paraphrasing and Appendix C for guidelines on summarizing.

Format of your summary paragraph:

- Your first sentences should both introduce the man being interviewed, Dr. Lee Berk, and contain the main idea of the interview. Because many people don't know Dr. Berk, it will be necessary to explain who he is by using an appositive: Dr. Lee Berk, *a doctor and researcher at the Loma Linda School of Medicine in Loma Linda, California,* . . .

- In subsequent sentences, include the main points and some of the details. Remember to use language of attribution because you will be giving the ideas of Dr. Berk and Norman Cousins.

LISTENING 2: LAUGH SESSIONS

 Getting Ready to Listen

You are about to listen to the same National Public Radio journalist, Scott Simon, conduct another interview related to the benefits of laughter. This time he interviews Dr. Madan Kataria, a physician in Bombay, India, who uses laughter in an unusual way. In the interview, references are made to *yoga, yogic exercises,* and *yogic principles. Yoga* refers to a Hindu system of exercises designed to free the self from the body, will, and mind.

The two men discuss a number of different types of laughs. You will hear the word *guffaw* mentioned, for example, which refers to a loud laugh. You will also hear reference to the word *giggle*, which refers to a high-pitched, silly form of laughter that is repeated in an uncontrolled manner, especially by young girls.

 Listen

Listening 2: Laugh Sessions

Listen for the Main Idea

Listen to the interview. Then write one sentence that summarizes the main idea:

_____

_____

_____

> **Humor is the only type of human communication that results in a physical response, specifically the contraction of fifteen facial muscles and altered breathing, in a pattern known as laughter.**
>
> **—JOEL ACHENBACH**

Listen for More Information

- Read the questions below.
- Listen to the interview again.
- As you listen, write short notes that answer each question.
- Listen again to check your answers.

1. Why does Dr. Kataria think that laughter is a useful exercise?

_____

_____

2. How are his laughter exercises based on yoga?

_____

_____

3. What are some of the kinds of laughs he uses?

_____

_____

4. Why does he think laughter exercise is similar to meditation?

_____

_____

In the interview, Scott Simon tells a joke that is *a play on words*. He says, "I'm wondering if you've heard the one about the yogi master who says to the hot dog vendor, 'Make me one with everything.' Simon begins the joke in the way that English speakers often begin a joke, which is to say, "Have you heard the one about the . . . ?"

Did you understand Simon's joke? When English speakers don't understand a joke, they often say, "I don't get it." If the joke teller thinks his listeners didn't understand, he will typically ask, "Did you get it?"

Talk About It

1. What is your reaction to what you have heard so far in this chapter about laughter and health? Do you believe in this link between laughter and health, or do you think it is overrated? If you believe that laughter can promote good physical health, what are some possible implications of this? Discuss your thoughts on this issue, giving concrete examples to support your ideas.

2. Look at the following cartoons, which have appeared in newspapers and magazines in the United States. Do you think they are funny? Use the scale below and rate each cartoon on how funny you think it is. Write your rating on the line next to each number. Discuss your ratings with your classmates.

1 = not funny at all   4 = very funny

2 = mildly funny   5 = extremely funny

3 = definitely funny

—— 1.

The Bizarro cartoon by Dan Piraro is reprinted by permission of Chronicle Features, San Francisco, California.

—— 2.

Drawing by Leo Cullum;
©1992, *The New Yorker* Magazine, Inc.

—— 3.

Source: The Bizarro Cartoon by Dan Piraro is reprinted by permission of Chronicle Features, San Francisco, California.

—— 4.

Source: Drawing by Donnelly;
©1992, *The New Yorker* Magazine, Inc.

After you have rated the cartoons, work with a partner or in small groups to categorize the kind of humor in each cartoon. Match each cartoon with one or more of the following types of humor.

- satire: humor that makes fun of the practices and institutions of society

- black humor: humor dealing with the unpleasant side of human life

- nonsense humor: humor that portrays an absurd, ridiculous situation

- word play or puns: humor that comes from the amusing double meaning of words

3. Newspaper writers sometimes unintentionally allow linguistic ambiguity (double meanings) in headlines. Can you see the double meanings in the following examples that the *Columbia Journalism Review* found?

- Police Help Murder Victims

- Suicide More Common Than Thought

- American Sentenced to Life in Scotland

LANGUAGE LEARNING STRATEGY

Develop an organized, systematic approach to learning vocabulary. Glossaries and vocabulary lists by themselves are not adequate study aids for acquiring new vocabulary. One method is to create vocabulary study cards that allow you to categorize, label, personalize, and apply new words.

Apply the Strategy

The following study system will help you expand your English vocabulary. Choose ten new words or phrases that you have learned so far in this chapter. Make a vocabulary study card for each.

(continued on next page)

Vocabulary Study Cards

new word

related word forms

Illiterate, adj.

literate, adj.
literacy, n.
illiteracy, n.

part of speech

1. "Many illiterate people in the United States are immigrants from cultures where education wasn't available or was denied."

original context

2. not literate; unable to read or write

dictionary definition

3. "About half the population is still illiterate."

dictionary example

4. "My grandmother is illiterate in English because she immigrated to the United States at age 70 and is afraid to go to school."

student's own sentence

Source: Kate Kinsella and ARC Associates, *Strategies Which Promote Academic Reading Comprehension and Retention for Diverse Leaders*.

◆ Language You Can Use

Starting a Conversation

Often, people start a conversation by describing something they have seen, heard, or read. Other people help continue the conversation by asking questions, giving their responses, sharing similar experiences, etc. Here are some opening conversation phrases:

I heard . . .	Did you hear . . . ?	Have you heard . . . ?
I saw . . .	Did you see . . . ?	Have you seen . . . ?
I read . . .	Did you read . . . ?	Have you read . . . ?

Using New Language

1. Imagine you are at a cafe talking to some friends. You want to tell them about some of the things you have learned about humor. Practice the following dialogue with a classmate:

   X: I heard an interesting interview on the radio this morning about the healing effects of humor. Did you know that laughter is actually good for you?

   Y: Well, I know that I enjoy laughing, and if I think about it, laughing does make me feel good. It relaxes me, makes me feel happy and cheerful. But what do you mean when you say laughter can have a healing effect?

X: Well, apparently [*explain how laughter has a physiological effect on the immune system*]:

_____

_____

_____

Y: That's really interesting. I guess that old saying about laughter being the best medicine is true. Did they say anything else?

X: Let me think. Well, the doctor being interviewed mentioned a writer named Norman Cousins who [*mention some of the things you learned about Norman Cousins in the interview*]:

_____

_____

_____

I'd like to read some of the stuff he's written. Have you ever heard of him?

Y: No, but you could go to a bookstore and ask about him. Or try searching the Web.

X: Good idea.

Y: Let me know what you find. I might want to read more about this myself.

X: Sure thing.

> Culture plays an important role in humor. For example, in the Navajo culture, the first person who makes a baby laugh has a special relationship with that child forever after.

2. Go back and analyze the dialogue. How does each speaker contribute to keeping the dialogue moving back and forth? What kinds of questions are asked?

3. Practice another conversation with a classmate about the second interview you listened to. One of you should begin by saying, "I heard something interesting on the radio today. It was about how some people in India use laughter as a kind of daily exercise. . . ." Explain the main points of Dr. Kataria's use of laughter as exercise. The other person should ask questions, share a related experience, or make appropriate comments to keep the conversation going.

4. Now start a conversation with a classmate using one of the following phrases. The words in brackets are just examples. You should substitute something appropriate from what is happening in your life.

I saw [an interesting movie last night; you working hard in the library over the weekend, etc.]

I heard [that you are getting married in June; that the concert has been canceled, etc.]

I read that [the President is coming here to give a speech; that the next Olympics will be in . . ., etc.]

Did you see/have you seen [the new movie at the Galaxy Cinema; the latest issue of *Time* magazine; the new exhibit at the museum, etc.]

Did you hear/have you heard about [the change in the foreign language requirement for graduation; that student who got caught cheating, etc.]

Did you read [the article in yesterday's paper about . . ., etc.]

Have you read [any good books recently . . ., etc.]

◆ The Sound of It: Pronouncing -*ed* at the end of Regular Past Tense Verbs

Read the following joke aloud and underline all of the regular past-tense verbs that end in *ed*. How many ways is the *ed* pronounced?

> A man was lost, so he got out of his car and walked up to a farmer's house to ask directions. As he approached the house, he saw a mean-looking dog sitting in the yard. The man wanted to know if the dog just looked mean or really was mean, so he stopped and asked the farmer, "Does your dog bite?" The farmer answered, "No," so the man continued walking toward the farmer. The dog suddenly jumped up, grabbed the man's leg in his mouth, and bit him. The man pulled away and shouted angrily, "I thought you said your dog doesn't bite!" The farmer smiled and replied, "That's not my dog!"

If you answered that the final *ed* in regular past-tense verbs can be pronounced in one of three ways, you were correct. The final *ed* that is used to form the past tense of regular verbs can have three sounds: the voiceless /t/, the voiced /d/, or a new syllable, /ɪd/.

To determine which sound to use, you need to know whether the last sound (not letter) is voiced or voiceless. All vowels are voiced.*

Past Tense Ending Rules				
Final Sound of Regular Verb*	**Pronunciation of -*ed* Ending**	**New Syllable Added?**	**Examples**	
voiceless	/t/	no	*looked* sounds like	/lʊkt/
voiced	/d/	no	*caused* sounds like	/kɔzd/
t or *d*	/ɪd/	yes	*needed* sounds like	/ní-dɪd/

*You can feel whether consonant sounds are voiced or voiceless by holding your hand against your throat and saying the sounds. If you feel a vibration, the sound is voiced.

/t/ ending	/d/ ending	/Id/ ending

Now insert the past-tense verbs from the joke about the dog in the appropriate column in this chart, and then practice pronouncing the verbs and telling the joke.

TUNING IN: "Dr. Clown"

You will watch a CNN video clip about doctors who dress as clowns when they make their rounds in the children's ward of a hospital.

Vocabulary in the Video

© CNN

1. You will hear the following idiomatic phrases in the video clip. Have you heard them before? What do you think they mean?

   a. His doctors have just **dropped by.** . . .

   b. We're **out of here.** . . .

   c. Researchers want to **get a handle on this.** . . .

2. You will hear the following medical-related vocabulary terms in the video clip. Try to guess their meanings with a partner.

   a. **Clinical trials** will begin at the hospital next month.

   b. The child is **in an uncomfortable state in surgery.**

   c. Among the things that will be measured are **physiological indices** such as heart rate.

Watch the Video

Watch the video at least two times. First, just watch. Second, write down some notes in each category below. From this information, you and your group will create two comprehension questions and two discussion questions to ask other groups.

Humor and Healing
How one hospital uses clowns
What happens when a clown doctor enters a room
Effectiveness of using clowns (older doctor's comments)
What the study will measure
Anecdotal evidence of clowns' effectiveness

◀**Talk About It**

With your group and using your notes, create four questions. Two should be comprehension questions, and two should be questions that get students to think about the subject discussed in the video clip. Write the four questions on one sheet of paper. Then exchange questions with another group. Follow these steps:

• Have a discussion as you and members of your group answer the other group's questions orally. Choose one student to write short notes on the paper with the questions.

• Combine the two groups. Tell the other group what your group said in answer to their questions. Refer to the notes if necessary.

ACADEMIC POWER STRATEGY

Talk to your instructors outside of class to find out what you need to do to improve your work. Communicating with your instructors early in the semester is especially helpful as it will give them a stronger understanding of your academic background, your academic goals, and any concerns you might have about your coursework. It will give you a clear picture of what is expected of you and what you need to do to succeed in your studies.

Apply the Strategy

Go to an instructor's office hour or make an appointment to get feedback on how you are doing so far. While you are meeting, take notes on what your instructor says you need to do to improve for this class.

PUTTING IT ALL TOGETHER

Public Speaking

Tell an Anecdote

Whether speaking in formal or informal situations, we often make a point or explain something by telling a story about something that happened to us or to someone we know, or by using an example from something we have read. The following anecdote makes an important point in an interesting way. What is the point it makes? Do you think this anecdote is effective?

> A young professor asked an elderly, well-known author how long it had taken to finish his most recent book. Instead of giving a long explanation, the old man used an analogy from his own life: "I was a soldier on leave in Paris, just after the Second World War and I stopped to watch a sidewalk artist painting. I asked the artist if one painting I particularly liked was for sale. He said, "Yes," and then quoted a price that seemed extremely high. I said to him, "But it took you only one hour to paint that picture!" He replied, rather indignantly, "But I have been preparing all my life!"

In an informal, conversational speech lasting 3 to 5 minutes, share an interesting or amusing anecdote with your classmates.

Preparation

1. Think of something interesting, surprising, or amusing that happened to you or to someone you know. If possible, try to choose

a story that makes a larger point or illustrates something. Make a list of the important elements of the story and the larger point that it makes.

2. Rehearse telling the anecdote. Practice it several times, but do not memorize it. Memorized speech often sounds artificial. You want to sound relaxed when you tell your anecdote. Begin your anecdote by using an opener such as one of these:

   • "Today I'd like to tell you about something I saw happen when I was . . ."

   • "Today I'm going to share with you an interesting experience I had . . ."

   • "Today I'm going to tell you what happened when . . ."

3. Tape yourself telling the anecdote, and then listen to the tape. Make a note of any words you mispronounced or anything you want to change. Pay special attention to pronouncing past endings clearly and correctly. Keep practicing until you feel comfortable telling the anecdote.

Presentation

Share the anecdote with your classmates, paying special attention to pronouncing past-tense endings correctly. After you finish telling the anecdote, tell your listeners what you think the story illustrates or what point it makes. Evaluate your presentation by using the speech self-evaluation form in Appendix G.

It is not uncommon in the United States for people to begin a formal speech by telling an anecdote or a joke as an ice breaker or to get the audience's attention. Many professors and public speakers like to energize their audience by including interesting stories or amusing jokes throughout their talk. Would this ever happen in your native country?

Listening Log Report

Bring your Listening Log to class and report on one entry in a small group.

Search the Web

Learn more about humor and health by searching the Web. Possible key words: humor, laughter, health, healing, endorphins, clowns in hospitals.

Test-Taking Tip

Try to anticipate test questions by:

- asking the instructor what areas will be covered on the test.
- paying particular attention to points the instructor brings up more than once.
- generating a list of possible test questions.
- reviewing previous tests given in the class.
- speaking with other students about what they feel will be covered in the test.

CHECK YOUR PROGRESS

On a scale of 1 to 5, rate how well you have mastered the goals set at the beginning of the chapter:

1 2 3 4 5   learn information on ways that laughter can promote health.

1 2 3 4 5   learn vocabulary related to the topics of laughter and the immune system.

1 2 3 4 5   learn how to analyze your strengths and weaknesses as a language learner.

1 2 3 4 5   learn an organized, systematic approach to learning vocabulary.

1 2 3 4 5   learn how to use personal experience in developing a conversation.

1 2 3 4 5   learn how to pronounce *ed* at the end of regular past-tense verbs.

1 2 3 4 5   talk to your instructors outside of class to find out what you need to do to improve your work.

If you have given yourself a 3 or lower on any of these goals:

- visit the *Tapestry* web site for additional practice.
- ask your instructor for extra help.
- review the sections of the chapter that you found difficult.
- work with a partner or study group to further your progress.

The students in this photo are taking a very important examination, perhaps one for entrance into a college or university. Have you ever taken an exam like this? If so, answer these questions:

- Did students have to show photo identification to enter the room where the test was being held?

- Were you warned about the consequences of cheating?

- What were the consequences of cheating?

- Were there many proctors? (Proctors are people who watch students to make sure that they aren't cheating.)

ACADEMIC DISHONESTY— HOW COMMON IS CHEATING?

*D*ishonesty. *Cheating. Lying. Corruption*. These are words that we hear day after day about politics, business, and education too. In this chapter, we will explore the types and extent of cheating in education. We will also talk about the reasons students break the rules and the different types of punishment that are used by academic institutions.

Setting Goals

In this chapter you will learn:

◈ about the problem of academic dishonesty, more commonly known as "cheating."

◈ vocabulary related to the subject of academic dishonesty.

◈ to use background knowledge to guess the meanings of unfamiliar words and phrases.

◈ to ask native English speakers the meanings of idioms and other expressions.

◈ about your school's policies on academic dishonesty.

73

◈Getting Started

It is said that a picture is worth a thousand words. Look at the picture below, and then answer these questions with a partner or group:

People Weekly, © 1991 Penny Wolin

- What is the student doing?
- Is this common in your native country?
- Do you think it is common in the United States and Canada?
- Do you think the student should be punished? Why or why not?
- What adjectives describe this kind of behavior?
- This student is looking at notes that he wrote on his hand. What are some other methods of cheating that students use?
- It has been said that people cheat because:

  a. It doesn't hurt anybody.

  b. They are desperate, perhaps because they didn't have time to write their own paper or to study for a test.

  c. Everyone does it.

What do you think of these excuses?

LISTENING: ACADEMIC DISHONESTY IN HIGHER EDUCATION

◈Getting Ready to Listen

Read the following excerpt from a *Washington Post* article titled "College Cribbers . . . Ethics May Be in, But So Is Cheating." The discussion in this article is about the results of an "Academic Honesty" survey conducted by Professor Donald McCabe, one of the speakers that you will soon be listening to in a National Public Radio interview.

> At the University of California at Berkeley, a new pilot program that uses computers to scan student papers turned up 35 cases of cheating in a class of 300 students.

"I haven't shocked anyone with my survey," asserts Donald McCabe, an associate professor of business ethics at Rutgers University Graduate School of Management who not long ago conducted a broad-scale study of college cheating. . . . In his four-page questionnaire filled out anonymously by 6,097 students from 31 of America's most scholastically elite schools, 67 percent admitted cheating at least once in college; 41 percent of undergraduates admitted cheating on exams and 19 percent admitted cheating on four or more tests. . . .

Source: *Washington Post,* January 6, 1992, p. C5.

Below are some of the actual questions from the academic honesty survey that Dr. McCabe is referring to. Try to answer these questions. Your answers should be based on either your high school or college experience.

1. In your opinion, what percentage of your classmates have cheated on a test, exam, or paper?

_____ None   _____ 1–5%   _____ 6–10%   _____ 11–20%

_____ 21–30%   _____ 31–40%   _____ 41–50%   _____ Over 50%

2. How frequently do you think any of the following occur?

	Never	Very Seldom	Seldom	Often	Very Often
*Stealing from the library	_____	_____	_____	_____	_____
**Plagiarism	_____	_____	_____	_____	_____
Cheating during exams/tests	_____	_____	_____	_____	_____

*Two students can be chosen to ask the school librarian about the frequency of library theft and report to the class at the next class meeting.

**Plagiarism is the act of copying material almost word for word from a source and turning it in as your own work.

3. Have you ever:

(Since this question is very personal, you don't have to answer in writing. Just think about your responses.)

	Never	Once	A Few Times	Many Times
used crib notes (cheat notes) on a test?	_____	_____	_____	_____
copied from another student during a test?	_____	_____	_____	_____
seen another student cheating on a test?	_____	_____	_____	_____
used unfair methods to learn what was on a test before it was given?	_____	_____	_____	_____
copied material almost word for word from any source and turned it in as your own work (plagiarized)?	_____	_____	_____	_____

4. What do you think the typical teacher would do if he or she knew someone had cheated on a test or an assignment?

_____ Probably nothing

_____ Refer the matter to the appropriate authority for handling

_____ Give the student a warning

_____ Give the student a failing grade on the test/assignment

_____ Give the student a failing grade in the course

_____ Other (specify): _____

Now answer these questions:

- Why do you think Professor McCabe conducted this study?

- Do you think that the subject of academic dishonesty should be discussed in classes? Why or why not?

- Dr. McCabe's findings were reported on the radio, on TV, and in newspapers and magazines. Why do you think there was so much interest in his research?

Words and Phrases You Will Hear

Often, seeing words and phrases before you hear them can help your listening comprehension. Take a look at the following list and briefly discuss any unfamiliar items with your teacher.

Cheating

charges of cheating

an epidemic of cheating

academic integrity

to counter cheating

cheating ranged widely in severity

padding a bibliography

explicit cheating

the extent of cheating

multiple offenses

Worries About Cheating

an increasing concern

the level of concern

the concern is well-founded

the situation is appalling

instill positive values

a substantial problem

Working with Others

rules concerning collaboration

conferring with other students

Phrases Used in Academic Settings

the college entrance exam

a pop quiz

a research paper

a term paper

an undeclared major

Useful Phrases

studies are underway

to have a different perspective

virtually nobody

what is at issue is

to have reason to believe

Listen (Part I)

Academic Dishonesty in Higher Education

1. Listen, and connect what you hear to the concept map on the next page. Then complete the empty circle in the middle.

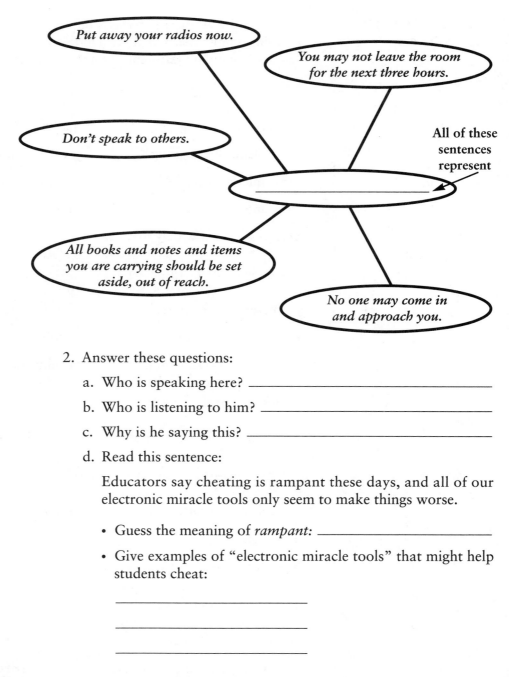

Put away your radios now.

You may not leave the room for the next three hours.

Don't speak to others.

All of these sentences represent

All books and notes and items you are carrying should be set aside, out of reach.

No one may come in and approach you.

2. Answer these questions:

a. Who is speaking here? _____

b. Who is listening to him? _____

c. Why is he saying this? _____

d. Read this sentence:

Educators say cheating is rampant these days, and all of our electronic miracle tools only seem to make things worse.

- Guess the meaning of *rampant*: _____

- Give examples of "electronic miracle tools" that might help students cheat:

    _____

    _____

    _____

Listen (Part II)

Academic Dishonesty in Higher Education

1. Write down one point that you remember most clearly. Compare what you wrote with a partner.

One point that I remember: _____

_____

2. Listen to Part II again, but this time focus on finding certain details. To do this, read the following questions *before* you listen. Then listen and try to answer the questions.

- Here's the "pop quiz" that the speaker gives to his listeners. What is the correct answer to his question about how many students admit to cheating?

    a. 1/4 of the student body

    b. 1/2 of the student body

    c. 1/3 of the student body

    d. 2/3 of the student body

    Guess what he means by "the student body." _____
    _____

- List the kinds of cheating that he mentions by completing these phrases:

    a. stealing _____

    b. copying _____

    c. groups of students joining together to _____

- What happened in India? _____
    _____

After You Listen

LANGUAGE LEARNING STRATEGY

Apply the Strategy

Use your background knowledge to guess the meanings of unfamiliar phrases. Think about the meanings of the individual words in a phrase, and also consider the context in which a phrase is used.

At the end of Part II, the speaker refers to "a how-to guide for would-be cheaters" called "Cheating 101." Use the knowledge that you already have to figure out what this phrase means by analyzing its separate words:

(continued on next page)

1. guide—think of a travel guidebook. What does it tell its readers?

   _____

2. would-be—think of conditional sentences such as "I would be happy if I got an *A* on the test." Compare this sentence to "They would be cheaters if they knew how to cheat."

   Would-be cheaters, then, are probably people who

   _____

3. At many colleges and universities in the United States, introductory courses are given the number "101." Why do you think, then, that the author of *Cheating 101* gave his book that title?

   _____

4. Now answer this question: What is a "how-to guide for would-be cheaters"?

   _____

◇ Getting Ready to Listen

Vocabulary Building

In Part III, you will hear a discussion with the interviewer, Professor Donald McCabe of Rutgers University, and Sally Cole, judicial affairs officer at Stanford University. Read the following sentences from the discussion, and then, in the matching exercise that follows, try to match the boldface words with their definitions. (The spaces at the left will be used later as you listen to Part III. Leave them blank for now.)

_____ 1. . . . the students who were participating in the surveys . . . were asked to indicate whether they had ever **engaged in** any of the following list of activities, each of which, um, was dishonest and therefore a form of cheating, though they certainly **ranged widely in severity** from **padding** a few items on a bibliography . . . to purchasing a term paper from a paper factory and submitting it with one's own name on it.

_____ 2. [Purchasing a term paper from a paper factory]: that's when you **hand in** a research paper that someone else has written and you . . . paid fifty **bucks** or something for it.

_____ 3. . . . I've become convinced after looking at the responses of the over six thousand students that responded to my survey that students have a somewhat different **perspective** on what **constitutes explicit cheating**. . . .

_____ 4. . . . there are many students out there, according to the results I found, that are cheating because everybody else is. It's a very **standard justification**, and as Sally said, that doesn't make it right. But I think I **can appreciate** more now that I've done the survey than I did before that students today, with all the pressures that graduate schools put on their **G.P.A.s** . . . feel it very difficult to sit in a class when they see other students cheating in a given course and not cheat themselves.

_____ 5. A lot of these . . . issues of what constitutes cheating depends . . . especially rules concerning **collaboration**, it will depend on what the instructor's guidelines are. . . .

_____ 6. How **widespread** do you think it ["classic cheating"] is?

Matching

Write the letter of the word or phrase on the right next to the word or phrase in bold on the left that it can replace.

_____ 1. **engaged in** activities

_____ 2. **ranged widely in severity**

_____ 3. **padding** a few items on a bibliography

_____ 4. **hand in** a research paper

_____ 5. paid fifty **bucks**

_____ 6. a somewhat different **perspective** on

_____ 7. what **constitutes explicit cheating**

_____ 8. It's a very **standard justification**

_____ 9. I **can appreciate** more now

_____ 10. **G.P.A.s**

_____ 11. rules concerning **collaboration**

_____ 12. **widespread**

a. dishonestly adding

b. dollars

c. view

d. is _real_ cheating

e. submit, give

f. participated in

g. working together

h. grade point averages

i. common

j. can understand

k. varied in seriousness

l. common excuse

Listen (Part III)

Academic Dishonesty in Higher Education

Listen for the Main Idea

Listen to Part III. Then write one sentence that summarizes the main idea:

_____

_____

_____

Listen for More Information

Have the Part III Vocabulary Building exercise (pages 80–81) in front of you as you listen to Part III again. As you listen, put check marks (✔) in the spaces next to the sentences that you hear.

Listen and Take Notes

Use the "split-page format" described on page 35 in Chapter 2 to take notes as you listen again to the material.

- Take out a piece of paper and copy what is written on the sample page below. The underlined headings are included to help you take notes. Copy them before you listen to the interview,

QUESTIONS/IDEAS	NOTES: ACADEMIC DISHONESTY
	Cole — Ex of Cheating
	McCabe — Reasons Students Cheat
	Cole re Buying Notes
	Alec — Classic Cheating
	Cole — Instructor's Responsibility
	McCabe — Extent of the Problem

and be sure to leave plenty of space after each heading so that you will have room to write details.

- As you listen, write *only* in the Notes column. Indent your notes to show the organization of what you hear. Main points should start farthest to the left. Specific information that comes after each main point should be below and indented a little bit to the right. Also, you can use capital letters and underlining to indicate the most important points.

For note-taking tips regarding abbreviations and signals, see Appendix A.

After You Listen

1. Reread your notes. Add ideas and questions to the left column.

2. Compare notes with a partner.

3. Using your notes, orally answer the following questions with your partner:

   a. According to Dr. McCabe, why do so many students cheat?

   b. Does Dr. Cole think that buying notes is a form of cheating? Explain.

   c. Does Dr. McCabe believe that one in eight students cheating is a large or small number?

4. Using only your notes, orally reconstruct Part III with a partner. Each of you should reconstruct half of Part III.

As you give the opinions and ideas of others, it is necessary to show that you are not giving your own ideas. Try to use some of these phrases as you speak:

According to Dr. Cole, . . .

From Dr. Cole's standpoint, . . .

In Dr. McCabe's view, . . .

From Dr. McCabe's point of view, . . .

Dr. Cole has found from her experience that . . .

In your own words, write a one-paragraph summary of Part III.

Write About It.

- Begin your first sentence as follows: "In the 'Academic Dishonesty' discussion, the speakers talk about. . . ." Complete that sentence with the main idea of the interview.

- Because two people are expressing their views, it will be necessary to pay special attention to "attribution." That is, you will need to indicate whose opinions you are giving, so be sure to use some of the phrases listed in number 4 in the After You Listen section.

- If you use a speaker's exact words, put them between quotation marks. Otherwise, you will be plagiarizing! For instructions on how to paraphrase, refer to Appendix B, and for instructions on how to summarize, see Appendix C.

◆Listening Focus

Listening Between the Lines

Listen once more to Part III. Now that you understand what the speakers are saying, focus on the *way* they communicate with one another. The following questions will be your guide:

1. When he introduces Professor McCabe, the host stumbles on two sounds when he says the words "business ethics." What two English sounds does he mix up?

   _____

   (The message to you: Even native speakers stumble in pronunciation.)

2. What phrase does the host use to get the discussion started after he finishes introducing the professor?

   I _____ (2 words total)

   (The message to you: When you want to start a conversation with someone, you might want to start with, "I understand [that] . . ." or "I've heard [that]. . . .")

3. When Sally Cole defines cheating, she gives a long definition. The most important words in her definition are said louder and stronger than the others, and those words are also given higher intonation. Can you catch some of those important words? Try to write five of them here:

   Hint: Most of the words are nouns or adjectives.

   _____

   _____

   (The message to you: The most important words—usually nouns, adjectives, adverbs, and main verbs—usually receive the strongest stress and intonation.)

4. After Sally Cole mentions purchasing a term paper from a "paper factory," the host needs some clarification, so he rephrases what

she said in a statement. Rephrasing is a method of putting what someone else said into your own words so that you can find out if you understood what you heard. Here is part of what the host said. Try to fill in the missing words:

That's when you hand in a research paper that _____

_____

and you've paid fifty bucks or something for it.

(The message to you: When you want to make sure that you understood what someone said, you can try to repeat the idea in your own words.)

5. What does Sally Cole say to the host to let him know that he understood what she meant?

    _____

    (The message to you: After you rephrase what people have said, they will let you know if you accurately caught their point. If your rephrasing is inaccurate, then you will probably hear an explanation.)

6. When the host asks Professor McCabe for his definitions of cheating, the professor expresses agreement with what Sally Cole said, but he needs to add an explanation. What does he say?

    I think I would generally agree with what Sally said, with possibly

    _____

    (The message to you: It's important to learn polite ways to express partial agreement and then add more details.)

7. When the host asks Sally Cole about how widespread "classic cheating" is on the Stanford University campus, she doesn't really understand the question. First, she pauses, and then what does she ask?

    _____

    (The message to you: When you don't understand a particular part of what someone has said, ask, "What do you mean by . . . ?")

    How does the host respond to this question?

    Well, _____, isn't it? Uh, I _____, uh. . . .

    (The message to you: Phrases such as *That's a good question* and sounds such as *uh* and *um* give the speaker some thinking time before answering an unexpected question.)

The Sound of It: Stressed and Unstressed Words

Certain types of words in English are usually (but not always) stressed in phrases and sentences. These words carry the most information. Native speakers of English stress words by making them stronger and a bit louder than other words.

The following indicates which types of words are usually stressed and unstressed:

Usually Stressed	Usually Unstressed
nouns	pronouns
main verbs	helping (auxiliary) verbs
adjectives	forms of *be*
demonstrative adjectives (*this, that, these, those*)	conjunctions
adverbs	prepositions
WH question words (*who, what, where, when, why, how,* etc.)	articles

Look at Part II of the listening, below. Underline the words that you expect the speaker to stress, and then listen to the tape to see if what he says actually matches your expectations. Then practice reading Part II aloud.

Part II

A pop quiz now. At top American universities, studies indicate that cheating on tests is practiced by:

> (a) a quarter of the student body
> (b) half
> (c) um, well, say, a third for (c)
> and (d) two-thirds

The mere fact that such studies are under way tells us of the level of concern about cheating and the answer to the question (d) two-thirds admit to cheating, shows that the concern is well-founded. Teachers, administrators, test developers, and students find increasing instances of stealing answers from others, and of copying research papers. And of groups of students joining together to share information in ways that they shouldn't.

At MIT two years ago, charges of cheating were brought against seventy-three students involved with just one assignment in one class. It's the worst known instance in the school's history.

And it's happening elsewhere in this country and abroad, too. An article on the Reuters newswire last year told of an epidemic of cheating in India. There, the report said, some students carried knives to threaten the exam watchers who were supposed to prevent cheating. We haven't heard of instances like that in this country, but the situation is appalling for many educators and students.

Others, however, see opportunity. A senior at Rutgers this year, the state university of New Jersey, published an eighty-six-page book with the title *Cheating 101*. This is not an exposé. It's a how-to guide for would-be cheaters. And traveling around by car, the student author managed to sell many thousands of copies of his self-published work.

Culture Note

It is common for colleges and universities in the United States to have academic honesty policies. These policies list activities that are considered to be cheating. The policies also explain the types of punishment that cheaters might face. Punishments usually range from getting a warning to being asked to leave the school. Do you know if it is common for schools in your native country to have academic honesty policies? Have you ever seen or heard about one? If so, how did you find out about it?

Talk About It

The Latin origin of *plagiarism* is *plagiarius*, which means "kidnapper, seducer, literary thief."

1. The following is an explanation of plagiarism given in a college policy statement on academic honesty:

    Plagiarism: Although difficult to define, plagiarism consists of taking the words or specific substance of another and either copying or paraphrasing the work without giving credit to the source. The following examples are only some of the many forms plagiarism may take:

    _____ a. Submitting a term paper, examination, or other work written by someone else.

    _____ b. Failure to give credit in a citation for ideas, statements of facts, or conclusions expressed by another.

    _____ c. Failure to use quotation marks when quoting directly from another, whether it be a paragraph, a sentence, or even a part thereof.

    _____ d. Inappropriate paraphrasing (e.g., over-reliance on sentence structure of the original author).

- Next to each letter, indicate whether or not you think these actions are acceptable in your native country. Write A for acceptable or U for unacceptable. Write a question mark (?) if you don't know.

- Explain any cases where you wrote *A*.

- Are you surprised that this is not always seen as acceptable behavior?

- What would you have to avoid doing when writing papers and making speeches in classes in the United States or Canada?

- Do you know what kinds of punishment are given to students who plagiarize in your native country? If so, tell your group or class.

ACADEMIC POWER STRATEGY

Apply the Strategy

Find out about your school's policies on academic dishonesty. They may be the same as the policies in your native country, but they may be different. If you are sure of the rules, you will be able to do your work with more confidence.

- Get a copy of your school's academic honesty policy or honor code. This may appear in your school's catalog or schedule of classes. If not, ask your teacher or librarian where you might locate the policy.

- Analyze the policy on your own or with a partner or group. Clarify new vocabulary you may come across, such as these words and phrases:

  to be (placed) on suspension   to suspend   to be suspended

  expulsion   to expel   to be expelled

  to be (placed) on probation

- Invite an administrator to come to your class as a guest speaker to talk about the academic honesty policy and the extent of cheating at your school. Follow the steps for inviting a guest speaker in Appendix E.

2. What do you think are the messages in these cartoons?

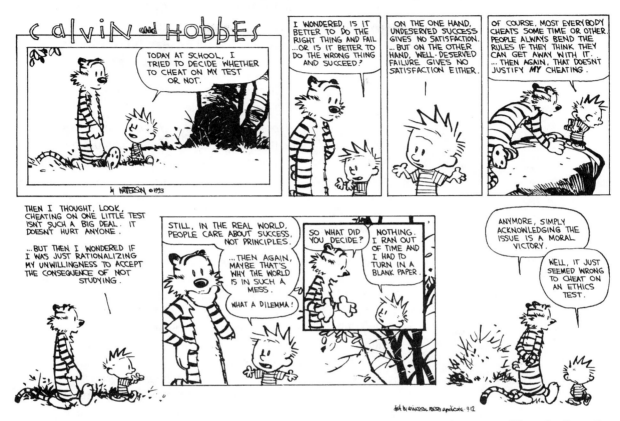

Source: Cartoon by Watterson; © 1993 Andrews and McNeel, A Universal Press Syndicate Co.

Source: Drawn by Jim Borgman, *Cincinnati Enquirer* © 1997 (from *SF Examiner* 12/7/97)

3. Read the following excerpt from an article that was written by a composition instructor who teaches at several California community colleges.

The Internet—A New Research Frontier or an Easy Way to Plagiarize?

····································

William Stevenson, Orange Coast College, Saddleback College, Fullerton College, Golden West College

1   A 1991 national poll involving thirty-one of the nation's most prestigious schools[1] found that "more than 50 percent of students had cheated during their college careers." In another survey, 26.1 percent indicated they had written a paper for one class and turned it in to another class without telling the professor it was an old paper, 14.6 percent indicated that they had handed in a paper written by a colleague, and 5.6 percent said that they had turned in a paper written by a research service. Several of the students wrote that they had never considered that there might be something wrong with this behavior.

2   Cheating by means of plagiarism is not a new phenomenon in academe.[2] Edward M. White tells of a colleague who "received from a student a copy of a paper that he himself had written a generation[3] earlier." Plagiarism comes in many forms, and now, with the proliferation of[4] student use of the Internet, a new source for plagiarism has emerged with students copying electronically-published documents and submitting them[5] as their own ideas. Because of the potential for academic dishonesty using this immense resource, institutions, departments, and instructors must expand existing policies and pedagogies[6] that already discourage student plagiarism to include this new source of information, which is fast becoming an integral component of[7] modern education and society.

3   With many students well versed at[8] "surfing the 'Net,'" finding myriad[9] information on nearly any topic is simple. With a home computer connected to the Internet, students don't even have to go to the library to access hundreds or thousands of Web sites on various subjects. . . . Although this convenient and easy access to such a vast amount of information appears ideal for student research, a serious underlying problem[10] exists with its use.

Source: *Inside English*, May, 1998.

[1]**prestigious schools:** very highly respected colleges and universities
[2]**academe:** the academic world
[3]**a generation:** approximately twenty years
[4]**proliferation of:** rapid increase of
[5]**submitting them:** turning them in, giving them to the instructor
[6]**pedagogies:** methods of teaching
[7]**an integral component of:** a basic part of
[8]**well versed at:** experienced at
[9]**myriad:** a vast amount of
[10]**underlying problem:** a problem that may not be easily seen

Discussion: The Internet and Plagiarism

Discuss the following in groups. Choose one person to be the leader, who will make sure that everyone understands the questions and participates. Choose another person to take notes and report the highlights of your discussion to your class.

1. Why do you think William Stevenson, a composition instructor, wrote this article?

2. If you were an instructor, would you encourage your students to do research on the Internet? Why or why not? What rules would you set about copying from the Internet?

3. In another part of his article, William Stevenson wrote, ". . . copying another's ideas diminishes one's capacity for developing the critical thinking skills necessary to form one's own opinions." Explain why you agree or disagree with this statement.

4. Are you aware of anyone who has copied material from the Internet and then handed it in as his or her own work? If so, what happened?

> If an author is once detected in borrowing, he will be suspected of plagiarism ever after.
>
> —WILLIAM HAZLITT

LANGUAGE LEARNING STRATEGY

Ask native English speakers to explain idioms and other expressions that you don't understand. This will not only help you learn the expressions, but it will also give you more opportunities to speak English with native speakers. If you don't understand an explanation, ask for a sample sentence with the expression. You might also ask about what age group commonly uses the expression and how to pronounce certain words.

Apply the Strategy

Individually or with a partner, ask native English speakers to explain the following idioms. Be sure to also ask for sample sentences. Then, in class, compare the sentences that students collected.

- to stretch the truth
- to bend the rules
- to take credit for something you haven't done
- to get away with something
- to keep your eyes on your own paper
- to watch someone like a hawk

(continued on next page)

- to be kicked out of school
- to turn someone in
- to tell on someone/to squeal on someone
- to copy something word for word

© CNN

TUNING IN: "Cheating in the Navy"

You will watch a CNN video clip about cheating at the Naval Academy in Annapolis, Maryland, where members of the Navy called "midshipmen" attend classes. First, you will read some sentences from the video and try to guess the meanings of some words and phrases.

Vocabulary in the Video

The following are sentences taken from the video clip. Try to guess the meanings of the boldface words and phrases. In many cases, the sentences themselves contain definitions or explanations.

1. One month before graduation, two dozen midshipmen got the final word—they're **getting the boot** for cheating on "**Wires**," a tough electrical engineering course required of all **middies**.

   a. What is "Wires"?

   _____

   b. What are "middies"?

   _____

   c. Two dozen midshipmen are "getting the boot" for cheating. Can you guess what "getting the boot" means?

   _____

2. NARRATOR: The cheating scandal, worst in the school's 149-year history, has caused **soul-searching** in the Navy's highest quarters.

   An example of "soul-searching" follows:

   ADMIRAL: I think that when there is a failure of a lot of people, like we saw at the Naval Academy, a lot of cheating, you don't just look at the people who cheated; you look inside at yourself and say, "What have I taught these young people?"

   Can you guess what "soul-searching" means?

   _____

3. CRITIC: I think **the root problem** has been basically **a blasé attitude** by the Navy Department as a whole towards honor at the Naval Academy.

What do you think a "root problem" is?

Hint: Think of the roots of a tree.

_____

NARRATOR: An independent panel concluded the cheating incident was **the culmination of decades of neglect** by the Navy.

The following is a paraphrase of what the critic and narrator said. After you read the paraphrase, try to guess the meanings of the words.

The cheating incident was a big event that came after years and years of the Navy not paying attention to cheating. In other words, there had been cheating for many years, but the Navy hadn't done anything about it.

• **a blasé attitude** is an attitude in which people _____

_____

• **the culmination of** something is _____

• **decades of neglect** are _____

Watch the Video

Watch the video at least two times. First, just watch. Second, write down some notes in each category below. From this information, you and your group will create two comprehension questions and two discussion questions to ask other groups.

Cheating incident
Role of the Navy

Talk About It

With your group and using your notes, create four questions. Two should be comprehension questions, and two should be for students' opinions about the cheating scandal. Write the four questions on one sheet of paper. Then exchange questions with another group. Follow these steps:

- Have a discussion as you and the members of your group answer the other group's questions orally. Choose one student to write short notes on the paper with the questions.

- Combine the two groups. Tell the other group what your group said in answer to their questions. Refer to the notes if necessary.

PUTTING IT ALL TOGETHER

Public Speaking— Panel Discussion

Imagine that you and your classmates are experts on the subject of ethics. You have come together as a panel on a CNN documentary to discuss cheating incidents at the Naval Academy and elsewhere.

Preparation for a Panel Discussion

1. Students should get into groups of five or six. The number of panel discussions that go on at the same time will vary according to the size of the class. (An alternative would be to have only one panel discussion while the rest of the class acts as the audience.)

2. Each group should choose roles for the participants. One student will need to take the role of "moderator." Other possible roles: a Navy officer, a student who has been caught cheating, a student who has never cheated, a psychologist, a teacher.

3. The group as a whole should brainstorm points that the different participants can make. Students should keep lists of points that they would like to make during the discussion.

4. Moderators should think of themselves as TV hosts. They should always keep in mind that they should not express their personal opinions in the discussion. Before the panel discussion they will:

   - plan an introduction that states the topic and why it is being discussed. They can also provide background information on the topic. In addition, moderators will need to plan how they will introduce each member of the panel.

   - prepare discussion questions to ask the different panel members.

   Moderators from the different groups may want to get together to discuss what they plan to say in their introductions and what discussion questions they plan to ask.

   For information for how to conduct your panel discussion, see Appendix F.

Listening Log Report

Bring your Listening Log to class and report on one entry in a small group.

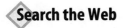**Search the Web**   Learn more about academic honesty by searching the Web. Possible key words: academic dishonesty, academic honesty, cheating, plagiarism, honor codes, academic honesty policies, UC Berkeley (Office of Student Conduct).

Test-Taking Tip

Pronunciation is usually an important factor in speaking tests. Before a speaking test, practice any pronunciation areas which you know are problematic for you. Make a list of words which include these difficult pronunciation areas. Practice these words whenever you get a chance. Ask a classmate who doesn't have trouble with the same pronunciation areas to listen to you practice and point out any mispronunciations.

CHECK YOUR PROGRESS
. . . .

On a scale of 1 to 5, rate how well you have mastered the goals set at the beginning of the chapter:

1 2 3 4 5   learn about the problem of academic dishonesty, more commonly known as "cheating."

1 2 3 4 5   learn vocabulary related to the subject of academic dishonesty.

1 2 3 4 5   learn to use background knowledge to guess the meanings of unfamiliar words and phrases.

1 2 3 4 5   learn the meanings of idioms and other expressions from native speakers of English.

1 2 3 4 5   learn about your school's policies on academic dishonesty.

If you've given yourself a 3 or lower on any of these goals:

- visit the *Tapestry* web site for additional practice.
- ask your instructor for extra help.
- review the sections of the chapter that you found difficult.
- work with a partner or study group to further your progress.

- What is your reaction to this photo?
- Does the existence of an American fast-food restaurant in a foreign city raise any issues for you?

EXPORTING AMERICAN CULTURE— MCDONALDIZATION OF THE WORLD?

An ongoing topic of discussion throughout the world today is the spread of "American popular culture" around the globe. Some people argue that this phenomenon is a threat to national cultures. Other people believe that the spread of Hollywood films, popular music sung in English, fast food restaurants, and CNN represents an emerging "world culture" that is not "true American culture." In this chapter, we will examine different viewpoints on this issue.

Setting Goals

In this chapter you will learn:

- about different points of view regarding the "exportation" of American culture.

- vocabulary related to the topic of the dominance of American culture.

- how to choose an English–English dictionary that works for you.

- how to pause between thought groups when speaking.

- to assess and improve your study habits by becoming aware of your learning style.

- to record yourself speaking as a way to get self-feedback on your presentations.

◆ **Getting Started**

Read the following paragraph on popular American culture:

> There are currently
> **23,346 McDonald's**
> restaurants in 110
> countries world-wide.
>
> —FRANCHISE NZ MARKETING

Aspects of American culture are becoming increasingly popular around the globe. One can find the icons of American culture nearly everywhere. Consider the worldwide presence of Coke and Pepsi, McDonald's and Pizza Hut, Mickey Mouse and Mickey Rourke, cowboys and jazz, American films and Disneyland. The spread of American culture has produced some very incongruous television scenes of Third World protesters (usually young men) burning the American flag or chanting anti-American slogans while dressed in T-shirts, Nike shoes, and blue jeans. Although some people consider American culture to be distasteful, the general population seems to like many of its forms. Even in Anglophobic France, the uniform of young upper-middle-class Parisian women in 1990 was pure Americana—Calvin Klein jeans, a white button-down oxford shirt, a navy blazer, Bass Weejuns penny loafers, and a Marlboro cigarette.

Source: Eric Felten, "Love It or Hate It, America is King of Pop Culture," *Insight,* March 25, 1991.

Can any of these aspects of American pop culture be seen in your native country? How do you feel about it?

LISTENING:
EXPORTING AMERICAN CULTURE

◆ **Getting Ready to Listen**

1. Read the following excerpt from an article on American cultural domination.

Culture Wars

1 Officials from France's Ministry of Culture are convinced that a rising tide of American popular culture is swamping[1] France. And they spend much of their working lives administering a complex

[1]**is swamping:** is filling

system of quotas[2] and subsidies[3] that are designed to protect French culture from total submersion.[4]

2   The ministry has almost uniform support for its position among a French cultural elite worried about the threat that America poses, particularly to French film. Their concern is . . . that Hollywood is a Trojan horse[5] bringing with it Disneyland Paris, fast-food chains and free advertising for American products from clothes to rock music. "America is not just interested in exporting its films," says Giles Jacob, the head of the Cannes Film Festival. "It is interested in exporting its way of life."

3   These French people lead a world guerrilla army[6] hoping to curb American cultural hegemony.[7] In 1989 the French government persuaded the European Community to decree that 40% of TV programs should be domestic. It also strengthened their complex system of support (which taxes French cinema tickets to help French film production) by extending it to television programs.

4   The French have found a powerful ally[8] in Canada, which has long been terrified of being swamped by its closest neighbors. Of the films shown on Canadian screens, 96% are foreign, primarily American. Three-quarters of the music on Canadian radio is not Canadian. Four in five magazines sold on news-stands in Canada, and six in every ten books, are foreign, mainly American.

5   In June Canada organized a meeting in Ottawa about American cultural dominance. Nineteen countries attended, including Britain, Brazil and Mexico; the United States was pointedly excluded.[9]

Source: *The Economist*, September 12th, 1998.

With a partner, talk about the reading. Is the issue of American cultural dominance an important issue for you? Do you think that France, Canada, and the other countries at the meeting were overreacting? Do you think that free trade, which allows goods to be imported and exported freely, is a threat to national cultures?

[2]**quotas:** limits

[3]**subsidies:** money paid by the government to make prices lower or to make the cost of production cheaper

[4]**total submersion:** the state of being completely covered

[5]**a Trojan horse:** in Greek mythology, a giant wooden horse that secretly contained Greek soldiers so that they could make a surprise attack on the enemy

[6]**guerrilla army:** an unofficial fighting group

[7]**to curb American cultural hegemony:** to reduce or stop American cultural dominance over other countries

[8]**ally:** supportive friend

[9]**was pointedly excluded:** was noticeably and purposely left out

Words and Phrases You Will Hear

Often, seeing words and phrases before you hear them can help your listening comprehension. Take a look at the following list and briefly discuss any unfamiliar items with your teacher

References to France

the river Seine
Jean Paul Sartre's book *Being and Nothingness*
Jeanne d'Arc (Joan of Arc)
Mon Dieu! (My God!)

U.S. Television Programs

The X-Files   *Baywatch*   *Star Trek*

Television Networks

CNN   BBC

Names of International Movie Directors

Ingmar Bergman (Sweden)   Luc Besson (France)
Alfred Hitchcock (England)   Kurosawa (Japan)

Actors/Actresses

Juliette Binoche (France)   Bruce Willis (United States)

Movies

The Fifth Element   *Godzilla*
The Full Monty   *Shall We Dance?*

Other Names, Organizations, and Companies

UNESCO (United Nations Educational, Scientific and Cultural
   Organization)
Benetton
VW (Volkswagen)
Esa-Pekka Salonen, conductor of the Los Angeles Philharmonic
   Orchestra

Film Culture

the latest Disney flick   a revival of the Irish film industry
you can make it in Hollywood

> The French are going to movies more than ever, but they are choosing Hollywood blockbusters over [films] in their own language. French movies accounted for less than 30 percent of the 170 million times people went to movies in France in 1999.
>
> —*LE FIGARO*

◆**Vocabulary Building**

In Part I of the listening, the people you will listen to use the boldface words and phrases that appear in the sentences below. Use background knowledge and context to help you guess their meanings.

1. There is a great concern over **so-called American culture,** but I think what people call American culture is not really American culture.

   so-called American culture = _____

2. How **pervasive** is American culture? Has it spread throughout the world as much as many people think?

   pervasive = _____

3. Certain aspects of American culture **predominate** in certain areas, such as American movies, which you find everywhere. You don't find films from other countries with the same dominance throughout the world.

   predominate = _____

◆**Listen (Part I)**

Exporting American Culture

Listen for the Main Idea

The interview you are about to listen to is divided into three parts. You will listen to each part and answer questions before moving on to the next part. After you have listened to and answered questions on all three parts, you will listen to the entire interview at one time and practice taking notes.

   Listen to the first part of the interview and write short answers to the following questions:

1. Alain Modoux doesn't believe that "true American culture" is being exported. What, in his opinion, is really being exported?

   _____

   _____

   _____

2. What does Ambassador Derek Shearer mean when he says we have a "world culture"?

   _____

   _____

   _____

Listen for More Information

- Read the sentences below.
- Listen to Part I again.
- Circle the answer to each question.

1. What was the purpose of the recent conference in Canada?
    a. To examine the decline of French culture worldwide.
    b. To promote the spread of a unified world culture.
    c. To discuss the impact of American popular culture.

2. What does Alain Modoux say about the "true" American culture?
    a. It is seen most clearly in Hollywood films.
    b. It differs from American industrial culture.
    c. It can be found in countries all over the world.

3. Why does Ambassador Shearer think the spread of American culture is not a big problem?
    a. Because we have a global economy with products from many countries available worldwide.
    b. Because the Hollywood film industry realizes that its worldwide success depends on using foreign talent.
    c. Because different cultures have been dominant worldwide at different times throughout history.

4. Why does Ambassador Shearer think we have a democratization of culture around the world?
    a. Because the cultures of many countries have influenced world culture.
    b. Because the United States imports cultural products from all over the world.
    c. Because the spread of American culture has created more democracy in the world.

5. What does Alain Modoux say about industrial culture coming from the United States?
    a. That it will spread throughout the world whether we like it or not.
    b. That it has become a mass culture seen worldwide.
    c. That it must be stopped before the world becomes one culture.

The English language contains many words borrowed from other languages. For example, in the interview you heard the interviewer describe a Frenchman wearing a *beret* (a small, round cloth hat) and eating a *baguette* (a long, thin loaf of crusty bread). Both words are borrowed from French. Do you know of any other words in English that have been borrowed from other languages?

◁Vocabulary Building

In Part II of the listening passage, the speakers use the boldface words and phrases that appear in the sentences below. Try to guess their meanings.

1. Instead of ignoring the fact that movies made in English reach a wider audience, one French company **has met the challenge head-on** and found a way to solve the problem.

   Hint: A head-on collision is one in which one car hits another car with the front parts meeting.

   has met the challenge head-on = _____

   _____

2. As we discuss this issue, what is **the key question** to ask?

   Hint: Think of a very important person with a key position in a company.

   the key question = _____

   _____

3. I spoke with Arab students who were complaining about Egyptian **cultural imperialism.**

   Hint: Imperialism often refers to the gaining of political or trade advantages over poorer nations by a powerful country that rules them or helps them with money.

   cultural imperialism = _____

   _____

Listen (Part II)

Exporting American Culture

Listen for the Main Idea

Listen to Part II. Then write one sentence that summarizes the main idea:

_____

_____

_____

Listen for More Information

- Read the following questions.
- Listen again and circle the correct answers to each question. Note: This time there may be more than one correct answer, so circle all answers that are correct.
- Compare answers with a partner.
- Listen again to check your answers.

1. According to Alain Modoux, why do American movies have an advantage over European movies?

   a. The United States has a large population that buys tickets to American films.

   b. Americans have more experience making films than Europeans do.

   c. American films have a larger audience for reasons of language.

2. What example does Ambassador Shearer give to show that countries other than the United States can make films that will have a worldwide audience?

   a. There is a French company that makes successful films in English.

   b. British films of Shakespeare's plays are popular throughout the world.

   c. Japan has produced a number of film classics over the years.

3. What does Alain Modoux consider to be the key question in this discussion of worldwide American dominance in the film industry?

   a. Should Hollywood distribute more international films made in foreign countries by foreign directors?

b. Will it help solve the problem if non-English-speaking countries refuse to import and show English-language films?

c. Can a nation's culture survive if it always produces films in a language that is not the national language?

4. What does Ambassador Shearer say about the widespread use of English?

a. It is a situation that will not change because English is already the national language of many countries in the world.

b. It does not indicate American dominance because English does not belong only to the United States.

c. It will most likely decrease once the Internet increases its use of other widely spoken languages such as Arabic, Chinese, and Spanish.

5. What examples does Alain Modoux give to illustrate important cultural power at the regional level?

a. India in Asia

b. Brazil and Mexico in Latin America

c. Japan in the Far East

d. Egypt in the Middle East

◆Vocabulary Building

In Part III of the listening passage, the speakers use the boldface words and phrases that appear in the sentences below. Use background knowledge and context to help you guess their meanings.

1. One of the recommendations that came out of the Canadian conference was **a global competitor** to CNN because it's seen as a dominant worldwide information source generated in the United States.

    a global competitor = _____

2. Part of this new world economy is how a small country can develop its strengths to meet specific needs of the global market. Small countries need to develop their **market niches,** to find the places where they can sell their products successfully.

    market niches = _____

3. Instead of being **on the defensive,** they have developed a strategy where they are open to the rest of the world.

    on the defensive = _____

Listen (Part III)

Exporting American Culture

- Read the following questions.

- Listen to Part III.

- Answer the questions with short answers.

- Compare answers with a partner.

- Listen again to check your answers.

1. According to Alain Modoux, what are the two times a European would be likely to watch CNN?

   a. _____

   b. _____

2. According to Alain Modoux, why has CNN been so successful?

   _____

3. What are three examples that Ambassador Shearer gives to show that Finland has a strong local culture that is able to compete on a worldwide level?

   a. _____

   b. _____

   c. _____

4. What point does Alain Modoux make about most countries that complain about the influence of other countries?

   _____

5. What point does Alain Modoux make about the free flow of information?

   _____

Listen and Take Notes (Parts I, II, and III)

Use the "split-page format" described on page 35 in Chapter 2 to take notes as you listen again to the entire interview.

- Take out a piece of paper and copy what is written on the sample page on the next page. The underlined headings are included to help you take notes. Copy them before you listen to the tape, leaving plenty of space after each heading so that you will have room to write details.

QUESTIONS/IDEAS   NOTES: EXPORTING AMERICAN CULTURE

Concern About Dominance of American Culture

World Culture as Opposed to American Culture

Losing Cultural Identity vs. Meeting the Challenge

Language Is Key Question

Reasons for CNN's Success

How Small Countries Can Compete Successfully

Problems for Countries with Censorship

- As you listen, write *only* in the Notes column. Indent your notes to show the organization of what you hear. Main points should start farthest to the left. Specific information that comes after each main point should be below and indented a little bit to the right. Also, you can use capital letters and underlining to indicate the most important points.

For note-taking tips regarding abbreviations and signals, see Appendix A.

After You Listen

1. Reread your notes. Add ideas and questions to the left column.

2. Listen again and add more details to your notes.

3. Using only your notes, orally reconstruct the interview with a partner. Each of you should reconstruct half of the interview.

Write About It.

Write a one-paragraph summary of the interview. Refer only to your notes. Be sure to use your own words. Refer to Appendix B for guidelines on paraphrasing and Appendix C for guidelines on summarizing.

- Your first sentence should both introduce the men whose ideas are referred to, Alain Modoux and Ambassador Derek Shearer, and contain the main idea of the interview. Because many people don't know these two men, it will be necessary to explain who they are by using appositives: "Alain Modoux, *Director of the Division of Free Expression and Democracy at UNESCO,* and Ambassador Derek Shearer, *a former U.S. Ambassador to Finland. . . .*"

- In subsequent sentences, include the main points and some of the details. Remember to use language of attribution because you will be giving the ideas of the two men.

⬥ Talk About It

1. Is there an identifiable thing you can sensibly label "American culture"?

2. Do you agree with Alain Modoux's distinction between "true American culture" and "American industrial culture"? In your opinion, is the spread of "American industrial culture" a threat?

3. Is Hollywood as powerful as its enemies imagine? Do Hollywood's films really reflect American culture or a more general, worldwide culture? Do you think that films made in non-English-speaking countries can have a wide international audience?

4. Does the domination of the United States extend to all aspects of the popular arts and entertainment (popular singers, rock music groups, art, theater, fashion, etc.)? Give examples to support your point of view.

LANGUAGE LEARNING STRATEGY

Choose a user-friendly English–English dictionary, and then be an *active* user of it. Some dictionaries are easier to use than others, so find one that works for you. If you have an English–English dictionary that you find easy to use, you will be more likely to consult it often.

Apply the Strategy

There are many different English dictionaries, and deciding which one to buy can be an overwhelming choice. Is a dictionary for native speakers a good one for you, or is a learner's dictionary a better choice? It all depends. There are several questions to consider when you buy an English–English dictionary:

1. What is the purpose of the dictionary—do you want a large desk dictionary to keep at home or in your office, or do you want a portable dictionary that you can carry around with you? A large dictionary will have more words, but if it is too large, you probably will not carry it around with you to use when you need it the most.

2. How easy are the definitions for you to understand? (When you read a definition, do you have to look up even more words, or is it clear and easy to understand?)

3. Do the definitions contain example sentences so you can see how a word is used?

4. Can you understand the particular phonetic alphabet used in the dictionary? (Not all dictionaries use the same system, and it is important that you be able to check how a word is pronounced.)

5. Does the dictionary come with a CD-ROM? Some dictionary CD-ROMS allow you to hear each word pronounced aloud.

6. Does the dictionary have a variety of appendices with information you will find useful?

7. Does the dictionary contain terms that reflect contemporary English usage (for example, *fanny pack, day-care center, on-line, web site*)?

The two examples below illustrate the different approaches taken by different dictionaries. Look at the word *pervasive*, which is a vocabulary word you learned in this chapter. How do the definitions differ? Is one of the dictionary examples more useful for you? If so, which one?

a.

> **per·va·sive** /pər'veɪsɪv/ *adj.* **1** tending to pervade or spread: *a pervasive odor* **2** widespread, common, influential: *There is a pervasive trend toward casual dress in businesses. -n.* **pervasiveness.**

b.

> **per·va·sive** /pərvāysiv. -ziv/ *adj.* **1** pervading. **2** able to pervade. **per·va·sive·ly** *adv.* **per·va·sive·ness** *n.*

(continued on next page)

Go to a bookstore or a library. Find several different dictionaries, including at least one for native speakers and at least one that is designed for learners of English. Choose two or three words. Look up each word in each dictionary and, using the questions on page 109 as a guide, decide which dictionary would work best for you. Also, choose at least one word you are not sure how to pronounce, and look it up to see which dictionary symbols are easiest for you to understand and use.

The Sound of It: Thought Groups

Look at the following paragraph from the interview. Notice the groups of words in parentheses. Each group expresses a thought. By saying the words within a group without pausing, we create a certain rhythm. At the end of each "thought group," we sometimes pause briefly. If you say each word equally with pauses between them, you won't be using English rhythm. This can make your English difficult to understand, even if you are using clear pronunciation of sounds and correct grammar and vocabulary.

(I think there's too much focus on movies.) (As I say,) (I can defend Hollywood movies) (and I gave you examples of small countries) (that make good movies,) (but where I just served in Finland,) (this is a small country of 5 million people,) (but they have an incredibly strong local culture.) (The best composers in the world) (are Finnish) (and in fact,) (the head of the L.A. Philharmonic,) (Esa-Pekka Salonen,) (is a Finn.) (Some of the best architects in the world are Finns,) (some of the best designers of,) (of furniture and plateware are Finns.) (So you have a small country) (that produces incredible amounts of culture broadly defined) (and they compete in the world market. . . .)

Question: How can you know what words make up a thought group?

Answer: What goes into a thought group can vary, so it's not possible to give rules for 100% of the time. But you can follow these general guidelines:

What May Be a Thought Group	Example
a short sentence	(I think there's too much focus on movies.)
a phrase	(the best composers in the world)
a clause	(that make good movies)
transition words	(and in fact,)

In writing, commas, periods, and other punctuation marks indicate the ends of thought groups. These markers help make written language more comprehensible to us. In speech, changes in pitch and short pauses make our spoken language more comprehensible to our listeners.

Practice reading the paragraph from the interview using the thought groups as marked. If some of the thought groups seem too long, try breaking them up into shorter thought groups.

ACADEMIC POWER STRATEGY

Assess and improve your study habits by becoming aware of your learning style. Understanding what your learning style is can help you and your teachers maximize use of the learning strategies that you are most comfortable with and can help you understand what works best for you.

There are four types of learning styles corresponding to the principal senses: auditory (hearing), visual (sight), kinesthetic (touch), and mixed modality (all three). You may favor one of these over the others.

Educators talk about differences in learning styles—the ways in which people acquire knowledge. Some students learn well by listening to lectures. Others learn better through reading, class discussion, hands-on experience, or researching a topic and writing about it. Thus, your particular learning style may make you more comfortable with some kinds of teaching and learning, and even with some kinds of subjects, than with others.

Apply the Strategy

1. To find out the ways you learn best, fill out the Learning Styles Survey (Appendix H) on page 247.

2. After you complete the survey, read about the four learning styles on page 248 for an explanation of what your scores mean.

Source: Adapted from *Learning Success*, 1st edition, by C. M. Wahlstrom and B. K. Williams. © 1996. Reprinted with permission of Wadsworth Publishing, a division of Thomson Learning. Fax 800-730-2215.

TUNING IN: "Toy Barriers and Thai Food Wars"

You will watch two short CNN video clips that illustrate the pervasiveness of what Alain Modoux calls American industrial culture. However, you will see that American "exports" don't always receive

© CNN

automatic consumer interest and approval. In the first video clip, you will see how American toy manufacturers have to adapt their products to reach an international audience, and in the second video clip you will see how Thai entrepreneurs have figured out a way to compete with American fast-food restaurants.

Vocabulary in the Video

Take a look at the following list and briefly discuss unfamiliar vocabulary with your teacher.

Phrases	Meanings
children reject this toy in favor of that one	
that toy bombed	
kids are still mystified	
some customers are reluctant	
a half-time show	
fast-food outlets	
American fast-food giants	
a very important step on the socioeconomic ladder	
as they gravitate from hawker food and local fare	

Phrases	Meanings
we sell a concept	
local entrepreneurs	
small individual food stands	
to capture the youth market	

Watch the Videos

Watch the two video clips at least two times. First, just watch. Second, write down some notes in each category below. From this information, you and your group will create four questions to ask other groups.

From the first clip	Notes
Identical toys around the world	
not all toys are multinational	
From the second clip	**Notes**
Western fast food in Thailand	
Fast-food—Thai style	
Thai-style fast food: advantages	

When Coca-Cola was introduced in China in the 1920's, the translated meaning of the brand name was "bite the wax tadpole!" Sales were not good, and the symbols were later changed to mean "happiness in the mouth."

—*CONSUMER BEHAVIOR AND MARKETING STRATEGY*

◆ **Talk About It**

With your group and using your notes, create four questions. Two should be comprehension questions, and two should ask for students' opinions on the topic discussed in the videos. Write the four questions on one sheet of paper. Then exchange questions with another group. Follow these steps:

- Have a discussion as you and the members of your group answer the other group's questions orally. Choose one student to write short notes on the paper with the questions.

- Combine the two groups. Tell the other group what your group said in answer to their questions. Refer to the notes if necessary.

PUTTING IT ALL TOGETHER

◆ **Public Speaking**

Information Speech

The purpose of this presentation is to give a 5–7-minute talk in which you teach your classmates about someone or something interesting from your native culture.

Preparation

1. Choose a topic that reflects some aspect of your native culture:

- Talk about a person from your culture—a popular author, musician, artist, dancer, etc., or a historical figure—and explain who that person is and why he or she is important.

or

- Talk about a particular custom or event that is important in your culture, and explain its significance.

2. Collect information about your topic. You may already know quite a bit, or you may need to do some research so that you will have enough information for your talk. Go to a library, search the Web, or interview appropriate people.

3. Prepare your talk. When you organize your information, ask yourself "What do I want my listeners to understand or know about the significance of the person, custom, or event I have chosen to talk about?"

4. Remember that people have different learning styles. Use appropriate aids to help you communicate effectively. Will you use an overhead transparency? The chalkboard? A written handout? Photographs or slides? A chart? A physical model? Will you show a video clip? Play something from an audiotape? Demonstrate how to do something?

LANGUAGE LEARNING STRATEGY

Apply the Strategy

Record yourself speaking as a way to get self-feedback on the content and delivery of your presentations. This will help you focus on areas you need to improve.

1. Record yourself as you practice your information speech. Time your speech.

2. Listen to the tape. Evaluate your speech by answering the following questions:

   a. Was the main idea of my speech clearly stated in the beginning?

   b. Did I give enough details to clarify the main idea?

   c. Was the information well organized?

   d. Did I speak clearly, at a moderate speed?

   e. Did I pause appropriately between thought groups?

   f. Did I use the time effectively? (Did I run out of time, or did I stop too quickly? Did I try to communicate too much information, too little information, or just the right amount? Did I balance well the amount of time I spent talking about each point?)

   g. Did I end the speech smoothly or abruptly? Was the ending effective?

   h. Did I sound prepared but natural?

   i. Did I communicate what I wanted to communicate? If not, why not?

3. Decide what changes you want to make, and practice your speech again.

Presentation

1. Present your information speech to your classmates. You should use notes, but do not read a prepared speech. Use the visual or audio aids that you decided will help you communicate the information.

2. After you finish, ask the audience "What questions do you have?"

3. Evaluate your presentation by using the speech self evaluation form in Appendix G.

Listening Log Report

Bring your Listening Log to class and report on one entry in a small group.

Search the Web

Learn more about issues related to American cultural dominance by searching the Web. Possible key words: McDonald's/France, popular American culture, exporting American culture, cultural imperialism.

Test-Taking Tip

Read test questions completely and carefully before giving an answer. If you answer a question that you have only read very quickly, there is a chance you will not answer the question to the best of your ability.

CHECK YOUR PROGRESS

On a scale of 1 to 5, rate how well you have mastered the goals set at the beginning of the chapter:

1 2 3 4 5   learn about different points of view regarding the "exportation" of American culture.

1 2 3 4 5   learn vocabulary related to the topic of the dominance of American culture.

1 2 3 4 5   learn how to choose an English–English dictionary that works for you.

1 2 3 4 5 learn how to pause between thought groups when speaking.

1 2 3 4 5 assess and improve your study habits by becoming aware of your learning style.

1 2 3 4 5 record yourself speaking as a way to get self-feedback on your presentations.

If you have given yourself a 3 or lower on any of these goals:

- visit the *Tapestry* web site for additional practice.
- ask your instructor for extra help.
- review the sections of the chapter that you found difficult.
- work with a partner or study group to further your progress.

- What qualities do you think are most important in a doctor/patient relationship?

- How important do you consider honesty to be?

MEDICAL ETHICS: SHOULD DOCTORS EVER LIE?

To tell or not to tell? Doctors continually debate various aspects of this question. Is it ever acceptable for doctors to mislead patients about their condition or about the treatment they are receiving? Is it acceptable for doctors to prescribe a placebo*? Who should have access to a patient's medical history and treatment? Do family members have the right to know? What about insurance companies and employers? In this chapter, we will examine these and related issues of medical ethics.

Setting Goals

In this chapter you will learn:

◈ about some of the ethical issues facing doctors and patients, including the use of placebos and genetic testing.

◈ vocabulary related to different aspects of medical ethics.

◈ how to use an English Use Record to help you set language learning goals.

◈ how to use intonation patterns for asking questions.

◈ how to present your ideas in a clear and organized manner.

◈ how you can expand your vocabulary on a specific topic.

*A placebo is a sugar pill or other treatment containing no medication that doctors give to reinforce a patient's expectation of getting medication to make him or her get well. The patient thinks that he or she is getting actual medication and does not know that the "medication" is not real.

◆**Getting Started**

Doctors do not know much about how or why placebos are effective with some patients. Many think that the expectation of a patient that a medication will work has a powerful effect on the body.

1. Do you believe in the power of placebos? Why or why not?

2. If a doctor gives a patient a placebo instead of a real drug, do you think the doctor is being dishonest?

LISTENING 1:
PLACEBOS—HOW EFFECTIVE ARE THEY?

◆**Getting Ready to Listen**

The following case study involving the use of a placebo with a patient has been given to doctors in training. Read the case and then, in small groups, discuss the questions that follow the reading. Designate one person to take notes and report the results of your discussion to the rest of the class.

Case

1 A seventeen-year-old girl visited her pediatrician, who had been taking care of her since infancy. She went to his office without her parents, although her mother had made the appointment for her over the telephone. She told the pediatrician that she was very healthy, but that she thought she had some emotional problems. She stated that she was having trouble sleeping at night, that she was very nervous most of the day. She was a senior in high school and claimed she was doing quite poorly in some of her subjects. She was worried about what she was going to do next year. She was somewhat overweight. This, she felt, was part of her problem. She claimed she was not very attractive to the opposite sex and could not seem to "get boys interested in me." She had a few close friends of the same sex.

2   Her life at home was quite disorganized and stressful. There were frequent fights with her younger brother, who was fourteen, and with her parents. She claimed her parents were always criticizing her. She described her mother as extremely inflexible and her father as a disciplinarian, who was quite old-fashioned in his values.

3   In all, she spent about twenty minutes talking with her pediatrician. She told him that what she thought she really needed was tranquilizers,[1] and that was the reason she came. She felt that this

[1]**tranquilizers:** drugs used for reducing anxiety and nervousness

> The word *placebo* comes from the Latin *placere*, which means "to please."

was an extremely difficult year for her, and if she could have something to calm her nerves until she got over her current crises, everything would go better.

4   The pediatrician told her that he did not really believe in giving tranquilizers to a girl of her age. He said he thought it would be a very bad precedent for her to establish. She got very insistent, however, and claimed that if he did not give her tranquilizers, she would "get them somehow." Finally, he agreed to call her pharmacy and order medication for her nerves. She accepted graciously. He suggested that she call him in a few days to let him know how things were going. He also called her parents to say that he had a talk with her and he was giving her some medicine that might help her nerves.

5   Five days later, the girl called the pediatrician back to say that the pills were working really well. She claimed that she had calmed down a great deal, that she was working things out better with her parents, and had a new outlook on life. He suggested that she keep taking them twice a day for the rest of the school year. She agreed.

6   A month later, the girl ran out of pills and called her pediatrician for a refill. She found that he was away on vacation. She seemed quite upset at not having any medication left, so she called her uncle who was a surgeon in the next town. He called the pharmacy to renew her pills and, in speaking to the druggist, found out they were only vitamins and that she could get them over the counter[2] and didn't really need him to refill them. The girl became very distraught, feeling that she had been deceived and betrayed by her pediatrician. Her parents, when they heard, commented that they thought the pediatrician was "very clever."

Source: Reprinted by permission of Dr. Melvin Levine

Discussion Questions

1. What choices did the pediatrician have in treating the teenage girl? What could the potential consequences of those choices be?

2. Do you think he handled the situation well?

3. Do you think the consequences of the pediatrician's actions were harmful or harmless?

4. What should he have done once he learned that the girl had discovered that the prescription was merely for vitamins?

◈ **Vocabulary Building**

The following sentences come from the short talk you are about to listen to. Use context and background to guess the meaning of the boldface words.

[2]**over the counter:** without a doctor's prescription

1. A placebo is an imitation medicine that a doctor may give to calm an anxious patient or **to placate a persistent patient** who continues to demand medicine that the doctor is reluctant to give.

   to placate a persistent patient = _____

2. By imitation, I mean that the so-called medicine looks authentic but in reality has no **pharmacological substances,** no drugs in it.

   pharmacological substances = _____

3. Doctors know that even more than the actual prescription, it's **the prescription slip**—that little piece of paper with the magic writing on it—that is the vital ingredient that helps many patients get rid of whatever is ailing them.

   the prescription slip = _____

4. Many patients who seek medical help are suffering from **disorders** that the body **can heal by itself.** They don't need anything extra to get well.

   disorders = _____

   can heal by itself = _____

5. After he got better, Mr. Smith read some medical reports that the treatment was a fake remedy. He **suffered a relapse,** and the tumors reappeared.

   suffered a relapse = _____

6. Researchers carried out controlled studies on heart patients. They gave them a new drug for **angina** and found that it was no better than a placebo.

   angina = _____

7. There was a study done in which patients with **identical symptoms**—they all had bleeding ulcers—were divided into two groups.

   identical symptoms = _____

Words and Phrases You Will Hear

Often, seeing words and phrases before you hear them can help your listening comprehension. Take a look at the following list and briefly discuss any unfamiliar items with your teacher.

Treatment and Recovery

painkillers

to get well

name-brand pill

serious medical intervention

therapeutic

to be hospitalized

serum

immunizations

injection

a fake remedy

to work wonders

to maximize the effect

to provide relief

experimental drug

General Terms

ailing

to seek medical help

to suffer from

disorders

on his deathbed

medical reports

to suffer a relapse

Medical Conditions

cancer

tumors

bleeding ulcers

Listen

Listening 1: Placebos—How Effective Are They?

Listen for the Main Idea

The short talk that you are about to listen to is divided into three parts. Listen to each section to find out the main idea. After each part, when you hear a beep, stop the tape and circle a, b, or c.

Part 1

a. Patients feel less anxious and worried when they know they are receiving a placebo.

b. Doctors recognize that placebos have a true therapeutic value.

c. Doctors believe common drugs are no longer effective in curing many diseases.

Part 2

a. Studies show that belief in recovery is a powerful force in helping a patient get well.

b. Placebos don't work in curing certain types of terminal illnesses.

c. There are many strange cases of recovery from an illness that science can't explain.

Part 3

a. Medical studies have been unable to determine why placebos are effective.

b. For a placebo to work, a doctor must have a neutral attitude towards the patient.

c. The doctor/patient relationship can influence the effectiveness of a placebo.

Compare your answers to those of a partner or your class.

Listen for More Information

Listen to the short talk again for more information about placebos. Write T (true) or F (false) in front of each sentence. Base your answers on what you hear in the passage.

Part 1

_____ 1. Doctors don't like to give placebos.

_____ 2. Placebos contain no drugs.

_____ 3. A patient's belief is as important as the actual drug received.

_____ 4. Most people who see a doctor need serious medical help.

_____ 5. A doctor sometimes prescribes placebos to make a patient less worried.

Part 2

_____ 1. Mr. Smith asked for a blood transfusion to get rid of his tumors.

_____ 2. After receiving an injection of horse serum, Mr. Smith's health improved.

_____ 3. After Mr. Smith read a second article saying the horse serum didn't work, his doctor convinced him that the information was unreliable.

_____ 4. The doctor gave Mr. Smith a second injection of horse serum.

_____ 5. Mr. Smith died after he was told that the doctor had not injected him with horse serum.

_____ 6. Most people respond to placebos at one time or another.

Part 3

_____ 1. A doctor's attitude can make a treatment work better.

_____ 2. The patients in the ulcer study had different symptoms.

_____ 3. The patients in the ulcer study were given the same instructions and information.

_____ 4. One group of patients was given a placebo, and the other group was given an experimental drug.

_____ 5. The patients who did better had more enthusiastic doctors.

_____ 6. A drug's usefulness depends on what drugs it contains.

Listen and Take Notes

Use the "split-page format" described on page 35 in Chapter 2 to take notes as you listen again to the same material.

• Take out a piece of paper and copy what is written on the following sample page. The underlined headings are included to help you take notes. Copy them before you listen to the tape, but leave plenty of space after each heading so that you will have room to write details.

QUESTIONS/IDEAS	NOTES: PLACEBOS
	What Is a Placebo?
	Reasons Doctors Give Placebos
	Power of Belief (Mr. Smith Story)
	Doctor's Role in Placebo Effectiveness
	Ulcer Study
	Conclusions

- As you listen, write only in the Notes column. Indent your notes to show the organization of what you hear. Main points should start farthest to the left. Specific information that comes after each main point should be below and indented a little bit to the right. Also, you can use capital letters and underlining to indicate the most important points.

For note-taking tips regarding abbreviations and signals, see Appendix A.

⬦ After You Listen

1. Reread your notes. Add ideas and questions to the left column.

2. Listen again and add more details to your notes.

3. Using only your notes, orally reconstruct the short talk in your own words. Work with a partner and take turns presenting your oral reconstruction.

Write a one-paragraph summary of the interview. Refer only to your notes. Be sure to use your own words. Refer to Appendix B for guidelines on paraphrasing and Appendix C for guidelines on summarizing.

- Your first sentence should contain the main idea of the passage.

- In subsequent sentences, include the main points and some of the details.

LANGUAGE LEARNING STRATEGY

Apply the Strategy

Keep track of when, where, and how much you use English by using an English Use Record. This will help you find ways to maximize your opportunities to use the language skills that you want to improve most.

1. First, look at the following English Use Record kept by one student who wants to improve her listening and speaking skills in English. What do you think she is doing well? What else could she be doing to improve her listening and speaking skills?

EXAMPLE OF ENGLISH USE RECORD

MONDAY:
—watched TV news (1 hr.); focused on announcer's intonation
—had coffee with classmates from Mexico and Japan (35 min.)
—computer science class; listened to lecture (50 min.)
—talked with an American classmate about homework after computer science class (15 min.)
—saw a free film at the Boston Public Library (1hr. 40 min.)

TUESDAY:
—asked librarian where to find information for class project (5 min.)
—ESL class (2 hrs.)
—worked on ESL class project with classmates (1 hr. 20 min.)
—watched evening news, took notes for listening log (20 min.)
—talked on phone to Brazilian, American, and French friends (45 min.)

WEDNESDAY:
—listened to tapes in the language lab (1 hr.)
—went to computer science class; took notes on lecture (50 min.)
—listened to NPR (1 hour) and later talked to friend about an NPR story about an alternative school (35 min.); monitored for past tense
—called airline company to make reservations (7 min.)

THURSDAY:
—listened to the radio news (30 min.)
—went to ESL class (2 hrs.)
—watched TV program about unsolved mysteries (1hr.); took notes on words I couldn't understand

FRIDAY:
—listened to news on radio (30 min.)
—went to computer science class and listened & took notes (50 min.)
—asked the professor some questions after class (10 min.)
—watched the movie "A Room With a View" (2 hrs.)
—talked with friends about movie (1 hr.)

SATURDAY:
—spent all day on Cape Cod with friends from ESL class; spoke English together (6 hours); talked to American on beach (45 min.)
—watched the movie "Star Wars" (2 hrs.)
—talked with my landlady (45 min.)

SUNDAY:
—worked on ESL class project w/classmates (2 hrs.)
—listened to the radio news (30 min.); focused on past tense (10 min.)
—watched "60 Minutes" on TV and took notes on one of the stories for my listening log (1 hr.); had difficulty w/vocabulary
—talked to American friend; tried to use new vocabulary (40 min.)

What I will try to do next week: try to increase by 15 min. the amount of time I speak English each day and try to begin conversations with some of the American students in my computer science class. Also monitor myself for correct use of past tense.

(continued on next page)

2. For one week, keep a daily record of the time you spend using English. Write down all the times you use English in any way, and describe what you did and for how long. At the end of the week, analyze your record and write down two or three things you can realistically do to increase the amount of time you *listen to and speak* English in the coming week. Each week, set a goal for how much time you intend to spend practicing your English.

3. Keep a record for several weeks. At the end of each week, review your record of when, where, and how much you used English and how well you met that week's goal.

LISTENING 2: NPR INTERVIEW— SHOULD DOCTORS EVER LIE?

Getting Ready to Listen

You are about to listen to an interview in which National Public Radio medical commentators Dr. Miriam Shuchman and Dr. Michael Wilkes give their views on whether or not doctors should ever lie to their patients. You have already read and discussed a case on the ethics of deceiving a patient and taken notes on and summarized a short talk on placebos. The reading and short talk have provided you with some background knowledge of the topics explored in the interview you are about to listen to. Before you listen, briefly discuss the following questions with a partner:

- Do you think prescribing a placebo is the same as lying to a patient?

- Do you think it is OK for a doctor to lie to a patient?

Vocabulary Building

The following sentences contain vocabulary that you will hear in the interview. Read through the sentences and guess the meanings of any words or phrases that you don't know from their context. In the space at the left, write the letter of the word or phrase from the list that can be substituted in each sentence.

_____ 1. There are actually several situations when a doctor might **be tempted to be** less than truthful with a patient.

_____ 2. There are times when a doctor might want **to paint a more optimistic or rosy picture of** a patient's condition so that the patient won't be unnecessarily frightened.

_____ 3. Some people believe that **to withhold** information from a person is the same as outright lying. In both cases, the doctor is **being paternalistic** by not allowing the patient the right to know and decide.

_____ 4. A patient came to see the doctor to get a refill of a prescription for a sleeping pill. The patient recognized that he was **addicted to** the sleeping medicine, but when he tried to stop taking the medicine, he couldn't sleep and **ended up** taking a sleeping pill. Later the doctor tried **to wean the patient from the medicine.**

_____ 5. Chemotherapy has several **side effects,** including physical weakness and loss of hair.

_____ 6. A doctor's cultural, religious, educational, and economic background shapes how she interprets the world around her. This background acts like a filter that changes and shapes how she **perceives** things.

_____ 7. An important issue is whether doctors are ever justified in telling little **white lies** to benefit a patient. Is it right to ever **deceive** a patient?

a. resulted in

b. understands

c. to describe in very positive terms

d. treating people in an overly fatherly way

e. to stop his dependency over a period of time

f. to keep

g. harmless untruths that don't hurt anyone

h. desire to be

i. undesirable effects in addition to the intended one

j. unable to free himself from the habit of taking

k. mislead

People in the United States use first names in addressing each other at times that might surprise you. For example, in the interview you will hear, the interviewer calls both doctors by their first names. She does this because they are colleagues of hers and appear regularly on the radio with her; thus, she is well acquainted with them. Would you ever call a colleague, a doctor, or another professional person by his or her first name in your native country? Why or why not?

Listen (Part I)

Listening 2: Should Doctors Ever Lie?

You will listen to the two doctors discussing the pros and cons of a doctor lying to a patient. After you listen to Part I, stop the tape and complete the chart.

WHY A DOCTOR MIGHT DECEIVE A PATIENT	WHY A DOCTOR SHOULDN'T DECEIVE A PATIENT

After You Listen

Compare your notes with a partner. Decide if there is anything you want to add or take out. Listen again, and add details you missed during the first listening.

Listen (Part II)

Listening 2: Should Doctors Ever Lie?

- Read the following questions.
- Listen to Part II. After you listen, answer the questions. Write short notes on the lines.

1. Why did the old man come to Michael for help?

_____

_____

2. Why did another doctor suggest that Michael give the old man a placebo?

_____

_____

3. What does Miriam think is the conflict for a doctor in Michael's situation?

_____

_____

4. Should people be concerned that their doctor might be giving them a placebo? Why or why not?

_____

_____

5. How often do doctors lie to their patients?

_____

_____

6. What kind of treatment did Michael end up giving the old man?

_____

_____

After You Listen

Compare your answers to those of a partner. Decide if there is anything you want to change. Listen again, and add information you missed during the first listening.

Talk About It

1. Imagine that you are telling a friend about the interview with the two doctors you just heard. Using your notes, summarize the main points made in the interview and give your opinion of what the two medical commentators said. Work with a partner and take turns presenting your summary reactions.

   • Begin your summary reaction by saying, "I heard an interesting interview on the radio today. Two doctors were discussing whether or not a doctor is ever justified in lying to a patient. . . ."

   • Explain briefly the main issues raised.

   • Give your opinion.

2. Look at this cartoon. What do you think makes it funny?

"If this doesn't help you don't worry, it's a placebo."

© 1999 P. C. Vey from cartoonbank.com. All Rights Reserved.

The Sound of It: Intonation Patterns in Questions

The interviewer uses two kinds of questions—information (*WH*) questions and Yes/No questions. Her intonation changes slightly for each type of question. Note also a third type of question, called a "tag" question.

INTONATION IN QUESTIONS

Information (*WH*) Questions

End with falling intonation. The stressed syllable of the last word that you want to stress should receive high intonation. After that, your voice will go down.

Yes/No Questions

End with rising intonation.

Tag Questions or

Start out with a statement and end with a short yes/no question. Use falling intonation if you are quite sure of the response you will receive, if you are expecting the listener to confirm what you have said. Use rising intonation if you are unsure.

Source: from *All Clear! Advanced* by Helen Kalkstein Fragiadakis, Heinle and Heinle Publishers, Copyright 1997.

---

1. Here are information and Yes/No questions that the interviewer asked. Using the guidelines above, mark where you need to use rising and falling intonation. The first one has been done for you.

   • When might a doctor choose not to tell the truth?

   • Have you ever been tempted to be less than perfectly honest with a patient?

- As an ethics specialist, what do you say? What does medical ethics tell us is right in this situation?

- Should people be concerned when they go to their doctor that the doctor might be prescribing a placebo?

- We talked about placebos, but what about lying? How often do doctors lie to their patients?

- What happened to the man who was hooked on the sleeping pill?

2. Practice asking the interviewer's questions with a partner.

3. Practice asking tag questions, using the content of the interview for your questions.

Examples

- Michael decided to stop giving the patient sleeping pills, didn't he?

- Miriam doesn't think it's wrong to lie to a patient, does she?

ACADEMIC POWER STRATEGY

When you must speak on the spot (i.e., without having a chance to prepare what you are going to say), use a framework that allows you to sound organized and competent. There are many ways to arrange your thoughts, but one of the most popular ways is called the PREP formula. Short for *preparation,* this plan requires you to give the following:

(P)   **Point of view:** Provide an overview—a clear direct statement or generalization with your opinion.

(R)   **Reasons:** Give the general reasons that you hold this point of view.

(E)   **Evidence or examples:** Present specific facts or data supporting your point of view.

(P)   **Point of view restated:** To make sure you are understood clearly, end with a restatement of your position.

Let's look at an example of how you might use the PREP formula to answer a question in class:

(continued on next page)

Professor Snodgrass: Do you think the world's governments are working together effectively to make sure we all live in a healthy environment?

You: **(P)**   After listening to yesterday's lecture, yes, I do.

          (R)   I was surprised at the efforts that the United Nations General Assembly has focused on the environment.

          (E)   For example, the industrialized nations have set strict goals on reducing air pollution and greenhouse gases for the year 2010.

          (P)   So yes, the world's governments seem to be concerned and working to improve the situation.

Using a device like the PREP formula, you sound logical, organized, and competent—whether you are communicating with other students in a discussion group, talking to an instructor during office hours, or answering a question in class.*

Apply the Strategy

Give your opinions and thoughts on the two listening passages you have heard. Practice answering the questions using the PREP formula. Work with a partner and take turns.

- Should Mr. Smith's doctor have given him the horse serum?

- Would you ever want to be a participant in a study of a new drug where half the participants get the drug and the other half get a placebo?

- Do you think it is ethical to give a placebo to patients participating in clinical trials of an experimental drug?

- Do you think the effectiveness of placebos might be higher in some cultures than in others?

- Do you agree that it's sometimes OK to lie to a patient?

- Do you think Michael did the right thing by not prescribing a placebo for the old man?

- Do you think doctors should ever lie to a patient?

- If you were a doctor, would you ever lie to a patient?

*Source: From *Your College Experience*, 3rd edition, by J. N. Gardner and A. J. Jewler. © 1997. Reprinted with permission of Wadsworth Publishing, a division of Thomson Learning. Fax 800-730-221.

TUNING IN: "Genetics and Privacy Issues"

© CNN

So far, this chapter has looked at some of the traditional issues of trust between a doctor and a patient. However, doctors and their patients face ever more complex issues of medical ethics with the rapidly growing number of discoveries about the human genome (the collection of all genes). For example, one area of growing concern and debate is that of genetic testing. Scientists are discovering more and more genes that cause specific diseases. However, having one of these genes does not necessarily mean that a person will develop a disease. As a result, there is much controversy surrounding the issues raised by testing for genes that cause diseases. People ask:

- Who should be tested?
- Is it necessarily a good thing for a person who is carrying a gene for a disease to know that he or she is a carrier?
- Who should have access to the information?
- Does genetic testing result in genetic discrimination and bias?

In the video clip you are about to watch, you will learn more about some of the issues involved in genetic testing.

Vocabulary in the Video

With a partner, try to guess the meanings of the following key phrases used in the video clip about genetic testing. If you do not know a word or phrase, try to guess its meaning from context when you watch the video clip.

Phrases	Meanings
if the results became public	
the fear of repercussions	
confiding to her boss	
a search and destroy mission	

PHRASES	MEANINGS
A coalition of government and advocacy groups	
A silent scandal	
To come forward	
The concerns are overblown	
Federal statutes	

Watch the Video

Ethics means the "science of morals." It has a Greek origin.

Watch the video at least two times. First, just watch. Second, write down some notes in each category below. From this information, you and your group will create four questions to ask other groups.

Reasons people are worried about genetic testing	
Suggested laws against genetic discrimination	
Genetic bias in the workplace	
Anti-gene discrimination laws exist	

◆Talk About It

With your group and using your notes, create four questions. Two should be comprehension questions, and two should be for students' opinions on the controversy about genetic testing. Write the four questions on one sheet of paper. Then exchange questions with another group. Follow these steps:

- Have a discussion as you and the members of your group answer the other group's questions orally. Choose one student to write short notes on the paper with the questions.

- Combine the two groups. Tell the other group what your group said in answer to their questions. Refer to the notes if necessary.

LANGUAGE LEARNING STRATEGY

Learn as many words as you can related to a particular topic. In this way, you can expand your vocabulary and express your ideas in precise and varied ways. When you read about a topic, pay special attention to the topic-specific vocabulary used. Learn these new words and use them when you talk or write about the subject.

Apply the Strategy

1. In this chapter you have encountered numerous words and phrases that are used when talking about illness and healing:

> placebo, medicine, patient, pills, painkillers, prescription, ailing, drug, disorders, heal, physician, doctor, therapeutic, to suffer from, illness, cancer, hospitalized, tumors, serum, immunizations, disease, injection, remedy, relapse, treatment, cure, symptoms, bleeding ulcers, relief, angina, to be diagnosed with, to undergo a treatment, addiction, behavior modification, pediatrician, tranquilizers, pharmacy, druggist, surgeon, over the counter, genetic testing, genetic discrimination, genetic bias

Choose 10 new words or phrases from the list that you want to make part of your active vocabulary. Make a vocabulary card for each word using the Vocabulary Study Card system you

(continued on next page)

learned in Chapter 3. Keep the cards handy and review them periodically.

2. Choose a story that is currently in the news. Read a newspaper article about it and make vocabulary cards for topic-specific words. Listen to the story the same day on the TV or radio news to reinforce vocabulary related to the topic. Practice telling the news story using the specific vocabulary.

PUTTING IT ALL TOGETHER

Guest Speaker

Invite a guest speaker from a nursing department, a local hospital, or a medical school to talk about medical ethics issues. Follow the steps for inviting a guest speaker in Appendix E.

Public Speaking

Speaking on the Spot

Bring five notecards to class with each one listing a question on which your classmates would have an opinion. For example:

- Should animals be used in experiments testing new drug treatments?

- Is telling a white lie ever justified?

Your instructor will collect the cards and place one card face down on each student's desk. One at a time, each student will turn over his or her card and answer whatever question is written there by using the PREP formula on page 133. You may not turn your card over until the person before you begins to speak.

Listening Log Report

Bring your Listening Log to class and report on one entry in a small group.

Search the Web

Learn more about medical ethics by searching the Web. Possible key words: medical ethics, Hastings Institute, gene therapy, placebos, genetic testing, genetic discrimination.

Test-Taking Tip

Use the following strategies for True/False questions:

- True/False questions that contain absolutes like a*lways, never, none,* or *all* tend to be false.
- True/False questions that contain qualifiers like *generally* or *often* are often true.
- If any part of the True/False question is false, the entire statement is false.
- If a True/False question contains a confusing double negative, cross out both negatives to simplify the question before you choose your answer.

CHECK YOUR PROGRESS

On a scale of 1 to 5, rate how well you have mastered the goals set at the beginning of the chapter:

1 2 3 4 5   learn about some of the ethical issues facing doctors and patients, including the use of placebos and genetic testing.

1 2 3 4 5   learn vocabulary related to different aspects of medical ethics.

1 2 3 4 5   learn how to use an English Use Record to help you set language learning goals.

1 2 3 4 5   learn how to use intonation patterns for asking questions.

1 2 3 4 5   learn how to present your ideas in a clear and organized manner.

1 2 3 4 5   learn how you can expand your vocabulary on a specific topic.

If you have given yourself a 3 or lower on any of these goals:

- visit the *Tapestry* web site for additional practice.
- ask your instructor for extra help.
- review the sections of the chapter that you found difficult.
- work with a partner or study group to further your progress.

- What is your reaction to this picture?
- Can you identify with its message? Why or why not?

7

THE TIME BIND— ARE TWENTY-FOUR HOURS A DAY ENOUGH?

School, work, kids, traffic. Stress. No time. So many people in modern society are in this *time bind*. What a surprise, after hearing for years and years that with modern inventions we would have more leisure time. In this chapter, we will talk about the stresses of work and family and look at time management as a way to deal with our busy lives.

Setting Goals

In this chapter you will learn:

◈ about how people today balance work and family.

◈ vocabulary related to work and time.

◈ how to be a more active and supportive member of a discussion group.

◈ to use a clear native-speaker model to practice and improve your pronunciation.

◈ to identify unstressed words in natural speech.

◈ to analyze how you manage your time.

◆**Getting Started**

1. Do you and your classmates have busy lives? Do you find your-selves exhausted at the end of the day? Find out about two of your classmates by completing the chart below.

	Student One	Student Two
How many classes are you taking?		
Do you have a job? If so, how many hours do you work a week?		
Do you have children? If so, how many? How old are they?		
When do you have free time?		
Do you get enough sleep every night?		
Do you have enough time to study and do homework?		
What is more relaxing for you—to be at work, at school, or at home? Why?		

2. The chart below relates to the last question. Write the chart on the board and add the necessary information. Discuss the results with your class.

REASONS

Students Who Said Work Is More Relaxing	
Students Who Said School Is More Relaxing	
Students Who Said Home Is More Relaxing	

People in the United States often refer to the "work ethic." This idea about the importance of work comes from early Protestant settlers. Hundreds of years ago, these settlers believed that hard work brought them closer to God. This belief about the value of hard work became an important part of American culture. It may even explain why so many people ask "What do you do?" when they meet someone new. For them, work helps explain who people are. How important is work viewed in your native culture?

How do the following proverbs reflect the American work ethic? Do you have any similar proverbs in your native language?

- Early to bed, early to rise, makes a man healthy, wealthy, and wise.
- Don't put off to tomorrow what you can do today.
- Keep your nose to the grindstone.
- Work never hurt anybody.
- Another day, another dollar.
- You never get anything for nothing.
- Anything worth doing is worth doing well.

LISTENING: THE TIME BIND

Getting Ready to Listen   Read the following review of a book by sociology professor, Arlie Hochschild.

Home Work Time

1 Why are we working more and spending less time at home? Arlie Hochschild has discovered some surprising reasons.
                                                        by Marilyn Snell

2 In her latest book, *The Time Bind: When Work Becomes Home and Home Becomes Work* (New York: Metropolitan Books, 1997), UC Berkeley sociologist Arlie Hochschild takes a detective's eye to the problem of what's keeping parents at work so long. What she discovered were men and women apparently happily married to their jobs and not the least inclined to[1] take advantage of family-

[1]**not the least inclined to:** not at all interested in

friendly company policies—programs that would have allowed employees to spend more time at home.

3   Hochschild, who made waves[2] with *The Second Shift*—her groundbreaking[3] 1989 book on gender roles[4] in two-career marriages—this time spent three summers observing employees of a Fortune 500 company[5] she calls "Amerco" to protect the privacy of those she studied. She chose the Northeastern manufacturer precisely for its reputation as a good place for parents to work: A 1991 survey by the Families and Work Institute named it one of the 10 most family-friendly companies in the U.S.

4   After visiting company-sponsored childcare centers, tagging along[6] on errands with stressed-out,[7] upper-management moms, and interviewing employees in all sectors of the company—from "Bill," a high-ranking corporate executive, to "Becky," a factory-line worker—Hochschild discovered myriad ways[8] in which the home is being invaded by the pressures of work, while the workplace is becoming a haven[9] from a hectic,[10] unrewarding home life. Her findings offer eloquent, sad, and sometimes chilling evidence of the "time bind"[11] many employees find themselves in and, more broadly, suggest a disturbing cultural transformation in the way Americans feel about home, family, work, and even time itself.

Source: May/June 1997 issue of *Mother Jones* © Foundation for National Progress

> According to lexicographer Harry Collis, one of the 101 proverbs most frequently used in the United States is "There's no place like home." Similar proverbs: "Home is where the heart is" and "Home, sweet home."

With a partner, paraphrase this sentence from the third paragraph by using some of the definitions provided after the reading. After you finish, discuss whether you agree or disagree with Dr. Hochschild's findings:

. . . Hochschild discovered myriad ways in which the home is being invaded by the pressures of work, while the workplace is becoming a haven from a hectic, unrewarding home life.

_____

_____

[2]**made waves:** caused a reaction
[3]**groundbreaking:** original, new
[4]**gender roles:** roles of boys and girls and men and women
[5]**a Fortune 500 company:** one of the top 500 American businesses
[6]**tagging along:** going with others, but as an extra person
[7]**stressed-out:** very nervous and tense
[8]**myriad ways:** a great deal of ways
[9]**a haven:** a safe place
[10]**hectic:** very busy
[11]**the time bind:** to be in a bind is to have a problem; to be in a "time bind" is to have a problem because you don't have enough time

Words and Phrases You Will Hear

Often, seeing words and phrases before you hear them can help your listening comprehension. Take a look at the following list and briefly discuss any unfamiliar items with your teacher.

Good Things About Work

recognition ceremonies

an affirming network of people

motivational programs

work in teams

a vanguard family-friendly company

job sharing

Problems We Face

a particularly frustrating predicament

it wasn't something we were conscious of

pink slip

the obstacle in the way

How We Face Problems

seek refuge

social supports

pals

 **Listen (Part I)**

The Time Bind

You will hear an interview of Dr. Hochschild conducted by Terry Gross, host of the radio program *Fresh Air*®. Listen first to Gross's introduction, and then try to explain in your own words what this means: ". . . now many mothers are also seeking refuge at work from the demands of family life."

_____

_____

_____

_____

Vocabulary Building

You will hear the following sentences in the interview. Try to guess the meanings of the boldface words and phrases. Use the hints to help you guess.

1. There were so many marriages breaking up. It seems you can get your **pink slip** at home. . . . Home doesn't mean security the way it once did.

   Hint: When people are laid off or fired at work, it is often known as being given the "pink slip."

   pink slip = _____

2. It was a . . . company that offered **paternity leave**. . . . It offered **flex-time**. . . . It offered **flex-place**.

   Hints: "Maternity leave" is (sometimes paid) time off given to women when they have a baby. And "flex" comes from the word "flexible."

   paternity leave = _____

   flex-time = _____

   flex-place = _____

3. For a lot of companies, family-friendly policies are **a fig leaf** on top of a highly **workaholic culture**.

   Hints: In the Bible, Adam and Eve used leaves from a fig tree to cover themselves in the Garden of Eden; an "alcoholic" is a person who is dependent on alcohol.

   a fig leaf = _____

   workaholic culture = _____

Listen (Part II)

The Time Bind

Listen for the Main Idea

Listen to the interview. Then write one sentence that summarizes the main idea:

_____

_____

_____

_____

Listen for More Information

Listen to the interview again. Write information that you can catch about work on the left side of the chart. Write information about home on the right side of the chart. Listen again if necessary, and then compare your chart with the chart of another student.

AT WORK	AT HOME

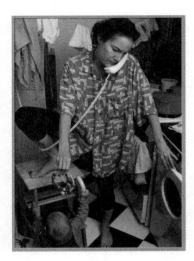

Listen and Take Notes

Use the "split-page format" described on page 35 in Chapter 2 to take notes as you listen again to the same material.

- Take out a piece of paper and copy what is written on the sample on the next page. The underlined headings are included to help you take notes. Copy them before you listen to the interview, but be sure to leave plenty of space after each heading so that you will have room to write details.

QUESTIONS/IDEAS	NOTES: TIME BIND
	Women at Home
	Women at Work
	What Companies Offer
	Marriages
	Family-Friendly Policies
	Surprising Findings

- As you listen, write *only* in the Notes column. Indent your notes to show the organization of what you hear. Main points should start farthest to the left. Specific information that comes after each main point should be written below and indented a little bit to the right. Also, you can use capital letters and underlining to indicate the most important points.

For note-taking tips regarding abbreviations and signals, see Appendix A.

After You Listen

1. Reread your notes. Add ideas and questions to the left column.

2. Compare notes with a partner.

3. Using your notes, orally answer the following questions with your partner:

   a. How did some of the women that Dr. Hochschild interviewed feel about work and home?

   b. According to Dr. Hochschild, what are some things that work can offer that can't be found at home?

   c. What surprised Dr. Hochschild about the use of family-friendly benefits?

> Hard work spotlights the character of people: some turn up their sleeves, some turn up their noses, and some don't turn up at all.
>
> —SAM EWIG

4. Using only your notes, orally reconstruct Part II with a partner. Each of you should reconstruct half of Part II.

Write a one-paragraph summary of the interview. Refer only to your notes. Be sure to use your own words. Refer to Appendix B for guidelines on paraphrasing and Appendix C for guidelines on summarizing.

- Your first sentence should both introduce Dr. Hochschild and contain the main idea of the interview. Because many people don't know Dr. Hochschild, it will be necessary to explain who she is by using an appositive: "Dr. Arlie Hochschild, *a sociology professor at the University of California at Berkeley, . . .*"

- In subsequent sentences, include the main points and some of the details. Remember to use language of attribution because you will be giving the ideas of Dr. Hochschild.

◈ Talk About It

LANGUAGE LEARNING STRATEGY

Become a more active and supportive member of your discussion group. Try to find a balance in the way you participate in a discussion rather than being too quiet or too dominant. Show the members of your group that you are actively listening to them by nodding, making eye contact, asking questions, and smiling when appropriate. If the speaking environment is not comfortable, people will have less courage and confidence to speak. It is important for all students in your group to be supportive, active listeners even if they are discussing an issue about which they disagree.

Apply the Strategy

Participate actively in a discussion of Dr. Hochschild's and others' views regarding the attitudes that people have about work and home. Read the following Group Work Questionnaire silently *before* you start the discussion. Then, after your discussion, complete the questionnaire to evaluate how well your group worked together.

(continued on next page)

GROUP WORK QUESTIONNAIRE

1. What one word would you use to describe how the group worked together? _____

2. What one word would describe the way you would have liked the group to work together? _____

3. Did everybody participate?

    Always   Usually   Occasionally   Rarely   Never

4. Did you try to help each other feel able to talk and say what each one thought?

    Always   Usually   Occasionally   Rarely   Never

5. Did you listen to each other?

    Always   Usually   Occasionally   Rarely   Never

6. Did you show you were listening by nodding at each other?

    Always   Usually   Occasionally   Rarely   Never

7. Did you use such expressions as "That's good" to each other when you liked something?

    Always   Usually   Occasionally   Rarely   Never

8. Did you ask each other questions?

    Always   Usually   Occasionally   Rarely   Never

9. Did you listen and really try to answer those questions?

    Always   Usually   Occasionally   Rarely   Never

10. Did you pay attention to each other?

    Always   Usually   Occasionally   Rarely   Never

11. Did your group stay on the assigned task?

    Always   Usually   Occasionally   Rarely   Never

12. Did any one person do most of the talking?

    Yes   No

13. Was any one person quiet most of the time?

    Yes   No

Source: Adapted from Scarcella and Oxford, 1992. *The Tapestry of Language Learning.* Boston, Mass: Heinle & Heinle, (p. 159); and Aronson, Blaney, Stephan, Sikes, and Snapp, 1978. *The Jigsaw Classroom.* Beverly Hills, California: Sage.

Discussion Topic

Dr. Hochschild found that many employees were not using the family-friendly policies of their company that would allow them to spend more time with their families. Her explanation for this is that

Men are spending more time with the kids than in 1977, but 70% of working mothers and fathers would like more time.

—ABCNEWS.COM

many people find work to be a refuge from the chaos at home, and that they often feel more appreciated at work: "As she sees it, home life has become more like an efficiently run but joyless workplace, while the actual workplace, with its new emphasis on empowerment and teamwork, is more like a family. Among employees she observed, home had become a place filled with incessant demands from noisy children, endless piles of laundry, few tangible rewards, and little time to relax." (Source: *U.S. News & World Report,* May 12, 1997.)

There are, however, people who disagree with Dr. Hochschild's research findings. Read the following opinions and comments from others. Then, in a group, discuss which opinions you agree and disagree with. When you present your opinion, you may want to use the PREP formula that is explained on page 133 in Chapter 6.

Opinions and Comments from Others

_____ Agree _____ Disagree 1. It's not that women are escaping chaos at home. They work long hours because they find their jobs to be very fulfilling: "Surveys have . . . consistently shown that employed women are happier, healthier and feel more valued, even at home, than women who are full-time homemakers." (Source: *Newsweek,* May 12, 1997.)

_____ Agree _____ Disagree 2. The reason employees at Amerco didn't use many of the family-friendly benefits was because they expected to be penalized for not being at work. It wasn't that they didn't want to spend time at home. It was that they were afraid that if they didn't have enough "face time" at work, they would have fewer opportunities for promotion and increased possibilities of being laid off if the company "downsized" (decreased its number of employees to save money).

_____ Agree _____ Disagree 3. Amerco is not a typical American business, so it is difficult to make a generalization about the work habits of American women.

_____ Agree _____ Disagree 4. Other research shows that men and women would work shorter hours if they could:

- Polls from 1985–1995 show that 15 to 17 percent of workers would prefer to work fewer hours even for less money, but they would have to change jobs. (Source: Juliet Schor in *Nieman Reports,* 1995.)

- Of 6,000 workers at Du Pont, 50 percent of women and 45 percent of men took some flex-time to give them more time with their families. (Source: Rosalind C. Barnett and Caryl Rivers in the Fall 1997 issue of *Dissent.*)

Language You Can Use: Discussion Phrases

Giving and Adding Reasons

First of all, . . .
The main reason is . . .
On top of that, . . .
Another reason why . . .
Not only that, but . . .

Asking for Clarification

I don't understand what you mean.
Can you explain . . .?

Arguing

That may be true, but . . .
Maybe, but . . .
Yes, but don't forget that . . .
But don't you think . . .?

Supporting Your Point

In my experience, . . .
In general, most people . . .

When you finish your discussion, choose one person from your group to report the highlights to your class. And remember to fill out the Group Work Questionnaire to evaluate how well your group worked together.

> Women's workday time on chores has decreased by about 1/2 hour per day, to 2.8 hours (since 1977), while men's time has increased by nearly 1 hour to 2.1 hours in 1997.
>
> —ABCNEWS.COM

The Sound of It: Recognizing Unstressed Words in Natural Speech

LANGUAGE LEARNING STRATEGY

Imitate clear native-speaker models to practice and improve your pronunciation. You might want to choose one character from a television program that you would like to imitate. Or you might want to use speakers on the tape that accompanies this book as your models. You can focus on stress, intonation, sounds, or word endings—whatever aspects of pronunciation that you would like to work on.

Apply the Strategy

Use Dr. Hochschild as a model to imitate for sentence stress. Listen to the following segment of the interview. You will notice that while she stresses nouns, verbs, adjectives, and adverbs, she does not stress prepositions and articles. Because these words are usually not stressed, they can be very difficult to hear.

Listen for the unstressed prepositions and articles in Dr. Hochschild's sentences, and write them in the blanks. When you finish, repeat what she says phrase by phrase, being sure not to stress prepositions and articles.

It's as if _____ village had gone _____ work, and when you asked them what it was like being _____ home, they would often say there's _____ lot to do. One woman, _____ example, said: "I come home and put _____ key _____ _____ door and one child hasn't talked _____ anybody all day." Another— _____ baby isn't _____ bed. The dishes are _____ _____ sink, and her husband just kind _____ felt like he was babysitting. He was waiting _____ her to come home, and as soon as she was home, it was all her job.

And she didn't feel appreciated. She didn't feel valued. There weren't any recognition ceremonies _____ her _____ home. So it wasn't something people were intending.

It wasn't something that people were really conscious _____, wasn't _____ sort _____ _____ way _____ seeing family and home life that I think we've been aware _____ before. But this was _____ theme, that home had become _____ kind of _____ workplace, and _____ some _____ _____ people some _____ _____ time, work had become _____ little bit _____ _____ home.

Using another segment of the interview as a dictation, try to write what you hear, one sentence at a time. Check what you have written by looking at the tapescript. Give special attention to whether or not you heard the unstressed words, including prepositions, articles, pronouns, helping verbs, forms of *be,* and conjunctions.

TUNING IN: "Busy Families"

You will watch a CNN video clip about the busy, but organized, Hartman family. They work hard to balance their jobs and family. Before you watch the video, think about how you spend your time.

© CNN

ACADEMIC POWER STRATEGY

Analyze how you manage your time and whether you have enough time to study. In this busy world, it can be very difficult to juggle family, school, work, and many more aspects of life. If you analyze how much time you spend on your various activities, you may find a way to make some useful changes.

Apply the Strategy

Complete the following chart, and then discuss in a group whether you would like to make any changes in the way you manage your time.

STUDYING DO NOT DISTURB!

ACTIVITY	HOURS PER DAY (TYPICAL WEEKDAY)
Class time	_____
Studying	_____
Employment	_____
Travel	
Home to school	_____
Between classes	_____
School to work	_____
Work to home	_____
Other	_____
Total Travel	_____

HOME RESPONSIBILITIES

Shopping   _____

Meals   _____

Housecleaning   _____

Laundry   _____

Other   _____

Total Home   _____

FAMILY RESPONSIBILITIES

General time   _____

Child care   _____

Care for elderly or disabled   _____

Other   _____

Total Family   _____

CIVIC RESPONSIBILITIES

Volunteer work   _____

Other   _____

Total Civic   _____

PERSONAL

Grooming/dressing   _____

Newspaper   _____

Exercise   _____

Rest   _____

Other   _____

Total personal   _____

Total Time for All Responsibilities   _____

Source: From *Your College Experience,* 3rd ed., by J. N. Gardner and A. J. Jewler. © 1997.
Reprinted with permission of Wadsworth Publishing Company, a division of Thomson
Learning. Fax 800-730-2215.

Vocabulary in the Video

With a partner, try to guess the meanings of the following key phrases used in the video clip about the busy Hartman family.

Phrases	Meanings
a race against time	
planning ahead	
the day's game plan (think of sports)	
quality time (versus "quantity time")	

Watch the Video

Watch the video at least two times. First, just watch. Second, write down some notes in each category below. From this information, you and your group will create two comprehension questions and two discussion questions to ask other groups.

Planning ahead
Quality time
Private time

Talk About It

With your group and using your notes, create four questions. Two should be comprehension questions, and two should be for students' opinions about the lifestyle of the Hartman family. Write the four questions on one sheet of paper. Then exchange questions with another group. Follow these steps:

- Have a discussion as you and the members of your group answer the other group's questions orally. Choose one student to write short notes on the paper with the questions.

- Combine the two groups. Tell the other group what your group said in answer to their questions. Refer to the notes if necessary.

PUTTING IT ALL TOGETHER

 **Guest Speaker**

If there is a sociology, psychology, or counseling department at your school, find out if a faculty member can visit your class to make a presentation on any of the issues covered in this chapter. Follow the steps for inviting a guest speaker in Appendix E.

Public Speaking

Problem/Solution Speech

More and more, students in college classes are expected to make pair or group presentations. In this activity, you and a partner will work together. One of you will present a problem, and the other will present possible solutions. It may be necessary for you to conduct research to gather information on your topic.

Use one or more visual aids (e.g., pictures, posters, objects, video clips, handouts, overhead transparencies, computer visuals) in your presentation. And when you are speaking, remember not to stress prepositions, articles, pronouns, helping verbs, forms of *be*, or conjunctions. Evaluate your presentation by filling out the speech self-evaluation form in Appendix G.

Choose a topic related to the theme of this chapter or another topic of interest to you.

Possible Topics:

- The Time Bind—Balancing Work and Family
- The Second Shift (women with jobs doing all or most of the work at home)
- Problems of Adjusting to a New Culture
- Bringing Up Bicultural Children
- Having the Courage to Speak English in Classes with Native English Speakers
- Other: _____

Format:

- One speaker introduces the topic and presents the problem.
- The other speaker offers solutions and concludes the speech.
- Both speakers take questions from the audience.

Language You Can Use

Today we face the problem of . . .
It seems to us that the major cause of this problem is . . .
There are a number of solutions to this problem . . .
One way to solve this problem is to . . .
Another solution is to . . .

Listening Log Report

Bring your Listening Log to class and report on one entry in a small group.

Search the Web

Learn more about the social issues related to the "time bind" by searching the Web. Possible key words: workaholics, mommy track, Families and Work Institute, Family and Medical Leave Act.

Test-Taking Tip

When taking a multiple choice listening test, use the process of elimination to select a correct answer. First, rule out any answers that are ungrammatical or which don't answer the question being asked. Then, if more than one apparently good answer remains, try to determine the one that answers the question most precisely.

CHECK YOUR PROGRESS

On a scale of 1 to 5, rate how well you have mastered the goals set at the beginning of the chapter:

1 2 3 4 5   learn about how people today balance work and family.

1 2 3 4 5   learn vocabulary related to work and time.

1 2 3 4 5   learn how to be a more active and supportive member of a discussion group.

1 2 3 4 5   learn to use a clear native-speaker model to practice and improve your pronunciation.

1 2 3 4 5   learn to identify unstressed words in natural speech.

1 2 3 4 5   learn to analyze how you manage your time.

If you've given yourself a 3 or lower on any of these goals:

- visit the *Tapestry* web site for additional practice.
- ask your instructor for extra help.
- review the sections of the chapter that you found difficult.
- work with a partner or study group to further your progress.

- Which of these two stores do you find more appealing?
  Why?

8

MARKETING TECHNIQUES—
ARE WE REALLY INFLUENCED?

Much has been written about the ways in which television and magazine advertisements use images to influence people to buy their products. But did you know that store design can also influence consumer behavior? In this chapter we will look at some of the latest techniques being used to influence shoppers to increase their in-store spending.

Setting Goals

In this chapter you will learn:

◈ about marketing techniques used to encourage consumer spending.

◈ vocabulary related to marketing.

◈ how to reinforce your language learning by reading, writing, listening, and speaking about current issues.

◈ how to reinforce vocabulary that you learn by using all four skill areas.

◈ the positive and negative connotations that words carry.

◈ how to pronounce the two *th* sounds correctly.

◈ how to cope with performance anxiety by practicing stress-reducing exercises.

◆**Getting Started**

Have you ever thought about how retailers get consumers to buy their merchandise? Marketing strategies are carefully designed to appeal to consumers on the basis of one or more of the following responses: *affective responses* (reactions based on consumers' feelings, moods, and emotions), *cognitive responses* (reactions based on consumers' knowledge and beliefs), and *behavioral responses* (consumers' reactions or behavior that can be observed and measured). The table below gives more information on these types of strategies and how they influence consumer behavior.

STRATEGIES DESIGNED TO INFLUENCE OVERT CONSUMER BEHAVIORS				
Type of Strategy	Description of Strategy	Strategic Focus	Sample Strategies	Ultimate Objective of Strategy
Affective	Strategies designed to influence consumers' affective responses	Consumers' emotions, moods, feelings, evaluations	Classically conditioning emotions to products	Influence overt consumer behaviors
Cognitive	Strategies designed to influence consumers' cognitive responses	Consumers' knowledge, meanings, beliefs	Providing information highlighting competitive advantages	Influence overt consumer behaviors
Behavioral	Strategies designed to influence consumers' behavioral responses	Consumers' overt behaviors	Positive reinforcement; modeling desired behaviors	Influence overt consumer behaviors
Combined	Strategies designed to influence multiple consumers' responses	More than one of the above	Information about product benefits with emotional tie-ins and rebates	Influence overt consumer behaviors

Source: J. Paul Peter and Jerry C. Olson, *Consumer Behavior and Marketing Strategy,* Copyright 1999 by The McGraw-Hill Company, p. 226.

Look at the following descriptions of ads and decide

- which strategy is used in each ad. Write that strategy in the space on the left.

- which strategy or strategies *you* are most likely to respond to.

1. _____ An advertiser includes coupons offering a rebate (a partial return of payment) of $5.00 off the product advertised.

2. _____ A tire ad features a cute baby sitting in a floating tire.

3. _____ An ad features a color picture of a little playhouse with two cute kids enjoying it, a product descrip-

tion, an age range of $1^{1}/_{2}$ to 4, the words "assembly required," and a sale price of $98.88.

4. _____ A clothing catalog includes extensive product information to help consumers decide whether particular clothing items are right for them.

LISTENING 1:
STORE DESIGN AND CONSUMER BEHAVIOR

◆ **Getting Ready to Listen**   Have you ever paid attention to how a store is designed? Just as advertisers do, retailers try to appeal to consumers' affective, cognitive, and behavioral responses when designing a store. Think about some of the stores you shop in frequently or have been in recently. What effect, if any, does the design and layout of a store have on you as a consumer? As you discuss your answers with your classmates, you might wish to consider how you respond to the following elements:

- lighting
- colors
- shelf space and displays
- music
- smell
- width of aisles
- amount of merchandise
- in-store ads, promotions, and signs
- appearance and behavior of sales staff

◆ **Vocabulary Building**   The short talk you will listen to contains the boldface words and phrases in the sentences below. Try to guess their meanings.

1. Shoppers move in predictable patterns. They respond predictably to **light and color stimuli** in a store.

   Hint: A stimulus is something that is the cause of activity.

   light and color stimuli = _____

2. The right store design can turn **a browser** into a shopper.

   Hint: To browse is to look around in a store.

   a browser = _____

3. The spacious look in the store **ignites** thoughts of exclusiveness and helps persuade customers to buy the expensive goods.

Hint: When wood ignites, it starts to burn.

ignites = _____

4. In The Gap stores, the table at the front of the store **is angled** so that it guides the customers to the right.

   Hint: If you hang a picture on the wall and it doesn't hang straight, it is at an angle.

   is angled = _____

5. The Disney stores are designed **to lure** customers and their children to the back of the store.

   Hint: A fisherman might place a worm or some food on a fishing hook as a lure to help catch a fish.

   to lure = _____

▷Words and Phrases You Will Hear

Often, seeing words and phrases before you hear them can help your listening comprehension. Take a look at the following list and briefly discuss any unfamiliar items with your teacher.

Words Related to Retail Stores

retailers

full-price specialty stores

fluorescent lights

luxury retailer

merchandise

exclusivity

high-priced goods

boutique

Store Improvement

renovation, remodeling, and attention to store design

renovating stores

to upgrade stores

redesigning stores

redoing its U.S. locations

cosmetic changes

Store Names

Sears

Kmart

JCPenney

Benetton

Bergdorf Goodman

The Gap

Disney stores

Listening 1: Store Design and Consumer Behavior

Listen for the Main Idea

Listen to the short talk. Then write one sentence that summarizes the main idea:

_____

_____

_____

Listen for More Information

- Read the following statements.
- Listen to the short talk again for more information.
- As you listen, write T (true) or F (false) in front of each sentence. Base your answers on what you hear in the passage.

_____ 1. Retailers have very little control over shoppers.

_____ 2. Shoppers move in predictable patterns.

_____ 3. Renovation, remodeling, and attention to store design are increasing.

_____ 4. Full-time specialty stores rarely hire store design consultants.

_____ 5. Sears and Kmart are spending billions of dollars in store improvements.

_____ 6. Most store improvements involve only cosmetic changes.

_____ 7. Eighty percent of shoppers use a particular pattern when entering a store.

———— 8. Retailers like to put sale items to the right of the store entrance.

———— 9. Stores like to use fluorescent signs that spell out the words "Good Value."

————10. Bergdorf Goodman sells very little of its merchandise because of the high prices.

————11. People will pay higher prices if a store has wide, spacious aisles.

————12. The interiors of The Gap stores are designed in a diamond shape.

————13. Disney stores give a video with each purchase over a set amount of money.

————14. Disney stores do three times as much business as competing mall stores.

Listen and Take Notes

Use the "split-page format" described on page 35 in Chapter 2 to take notes as you listen again to the same material.

- Take out a piece of paper and copy what is written on the sample page below. The underlined headings are included to help you take notes. Copy them before you listen to the tape, but be sure to leave plenty of space after each heading so that you will have room to write details.

QUESTIONS/IDEAS	NOTES: MARKETING AND CONSUMER BEHAVIOR
	Control Over Consumers
	Attention To Store Design Increasing
	Science of Store Design
	Wide Aisles = High Prices
	High-Profile Success Stories

- As you listen, write *only* in the Notes column. Indent your notes to show the organization of what you hear. Main points should start farthest to the left. Specific information that comes after each main point should be below and indented a little bit to the right. Also, you can use capital letters and underlining to indicate the most important points.

For note-taking tips regarding abbreviations and signals, see Appendix A.

After You Listen

1. Reread your notes. Add ideas and questions to the left column.

2. Compare notes with a partner.

3. Using your notes, orally answer the following questions with your partner:

   a. What does Joseph Weishar mean when he says, "Retailers can have absolute control over the response of their customers"?

   b. What does Weishar mean when he says that there is a science to store design?

   c. How does Bergdorf Goodman exemplify the "wide aisles = higher prices" theory?

   d. Why is The Gap store design so effective?

   e. Why are Disney stores effective?

4. Using only your notes, orally reconstruct the short talk with a partner. Each of you should reconstruct half the talk.

Write About It.

Write a one-paragraph summary of the short talk. Refer only to your notes. Be sure to use your own words. Refer to Appendix B for guidelines on paraphrasing and Appendix C for guidelines on summarizing.

- Your first sentence should both introduce the man whose ideas are referred to, Joseph Weishar, and contain the main idea of the short talk. Because many people don't know Mr. Weishar, it will be necessary to explain who he is by using an appositive: "Joseph Weishar, <u>author of the book *Design for Effective Selling Space*</u>, . . ."

- In subsequent sentences, include the main points and some of the details. Remember to use language of attribution because you will be giving the ideas of Mr. Weishar.

Consumer behavior in every society is influenced by the basic values held by the people in that society. The table below presents basic core values that are shared by many people in the United States and how these values relate to consumer behavior. Do you think the core values and relevant consumer behavior for people in your native culture are any different?

CORE VALUES SHARED BY MANY AMERICANS		
Value	**General Feature**	**Relevance to Consumer Behavior**
Achievement and success	Hard work is good; success flows from hard work	Acts as a justification for acquisition of goods ("You deserve it")
Activity	Keeping busy is healthy and natural	Stimulates interest in products that save time and enhance leisure-time activities
Efficiency and practicality	Admiration of things that solve problems (e.g., save time and effort)	Stimulates purchase of products that function well and save time
Progress	People can improve themselves; tomorrow should be better	Stimulates desire for new products that fulfill unsatisfied needs; acceptance of products that claim to be "new" or "improved"
Material comfort	"The good life"	Fosters acceptance of convenience and luxury products that make life more enjoyable
Individualism	Being one's self (e.g., self-reliance, self-interest, and self-esteem)	Stimulates acceptance of customized or unique products that enable a person to "express his or her own personality"
Freedom	Freedom of choice	Fosters interest in wide product lines and differentiated products
External conformity	Uniformity of observable behavior; desire to be accepted	Stimulates interest in products that are used or owned by others in the same social group
Humanitarianism	Caring for others, particularly the underdog	Stimulates patronage of firms that compete with market leaders
Youthfulness	A state of mind that stresses being young at heart or appearing young	Stimulates acceptance of products that provide the illusion of maintaining or fostering youth
Fitness and health	Caring about ones's body, including the desire to be physically fit and healthy	Stimulates acceptance of food products, activities, and equipment perceived to maintain or increase physical fitness

Source: *Consumer Behavior*, 4th ed. by Schiffman/Kanuk, © 1991. Reprinted by permission of Prentice-Hall, Upper Saddle River, NJ.

LISTENING 2: HOW DO SMELLS INFLUENCE OUR BEHAVIOR?

◆ **Getting Ready to Listen**

In the first listening passage, you learned about ways in which a store's layout can influence consumer spending. Other elements of store design are important as well. Stores have many stimuli that influence consumers, including lighting, noises, smells, temperature, shelf space and displays, signs, colors, and merchandise. Now you will learn more about how smells can influence how much we spend by first reading a newspaper article on the subject and then listening to a radio interview.

LANGUAGE LEARNING STRATEGY

Reinforce your language learning by reading, writing, listening, and speaking about a current issue you are following in the news. The more ways you expose yourself to language, the more chances you have of increasing both your passive understanding and active use of vocabulary that can help you express your ideas more precisely and effectively.

Apply the Strategy

• Read the following excerpt from a *New York Times* article called "The Smell of Money" by N. R. Kleinfield. The article contains information related to the interview you will listen to.

• As you read, take notes to answer the following questions:

1. Who is Alan Hirsch? Where does he work? What kind of work and research does he do?

2. How did Dr. Hirsch test the effect of smells on gamblers at a Las Vegas casino?

3. What were the smells he used?

4. What were the results of the casino study?

5. Why are so many businesses interested in his research?

The Smell of Money

1 Dr. Alan Hirsch is a neurologist and psychiatrist who calls himself the "Jacques Cousteau of the nose" and once wore a watch that ran backward. Eight years ago, he started the Smell and Taste Treatment and Research Foundation in Chicago, where he and his colleagues treat patients with smell disorders and pursue research. He thinks he became curious about smell after he was hit by a car while he was a medical student and found that for a week afterward everything smelled like cigarettes.

2 His foundation is probing[1] whether the scent of green apples can soothe migraine headaches and whether the smell of Fritos can bring on weight loss. What has gained Dr. Hirsch the most attention, though, is his untiring promotion of the commercial applications of smells. In particular, he did two studies that have had an electric reception among marketers.

3 The first was the sneaker study. About two years ago, Dr. Hirsch asked 31 shoppers to inspect Nike sneakers in two identical-looking rooms. One room was filled with purified air, the other with a mixed floral scent. Afterward, Dr. Hirsch said, 84 percent of the subjects[2] said they were more inclined to[3] buy the sneakers in the scented room.

4 Dr. Hirsch said throngs[4] of retailers got in touch with him, and several retail stores and athletic shops bought the scent's formula for about $3,000. Nike did not. "The big thing we try to do is get athletic shoes not to smell," said Liz Dolan, Nike's director of communications. "We never think about adding a smell."

5 Dr. Hirsch's second venture[5] came a year ago, when he went to Las Vegas, Nevada to scent a casino. He is no gambler himself (on his last visit, he risked all of 35 cents, losing it). Yet, he went to the Las Vegas Hilton and picked out three slot-machine[6] zones[7] to study for a weekend. One zone was left unscented, while each

---

[1]**probing:** investigating
[2]**subjects:** people being tested or studied
[3]**were more inclined to:** felt a greater wish to
[4]**throngs:** crowds
[5]**venture:** an attempt
[6]**slot-machine:** a machine at a gambling casino in which you put coins in order to win more money than you put in
[7]**zones:** areas

of the other two was misted[8] with a different agreeable odor.[9] Dr. Hirsch is vague about describing the odors. Using numbers furnished by the Hilton, he compared the play at the slots with the previous and subsequent[10] weekends. He found little change in the neutral zone or in one scented zone, he said, but in the other scented area the amount of money gambled soared[11] by 45 percent. And the more intense the smell, the more people bet.[12]

6   Dr. Hirsch announced these results last month and has heard from 20 casinos around the world that feel their dreams have come true. The Las Vegas Hilton, among others, has asked him for a proposal and cost estimate. He has also been approached by 150 other businesses—clothes stores, shopping malls, health clubs, restaurants—praying that the smell may induce[13] their clientele[14] to spend more, too. Dr. Hirsch said he would probably start selling the Las Vegas Odor by January, though he had no idea why it worked.

7   Dr. Hirsch charges up to $50,000 to produce a smell. Chicago Transparent Products bought a "fresh linen" scent for its new Brawny plastic trash bags that supposedly makes consumers feel healthy and clean. A women's clothing maker, which Dr. Hirsch would not identify, hired him to come up with a smell that can be blended into garments and will supposedly make young women more inclined to buy them.

Source: Copyright © 1992 by The New York Times Company. Reprinted by permission.

Listen

Listening 2: How do Smells Influence our Behavior?

Listen for the Main Idea

Listen to the NPR radio interview with Dr. Hirsch. Then write one sentence that summarizes the main idea:

_____

_____

_____

[8]**misted:** sprayed
[9]**agreeable odor:** pleasant smell
[10]**subsequent:** follow-up
[11]**soared:** greatly increased
[12]**bet:** risked money with the hopes of gaining more money, gambled
[13]**induce:** cause
[14]**clientele:** customers

Listen for More Information

Now you will listen to the interview again for more information.

- First, read the questions below.
- As you listen, take short notes that answer each question.

a. What were the results of Dr. Hirsch's research at a Las Vegas casino?

_____

_____

b. What was the smell that Dr. Hirsch used in his casino study?

_____

_____

c. How does Dr. Hirsch envision smells as part of our life in the future?

_____

_____

_____

d. What can you guess about the interviewer's attitude towards having smells added to our environment?

_____

_____

> Memories, imagination, old sentiments and association are more readily reached through the sense of smell than through any other channel.
>
> —OLIVER WENDELL HOLMES

◆ **After You Listen**

How did reading about Dr. Hirsch's research before you listened to the interview affect your understanding of the material? It probably helped you. Practice this same strategy at home by first reading an article in the newspaper and then listening to the same story later in the day on the radio or TV news. It is a useful strategy to practice because students in academic lecture classes often listen to material closely related to the assigned readings.

◆ **Talk About It**

1. Now that you have heard and read about the implications of Dr. Hirsch's research, what is your reaction? Do you think you can be influenced by smells? What do you think are the implications of using smells to control consumer behavior? Do you think consumers should be "left alone," or do you think using smell to influence shoppers is acceptable?

2. Do you feel manipulated by marketing in general? Why or why not?

3. What do you think is the point of this cartoon?

"*Your magazine smells fabulous. May I kiss you?*"

Source: Drawing by Weber; © 1992, *The New Yorker* Magazine, Inc.

Basil is a scent that is said to improve memory.

4. Marketing strategies of international corporations vary from country to country in order to make a product appeal to a local culture. What are some differences in how a particular global product is marketed in your native country and in the United States? How do these differences reflect what is important to the local consumer? You might wish to consider the marketing of soft drinks, fast food, cigarettes, automobiles, breakfast cereals, and other products that are sold throughout the world.

5. Here are some difficult ethical situations that marketers could face during their careers. If marketers choose immediate sales-producing actions in all of the cases, their marketing behavior might be criticized for being unethical. However, if they refused to go along with any of the actions, they would be criticized for being ineffective marketing managers. What would you do in each case?

   a. Your research and development department has changed one of your products slightly. It is not really "new and improved," but you know that putting this statement on the package and in advertising will increase sales. What would you do?

b. You are thinking of hiring a product manager who just left a competitor's company. She would be more than happy to tell you all the competitor's plans for the coming year. What would you do?

c. You have to choose between three ad campaigns outlined by your agency. The first (A) is a soft-sell (low pressure), honest information campaign. The second (B) uses sex-loaded emotional appeals and exaggerates the product's benefits. The third (C) involves a noisy, irritating commercial that is sure to gain audience attention. Pretests show that the campaigns are effective in the following order: C, B, and A. What would you do?

d. You are interviewing a capable female applicant for a job as a salesperson. She is better qualified than the men just interviewed. Nevertheless, you know that some of your important customers prefer dealing with men, and you will lose some sales if you hire her. What would you do?

Source: Adapted from *Marketing: An Introduction,* 4th ed. by Philip Kotler and Gary Armstrong, © 1999, Prentice-Hall, Upper Saddle River, NJ.

LANGUAGE LEARNING STRATEGY

Learn the positive and negative connotations that words carry. Connotations are the meanings or ideas suggested by a word in addition to the formal meaning. Expanding your vocabulary by becoming aware of subtle distinctions in the meanings of related words can help you become more articulate and precise.

Apply the Strategy

In the *New York Times* reading and the interview with Dr. Hirsch, you came across a number of words related to smell. They are all useful words with different shades of meaning. The following lists contain those words plus a few more.

Nouns

smell	stink	stench	perfume
odor	fragrance	odorant	bouquet
scent	aroma	fumes	

Adjectives

smelly   scented   fragrant   stinky   aromatic

Verbs

to smell	to deodorize	to smell up	to reek
to odorize	to stink	to stink up	to fumigate

What is the difference in their meanings? Do they have a positive, negative, or neutral connotation? Which of the words are interchangeable? Use a dictionary or ask a native speaker, and put the words into the chart below.

WORD CONNOTATIONS

POSITIVE	NEUTRAL	NEGATIVE

TUNING IN: "In-Floor Ads"

© CNN

You will watch a CNN video clip about yet one more way that advertising surrounds us. Before you watch the video clip, read the following excerpt about support for and criticism of the marketing system.

Critics: The marketing system creates cultural pollution. Our senses are constantly being attacked by advertising. Commercials interrupt serious programs; pages of ads obscure printed matter; billboards ruin beautiful scenery. These interruptions constantly pollute people's minds with messages of materialism, sex, power, or status. Although most people do not find advertising too annoying (some even think it is the best part of television programming), some critics call for major changes.

Supporters: Marketers hope that their ads primarily reach the target audience. But some ads will still reach people who have no interest in the product and are therefore bored or annoyed. People who buy magazines about their interests—such as *Vogue* or *Fortune*—rarely complain about the ads because the magazines advertise products they are interested in. Second, ads make it possible for most television and radio stations to offer free broadcasts, and ads keep down the costs of magazines and newspapers. Many people think that commercials are a small price to pay for these benefits.

Source: Adapted from *Marketing: An Introduction,* 4th ed. by Philip Kotler and Gary Armstrong, © 1999, Prentice-Hall, Upper Saddle River, NJ.

You have read the two sides of the argument.

- With which do you agree?
- Why?

Vocabulary in the Video

With a partner, try to guess the meanings of the following key phrases used in the video clip:

Phrases	Meanings
to buy on impulse	
advertising becomes critical	
2-foot-by-2-foot panels	
space-age plastic	
advertising copy	
a soft drink aisle	
it caters to impulse buyers	
the firm that patented this technique	

Campbell's Soup has "planograms" that show grocery stores how the soups ought to be arranged. New soups that need exposure are put at eye level.

Watch the Video

Watch the video at least two times. First, just watch. Second, write down some notes in each category below. From this information, you and your group will create two comprehension questions and two discussion questions to ask other groups.

Importance of impulse buying for advertisers
What is in-floor advertising?
Effectiveness of in-floor advertising
Future plans of in-floor advertising

 **Talk About It**

With your group and using your notes, create four questions. Two should be comprehension questions, and two should be for students' opinions about the issues raised by in-floor ads. Write the four questions on one sheet of paper. Then exchange questions with another group. Follow these steps:

- Have a discussion as you and the members of your group answer the other group's questions orally. Choose one student to write short notes on the paper with the questions.

- Combine the two groups. Tell the other group what your group said in answer to their questions. Refer to the notes if necessary.

The Sound of It: Pronouncing the Two /th/ Sounds Correctly

Many non-native speakers of English have difficulty correctly pronouncing the two *th* sounds: /θ/ as in **th**ink and /ð/ as in **th**is. Often, learners of English substitute /t/ or /s/ for /θ/, and /d/ or /z/ for /ð/. To produce the two *th* sounds correctly, it is necessary to put your tongue out slightly between your teeth. To produce the voiceless *th*, blow air without using your voice. To produce the voiced *th*, use your voice but don't blow air. If you don't put your tongue between your teeth, you will get a /t/ or /s/ sound for the voiceless *th* and a /d/ or /z/ sound for the voiced *th*.

Practice reading aloud a different excerpt from the *New York Times* article about Dr. Hirsch that you read earlier. Pay attention to pronouncing *th* correctly. Work with a partner and take turns reading aloud and correcting each other's pronunciation:

It was bound to happen. Someone **th**inks he is about to create **th**e Honest Car Salesman in a bottle.

A year ago, one of Detroit's Big **Th**ree auto makers hired Dr. Alan R. Hirsch, a quirky smell researcher in Chicago, to devise a ra**th**er exceptional scent. **Th**e hope was **th**at when **th**e odor was sprayed on a car salesman, he would—yes—smell honest.

It sounds absurd. In fact, after she was done laughing, Dr. Susan Schiffman, a smell researcher and professor of medical psychology at **th**e Duke University Medical School, remarked, "I was not aware **th**at honesty had a specific smell associated wi**th** it."

But Dr. Hirsch, who refuses to name his Detroit client, is confident **th**at he will have **th**e Honest Car Salesman Odor devised wi**th**in a year. If he succeeds, he said, **th**e auto maker will entrust **th**e smell to its dealers, who will spray it on **th**eir salesmen, and **th**en customers will catch a whiff and cars will fly off **th**e lots.

ACADEMIC POWER STRATEGY

Cope with performance anxiety by practicing stress-reducing exercises recommended by experts. It is normal to feel performance anxiety in certain situations like public speaking, job interviews, test taking, and acting. Actors in the theater know that a few simple exercises can often relieve the physical and psychological symptoms of performance anxiety.

The best strategy for dealing with feelings of panic is to be prepared. Beyond that, there are various techniques for coping with stress. Following are five techniques for handling performance anxiety in the classroom:

1. **Press fists against your closed eyes and squint.** This exercise will give you a moment to blank out tensions and distractions. Here's how it works (best not to try this if you wear contact lenses):

   Press your fists against your closed eyes.

   Squint or tightly close your eyes at the same time.

   After a few seconds, take your hands away and open your eyes.

2. **Drop your head and slowly roll it left and right.** Do the following exercise five times:

   Drop your head forward on your chest.

   Roll it slowly over to your left shoulder, then slowly over to your right shoulder.

3. **Alternately tense your muscles and then let go.** If a particular part of your body, such as your shoulders, is tense, try this tense-and-relax activity. The effect is to make you aware of the relaxed feeling after you have released the tension.

   Take a deep breath and hold it.

   Make the muscles in the tense place even more tense. Hold tightly for a few seconds.

   Then let out your breath and release the tension.

   You can do this for other parts of your body (chest, neck, and so on) or for all parts simultaneously.

4. **Concentrate on breathing slowly in and out.** This activity will calm some of the physical sensations in your body. Do this for 2–5 minutes.

   Focus your mind on your breathing.

   Breathe slowly through your nose.

   Deeply and slowly inhale, filling your lungs.

   Then slowly exhale through your mouth.

   Avoid taking short breaths.

   Once your breathing is calm and regular, you can concentrate on what you are about to do (take a test, give a presentation, have an interview, and so on).

(continued on next page)

5. Try positive self-talk. If a voice inside you says, "You're going to fail!" make an effort to replace this and other negative thoughts with positive ones. Say to yourself: "Nonsense! I prepared enough, so I know I'll be OK."

Apply the Strategy

Practice the five techniques so that you feel comfortable with them. Then, before your next test or public speaking activity, use any or all of the five techniques to lessen your anxiety.

Source: Adapted from *Learning Success*, 1st edition, by C. M. Wahlstrom and B. K. Williams. © 1996. Reprinted with permission of Wadsworth Publishing, a division of Thomson Learning. Fax 800-730-2215.

PUTTING IT ALL TOGETHER

Guest Speaker

If there is a business, psychology, or communications department at your school, find out if a faculty member can visit your class to make a presentation on any of the issues covered in this chapter. Follow the steps for inviting a guest speaker in Appendix E.

Public Speaking

Group Report

In the first short talk, you heard about some of the successful in-store marketing strategies of several nationally known retail stores. For this public speaking activity, you will give a group oral report based on your own observations.

Preparation

1. With a team of one or two classmates, conduct your own field research. Take a trip to your local mall or shopping center. Find the directory sign and make a list of several major categories of stores. List the competing stores in each category. Then choose one category and visit several of the stores and observe their merchandising strategies. Take notes on your observations. In your notes you may wish to address some of the following questions:

   • How did the shopping environments and marketing strategies you observed differ?

- How were they similar?

- Did the shopping environments you observed differ from shopping environments in your native country?

- Did you see any examples of marketing based on the core values and consumer behavior described in the table on page 168? If so, what were they?

- What marketing strategies did you think were effective? Not effective?

- At whom were the marketing strategies aimed?

- Which store did you think had the most effective environment and marketing strategy in terms of getting people to spend money? Why do you think it was more effective than the other stores you visited?

- Did you see any marketing practices you disapprove of or consider unethical? Is so, what were they?

2. Prepare a 10–15-minute oral report in which your group presents its findings. Your report should contain the following:

   a. an attention-getting introduction (an anecdote, a quotation, a question to the audience, etc.)

   b. a logically organized body of information

   c. an action-oriented conclusion that encourages the listener to apply the message in some way

   d. if possible, appropriate visuals to illustrate your report

Presentation

1. Take turns with the others on your team when presenting your results. You should use notes, but do not read a prepared report. You might want to list your notes on 3 × 5 cards.

2. After your report, invite audience participation by asking for questions. Do not end your report by saying "That's all." And do not ask "Are there any questions?" because it is too easy for your audience to say no. Instead, ask "What questions do you have?"—which is phrasing that implies that you expect your listeners to have questions.

3. Evaluate your presentation by using the student self-evaluation form in Appendix G.

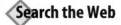

Listening Log Report   Bring your Listening Log to class and report on one entry in a small group.

Search the Web   Learn more about issues related to marketing by searching the Web. Possible key words: marketing, ethics, international, consumers. Or choose an international company and visit its web site to learn more information about the various aspects of its businesses around the world. For example, take the World Tour on the McDonald's web site at **www.mcdonalds.com** to learn more about the company's various marketing approaches.

Test-Taking Tip

After your test, make an appointment with your instructor to discuss how you did on the test. The grade you receive on your test doesn't give you detailed information about what you did particularly well or where your problem areas are. You should ask your teacher for his or her assessment of your performance and ask for advice on areas for improvement.

CHECK YOUR PROGRESS

On a scale of 1 to 5, rate how well you have mastered the goals set at the beginning of the chapter:

1 2 3 4 5   learn about marketing techniques used to encourage consumer spending.

1 2 3 4 5   learn vocabulary related to marketing.

1 2 3 4 5   learn how to reinforce your language learning by reading, writing, listening, and speaking about current issues.

1 2 3 4 5   learn how to reinforce vocabulary that you learn by using all four skill areas.

1 2 3 4 5   learn the positive and negative connotations that words carry.

1 2 3 4 5   learn how to pronounce the two *th* sounds correctly.

1 2 3 4 5   learn to cope with performance anxiety by practicing stress-reducing exercises.

If you have given yourself a 3 or lower on any of these goals:

- visit the *Tapestry* web site for additional practice.
- ask your instructor for extra help.
- review the sections of the chapter that you found difficult.
- work with a partner or study group to further your progress.

Immigration around the world is increasing at a fast pace today.

- What are some of the advantages and disadvantages of immigrating to another country?
- What are some advantages and disadvantages for the host country?

BEING AN IMMIGRANT— CULTURE SHOCK AND ADAPTATION

Culture shock can strike anyone who travels, both new immigrants and tourists. They are constantly comparing what they see with what they know. When it is necessary to stay in a new country, they need to decide which aspects of the new society they will adopt and which aspects of their original culture they will keep. In addition, they often face stereotyping by the majority culture. In this chapter, we will discuss these issues as we read about and listen to the stories of a Vietnamese immigrant in the United States.

Setting Goals

In this chapter you will:

◈ learn about factors related to immigration, adaptation, and assimilation.

◈ learn vocabulary related to stress, wastefulness, immigration, and voting.

◈ learn to take advantage of the different kinds of services and opportunities designed to give you added support at your school.

◈ learn to find a writer's or speaker's point by using your ability to infer.

◈ develop the ability to monitor your pronunciation as you speak.

◈ learn to stress the first part of a noun compound.

185

◆**Getting Started**

Answer Numbers 1, 2, and 3 if you are currently in the United States, Canada, or another English-speaking country. Answer Numbers 2 and 3 if you are currently in your native country.

1. Complete the chart below. In the first column, fill in the information about yourself. Use the other columns for interviews of two of your classmates.

	Student 1 (myself)	Student 2	Student 3
Name	Me		
What are some of the things you expected before you arrived in this country?	*Before I came, I expected . . .*		
What did you find?			
Were you surprised?			

2. What are some stereotypes of people from your native country? List them on the left. Then, on the right, indicate what people will really see or find if they visit your native country.

STEREOTYPES PEOPLE HAVE OF _____ (NATIONALITY)	THE REALITY

3. Keeping these exercises in mind, write a general sentence about people's expectations about a place and the reality that they actually find.

_____

_____

_____

LISTENING 1: WASTED FOOD, DISCOVERED SOULS

Getting Ready to Listen

Listening 1 is about a newcomer's reaction to the waste that he sees in the United States. Before you listen, read this excerpt from an article titled "Stressed Out in a Strange Land" by Andrew Lam. When you finish, answer the questions that follow the article.

1   One of the first words I learned when I arrived in America from Vietnam was, strangely, *stress*. An eccentric[1] aunt of mine, who probably had the gift of prescience[2] and came to America a few years before Vietnam fell in 1975, when my family came, taught me the word.

2   Many words, such as *bus* and *accident,* I understood immediately, having had a French education. But *stress* left me hanging.[3] Its meaning was ambiguous;[4] its pronunciation sounded like the hissing[5] of a poisonous snake.

[1]**eccentric:** unusual
[2]**the gift of prescience:** the gift of being able to predict the future
[3]**left me hanging:** left me still not understanding
[4]**ambiguous:** having several possible meanings
[5]**the hissing:** the *ssss* sound

3   *"Sss...stressss,"* I repeated after her, giggling. Yet, eager to learn everything—I was 11—I asked her to define the term in Vietnamese. As eloquent[6] as she was, the poor woman couldn't find its equivalent in her native language. "Going crazy" was all she came up with. She insisted, however, that I should learn the word, for I needed to understand its meaning sooner or later to live in America.

4   For a while, equipped with a generic[7] if not "chop suey" vocabulary,[8] I applied *stress* to practically everything. Sharing the two-bedroom apartment on Mission Street with another Vietnamese family made us all "stress." There were 13 of us huddling together[9] and wearing look-alike used ski jackets donated by a religious charity. The kid who one morning punched me in the chest for no reason, was he himself "stress"? The arguments between my aunt and my mother over the Vietnamese restaurant where they worked laboriously[10] night and day were "stress...."

5   But in school I expanded my vocabulary and redefined words I previously had misunderstood....That kid who hit me wasn't "stress," he was just showing off his brute strength by using me as a punching bag. My mother and my aunt, however, were under a lot of it. So were we all who endured the shortage of space and of clothing, and who initially feared venturing out of[11] the crowded apartment into a world of "foreign" strangers who might beat and rob us.

6   Though I did not fully grasp its entirety, I came to recognize stress in my mother's sunken eyes[12] as she scraped the skillets[13] in the restaurant each night. It manifested itself[14] in my father's trembling hands as he turned the pages of the newspaper, searching for work. And stress burned my cheeks and itched my skin as it set my heart beating wildly every time I failed to understand a teacher's question. Under stress, I kept my silence, while classmates giggled. *"Sstressss."* I whispered the word and felt its sting.

Andrew Lam is an associate editor of Pacific News Service. He came to America when he was eleven years old.

[6]**eloquent:** having the ability to use language very well
[7]**generic:** general
[8]**"chop suey" vocabulary:** a mixed vocabulary, like the dish "chop suey," which has a mixture of ingredients
[9]**huddling together:** crowding together closely
[10]**worked laboriously:** worked extremely hard
[11]**venturing out of:** taking the risk to go out of
[12]**sunken eyes:** eyes that seem to have gotten lower or deeper into the face
[13]**scraped the skillets:** washed the pans
[14]**manifested itself:** revealed itself

1. Why did the people Lam mentioned in the article feel stressed? Give the reasons in the column on the right.

REASONS FOR STRESS

The two families

His mother and aunt

His father

Himself

2. The time that Lam describes in the article is 1975. Discuss whether you think that the stress and problems that immigrants face today are the same or different, and give specific examples if you can.

3. When people move to a new country, they try to *adapt to* or *adjust to* the language and culture. That means that they change their behavior to fit the new situation. For example, if in their native country people drive on the left, but in the new country people drive on the right, they need to adapt to or adjust to the different way of driving.

   Over time, when an immigrant who has adapted to a new culture starts becoming part of the new culture, that person has *assimilated into* the new culture. This follows the process of *assimilation*.

   Give examples of what people have to adapt to when they move to a new culture. Do you think that assimilation into the majority culture should be the desired goal of people who immigrate? Why or why not?

ACADEMIC POWER STRATEGY

Take advantage of the different kinds of services and opportunities designed to give you added support at your school. International students today are often under a lot of pressure because many of them have to deal with family responsibilities and jobs in addition to going to school. The following are three kinds of support that may be of help to you:

(continued on next page)

- A mentor. A mentor is a person whom you respect and hope to be like in the future. This person may be in the profession that you would eventually like to have. A mentor can become your role model and advisor, and should be available to you to talk about your hopes and concerns.

- Study groups. Study outside of class with other students: "Research shows that students who study in groups often get the highest grades. The reasons are many. Students in a group fight isolation by being members of a social circle. They give each other support and encouragement. They help each other by working through lecture notes and readings and preparing for exams." (*Learning Success—Being Your Best at College & Life.*) In study groups, students can also quiz each other on class material.

- Clubs. Clubs are organizations designed to attract students with common backgrounds or interests. For example, your school may have a Latino Students Club, a Chinese Students Association, a Drama Club, political clubs, etc. The following are six reasons to join a campus organization:

1. You'll meet people with interests and ideas similar to yours.

2. You'll gain experience.

3. You'll improve your communication skills.

4. You'll improve your résumé.

5. You'll meet advisors who may be helpful to you in other areas of your educational experience.

6. There's more to life than working.

Apply the Strategy

Take advantage of the support available at your school:

- Find out if there is a mentor program and if you are eligible to participate. Join the program if you are eligible.

- Form or join a study group. Meet about one week before an exam, before each of you has studied alone. Share notes and ideas, and together create a list of potential questions for review. Then spend time studying alone, developing answers, outlines, etc. Meet again to share answers and prepare one another for the exam.

- Find out where you can get a list of campus clubs and any other student organizations. Analyze the list and call two or three clubs to find out about their meeting dates. Attend these meetings, and join one or more clubs if you are interested.

Sources: Adapted from *Learning Success—Being Your Best at College & Life*, by Carl Wahlstrom and Brian K. Williams. © 1996, and *Your College Experience*, 3rd edition, by J. N. Gardner and A. J. Jewler. © 1997. Both reprinted with permission of Wadsworth Publishing, a division of Thomson Learning. Fax 800-730-2215.

◆ Vocabulary Building

Look for the meanings of the boldface words in the column on the right. Make sure that the words you choose from the right would fit meaningfully and grammatically into a sentence on the left.

_____ 1. **The bulk of** the food that's lost simply goes bad in people's refrigerators.

_____ 2. It is left uneaten on the plate and **gets tossed out.**

_____ 3. I felt **a slight tug** of guilt.

_____ 4. I am not unfamiliar with his feelings of **indignation.**

_____ 5. I, too, came from that **agrarian-based ethos** in which land is sacred.

_____ 6. What I throw away today would have **astounded** me years ago.

_____ 7. Perhaps a sure sign of successful **assimilation** . . .

_____ 8. is when an immigrant tosses away his sense of **frugality.**

_____ 9. At home after our **excursion,** my cousin helped me prepare dinner.

_____ 10. I am watching farmers **stoop** to gather rice.

_____ 11. I had wanted to show my cousin America's **grandeur,** but he showed me something else far lovelier.

a. strongly surprised

b. short trip

c. agricultural spirit/belief

d. the majority of

e. strong displeasure at something unjust

f. splendor (magnificence/greatness)

g. gets thrown away

h. bend over

i. carefulness in saving and not wasting

j. a small pull

k. absorption or incorporation into a culture

◇ Words and Phrases You Will Hear

Often, seeing words and phrases before you hear them can help your listening comprehension. Take a look at the following list and briefly discuss any unfamiliar items with your teacher.

About Waste and Throwing Things Away

the amount of waste

goes to waste

discarded food

outdated pizzas

Values

an environmentalist

frugal background

land is sacred

The proverb "Waste not, want not" means that the less we waste, the less we will lack in the future.

Feelings

overwhelming high-rises

a long-cherished memory

Wealth and Success

America's opulence

successful assimilation into an overdeveloped society

Wall Street

stock market

Expressions

comes as no surprise

take it for granted that

there's plenty more where that came from

Listen

Listening 1: Wasted Food, Discovered Souls

Listen for the Main Idea

Listen to Andrew Lam's commentary. Then write one sentence that summarizes the main idea:

_____

_____

_____

> Some of the most common stereotypes of Americans: outgoing, friendly, informal, loud, rude, boastful, immature, hardworking, wasteful, disrespectful of authority, racially prejudiced, ignorant of other countries, wealthy, generous, always in a hurry.
>
> —L. ROBERT KOHLS, *SURVIVAL KIT FOR OVERSEAS LIVING*

Listen for More Information

Read the following before you listen again to Lam's commentary. Circle the letters of the answers that you already know. Then listen to find the answers that you are still unsure of.

1. The majority of the food wasted in the United States
   a. goes uneaten in people's homes.
   b. goes unsold in grocery stores and restaurants.

2. Andrew Lam took his cousin for a tour of San Francisco to show him
   a. the big amount of waste in the United States.
   b. the impressive buildings of the city.

3. When Lam was a child in San Francisco,

 a. his parents expected him to get expired food from a supermarket garbage bin.

 b. he and his brother stole food from a supermarket without their parents' knowledge.

4. What was Lam's "long-cherished memory"?

 a. being a five-year-old gathering rice in Vietnam.

 b. being a five-year-old watching people gather rice in Vietnam.

5. From his experience with his cousin, Lam

 a. becomes much more careful about throwing things away.

 b. now realizes how assimilated he has become, without even being aware of it.

Listen and Take Notes

Use the "split-page format" described on page 35 in Chapter 2 to take notes as you listen again to the same material.

- Take out a piece of paper and copy what is written on the sample page below. The underlined headings are included to help you take notes. Copy them before you listen to the commentary, but be sure to leave plenty of space after each heading so that you will have room to write details.

QUESTIONS/IDEAS	NOTES: LAM: WASTED FOOD
	Intro — Food Waste
	Lam's Cousin's Surprise
	Lam's Childhood Experience in SF
	What Lam Realized

- As you listen, write *only* in the Notes column. Indent your notes to show the organization of what you hear. Main points should start farthest to the left. Specific information that comes after each main point should be below and indented a little bit to the right. Also, you can use capital letters and underlining to indicate the most important points.

For note-taking tips regarding abbreviations and signals, see Appendix A.

After You Listen

1. Reread your notes. Add ideas and questions to the left column.

2. Compare notes with a partner.

3. Using your notes, orally answer the following questions with your partner:

   a. What did Lam originally plan to show his cousin, and what did his cousin see?

   b. What did Lam and his brother use to do at a supermarket when they first came to the United States? Why do you think they did this?

   c. What does Lam realize about himself today? How does he feel?

4. Using only your notes, orally reconstruct Lam's commentary with a partner. Each of you should reconstruct half of the commentary.

Talk About It

1. Look at this cartoon. How does it relate to Andrew Lam's cousin's reaction to the waste he saw in San Francisco? Could your native country also be called a "throwaway society"? Why or why not?

"We've certainly become a throwaway society."

2. In your native country, how do people get rid of things? Do they make donations? Do they have garage or yard sales? Do they sell things at flea markets? Do they recycle?

3. What do you think this title means: "Wasted Food, Discovered Souls"?

4. Andrew Lam's cousin was shocked by the waste he saw as he took one of his first walks around San Francisco. What were some of the cultural shocks you experienced when you first arrived in United States? (If you are currently in another country but have traveled in the past, describe any shock that you might have experienced.) Were you "stressed out in a strange land" when you first arrived?

Write a one-paragraph summary of the commentary. Refer only to your notes. Be sure to use your own words. Refer to Appendix B for guidelines on paraphrasing and Appendix C for guidelines on summarizing.

- Your first sentence should both introduce Andrew Lam and contain the main idea of his talk. Because many people don't know Mr. Lam, it will be necessary to explain who he is by using an appositive: "Andrew Lam, *a writer and editor,* . . ."

- In subsequent sentences, include the main points and some of the details. Remember to use language of attribution because you will be giving the ideas of Mr. Lam.

LISTENING 2: WHAT'S IN A NAME?

Getting Ready to Listen

Using the four questions below, interview three to five of your classmates. As they answer the questions, take very short notes on a sheet of paper.

1. What is your first name in your native language?
2. What does it mean?
3. Do you use an English first name? If yes, why? If no, why not?
4. If you use an English name, do you know what it means?

Vocabulary Building

You will hear the following sentences in the interview. Try to guess the meanings of the boldface words and phrases. Use the hints to help you guess.

> What's in a name?
> That which we call a
> rose by any other name
> would smell as sweet.
>
> —WILLIAM SHAKESPEARE

1. Vietnamese names are often turned ugly in America, their magic **snuffed out** like a birthday candle.

   Hint: What do people do with birthday candles?

   snuffed out = _____

2. Van, Truc, and Trang, the three pretty girls who walk down the high school hallway, suffered constant **pestering** from classmates.

   Hint: A "pest" is a person who bothers others.

   pestering = _____

3. Van, Truc, and Trang, after **leafing through** *Vogue* and *Mademoiselle* magazines, emerged Yvonne, Theresa, and Tanya.

   Hint: A leaf can be a piece of paper, as in a "loose-leaf binder."

   leafing through = _____

4. And there's Qua, . . . who wanted to finalize his **naturalization process**.

   Hint: "Naturalized citizens" are people who were not born in their new country, but who have earned the rights of citizens.

   naturalization process = _____

5. . . . it was Hoai who . . . amid exploding B-52 bombs **mourned for** slain relatives.

   Hint: "Slain relatives" in this case are relatives who died from bombing.

   mourned for = _____

Listen

Listening 2: What's in a Name?

Listen for the Main Idea

Andrew Lam gives a lot of examples throughout his commentary, and then he comes to his point near the end. Listen and then write his point, the main idea, below:

_____

_____

_____

LANGUAGE LEARNING STRATEGY

Apply the Strategy

Find a writer's or speaker's point by using your ability to infer. People frequently make their points indirectly and leave it up to the reader or listener to figure out what is being said "between the lines."

Use your inference skills to answer the questions in the "Listen for More Information" exercise below. You will need to listen to Andrew Lam carefully and then figure out what he means, but is not saying directly.

> In English my name means hope. In Spanish it means too many letters. It means sadness, it means waiting. . . . At school they say my name funny as if the syllables were made out of tin and hurt the roof of your mouth. But in Spanish my name is made out of a softer something, like silver. . . .
>
> —Esperanza in *House on Mango Street* by SANDRA CISNEROS

Listen for More Information

First, read the questions below. Then listen to Listening 2 again and write your answers. You will have to infer the answers because Lam does not state them directly. When you finish, discuss your answers with a partner or your class.

1. What does Lam mean when he says that Vietnamese names in English are "twisted into a funny word, a grunt, or even a cough"?

   _____

2. Why did the three Vietnamese girls change their names?

   _____

3. When Lam talks about the ways in which Nancy and Kevin got their English names, what is Lam's point?

   _____

4. Who is Hoai? Who is Lucy?

   _____

5. Christine, whose father sold fruit at a market, was expected to follow in her mother's footsteps. In other words, she was expected to live a life like her mother's. What kind of life do you think that was?

   _____

6. What kind of market does Christine work in today?

   _____

◆ The Sound of It: Stress in Noun Compounds

LANGUAGE LEARNING STRATEGY

Develop the ability to monitor your pronunciation as you speak. This will help you to speak English more clearly. To do this, you will need to speak slowly and carefully, and self-correct when possible. The more you do this, the more you will "self-monitor" and eventually improve your pronunciation.

Andrew Lam has done this quite successfully. While he still has an accent, his English is so clear that he gives radio commentaries and makes speeches around the United States.

Apply the Strategy

Choose one aspect of your pronunciation to monitor and self-correct. You may want to choose a vowel or consonant sound, the -*ed* or -*s* ending, stress in two-word verbs, stress in noun compounds, sentence stress, intonation in statements or questions, etc. When you speak, try to catch yourself using this one aspect of pronunciation, and correct yourself when possible. Also, try to notice when you hear this pronunciation used by other speakers in person, on the radio, on TV, etc. As you do this, you will eventually find yourself paying attention not only to that one pronunciation point, but to many other aspects of pronunciation and even grammar.

Imagine that you have decided to monitor your use of stress in noun compounds (also called "compound nouns").

Noun compounds are nouns that are made up of two words. These two words together create a noun with a special meaning. The first word in a noun compound receives the most stress (called "primary stress") and highest intonation. The second word receives secondary stress and lower intonation. Noun compounds can be in the form of two words together, or two separate words.

1. The following is a list of noun compounds that Andrew Lam uses in the two listening pieces in this chapter. Practice saying each noun compound aloud.

Ágriculture Depàrtment	bírthday càndle
grócery stòres	máke-ùp
hígh-rìses	lándlòrd
gárbage bìn	naturalizátion pròcess
súpermàrket	mílk càrton
cóokie dòugh	fóotstèps
párking lòt	compúter lìnkups
polícemàn	stóckbròker
hárvest tìme	tíme zònes

2. Become aware of more noun compounds by answering these questions and paying attention to how you pronounce the answers. Add your own question to the end of the list, and see if your classmates can provide the answer with a noun compound.

    a. What is the name of the house that the President of the United States lives in?

    b. What do you call the work that a student does at home?

    c. What do you call the cleaning that someone does in a house?

    d. What kind of paper do a lot of people around the world like to read every day?

    e. What kind of book do students use in class?

    f. _____

        _____ ?

3. In the next exercise, you will have the opportunity to talk about the ideas in the commentaries. Try to monitor yourself if and when you use any of the noun compounds listed above. If you find yourself making a mistake regarding where you place the most stress, slow down and self-correct.

◆ Talk About It

> Our identities, who and what we are, how others see us, are greatly affected by the names we are called. . . .
>
> —HAIG BOSMAJIAN

1. In an essay from *Word Play: What Happens When People Talk*, Peter Farb talks about how insulting and hurtful "name-calling" by children can be. Farb mentions the untruthfulness of the old saying, "Sticks and stones may break my bones, but names will never hurt me."

    Farb classifies name-calling by children into four categories: (a) names based on physical characteristics, (b) names based on a pun or joke about a child's own name, (c) names based on social relationships, such as "Baby," and (d) names based on mental characteristics.

    Answer the following questions about name-calling and names:

    a. In Listening 2, Andrew Lam talks about the name-calling that occurred with three Vietnamese high school students named Van, Truc, and Trang. Which of Farb's four categories would this name-calling fit into?

    b. Have you ever seen or experienced name-calling? What happened?

    c. Do you think that people change their first names when they move to a new country because of name-calling? Are there other reasons why people change their names?

2. What are the naming customs in your native country? In other words, how are babies' names chosen? Is it common for people to be named after someone?

Many women in the United States now hyphenate their last name with their husband's last name. For example, if a woman with the maiden name of King married a man whose last name was Martin, the woman's new last name would be King-Martin. The desire to hyphenate last names grew out of the women's liberation movement of the 1960s. Some women did not want to give up their maiden names entirely when they got married. In your native country, do women change their last name when they get married?

3. In both commentaries, Andrew Lam talks about pieces of his old identity. First, he talks of his early years, treasuring everything from the good earth and watching farmers stoop to gather rice. In the second passage, he talks about the beauty and magic of his native language. While he shows love for his past, he does not criticize people's efforts to assimilate into the new society. Do you think that it is possible to assimilate and still keep part of your past? Why or why not?

TUNING IN: "New Citizens and the Vote"

You will watch a CNN video clip about new citizens and voting. Which group do you think has a higher voter turnout rate (votes more)—naturalized citizens or citizens who were born in the United States?

© CNN

Vocabulary in the Video

With a partner, try to guess the meanings of the following key words and phrases used in the video clip about immigrants and the vote.

The word *ballot* comes from the Italian *ballotta* which means "small ball." Centuries ago voting was done by dropping small balls into a box or other receptacle. A white ball represented a "yes" vote, while a black ball indicated "no."

—*MORRIS DICTIONARY OF WORD AND PHRASE ORIGINS*

Words and Phrases	Meanings
cast their ballots	
a basic obligation as a citizen	
a sacred right	
harassment	
polls	
increasingly apathetic	

Watch the Video

Watch the video at least two times. First, just watch. Second, write down some notes in each category below. From this information, you and your group will create two comprehension questions and two discussion questions to ask other groups.

Voting	
Russian example	
Harassment	

Turnouts
Debate about immigration

◄Talk About It

With your group and using your notes, create four questions. Two should be comprehension questions, and two should be for students' opinions about the video clip. Write the four questions on one sheet of paper. Then exchange questions with another group. Follow these steps:

- Have a discussion as you and the members of your group answer the other group's questions orally. Choose one student to write short notes on the paper with the questions.

- Combine the two groups. Tell the other group what your group said in answer to their questions. Refer to the notes if necessary.

PUTTING IT ALL TOGETHER

◄Public Speaking

Information Speech

Imagine that you are speaking to a group of people from the United States or Canada who will be living in your native country. Your job is to prepare them for the cross-cultural differences that they will experience.

First, tell them what surprised you most when you first arrived in the United States or Canada. Give details and use anecdotes if possible. Then explain how things are different in your native country.

Students who are from the same native country may wish to work together and then share their presentation.

Be sure to use at least one visual aid (e.g., a picture, a poster, an object, a video clip, a handout, or an overhead transparency). And when you are speaking, remember to choose one specific aspect of pronunciation to monitor. Evaluate your presentation by using the speech self-evaluation form in Appendix G.

Language You Can Use

Expressing Surprise

It came as a great surprise to find/see that . . .

I was shocked to find out/see . . .

I have to admit that I expected . . .

I had expected . . ., but found . . .

◈ **Listening Log Report**   Bring your Listening Log to class and report on one entry in a small group.

◈ **Search the Web**   Learn more about immigration, culture shock, and other issues mentioned in this chapter by searching the Web. Possible key words: immigrants, immigration, INS (Immigration and Naturalization Service), names, stress, USDA (U.S. Department of Agriculture).

Test-Taking Tip

When you have no idea of the answer on a multiple choice test question, use these techniques to make a guess:

- If two answers are similar except for one or two words, choose one of these.
- If two answers have similar sounding/looking words, choose one of these.
- Eliminate grammatically incorrect answers.
- If two quantities are almost the same, choose one of these.

CHECK YOUR PROGRESS

On a scale of 1 to 5, rate how well you have mastered the goals set at the beginning of the chapter:

1 2 3 4 5   learn about factors related to immigration, adaptation, and assimilation.

1 2 3 4 5   learn vocabulary related to stress, wastefulness, immigration, and voting.

1 2 3 4 5   learn to take advantage of the different kinds of services and opportunities designed to give you added support at your school.

1 2 3 4 5   learn to find a writer's or speaker's point by using your ability to infer.

1 2 3 4 5   develop the ability to monitor your pronunciation as you speak.

1 2 3 4 5   learn to stress the first part of a noun compound.

If you've given yourself a 3 or lower on any of these goals:

- visit the *Tapestry* web site for additional practice.
- ask your instructor for extra help.
- review the sections of the chapter that you found difficult.
- work with a partner or study group to further your progress.

"I'm beginning to think I need a three–million–year sabbatical from humankind to recover my health."

What does this cartoon suggest to you? Do you think the earth has any reason to look so sad and exhausted?

10

CHANGES ON EARTH— IT'S NOT WHAT IT USED TO BE

We hear all the time about the variety of ways in which the earth is changing, particularly in terms of plant and animal species that are disappearing. In this chapter we will expand this theme by exploring three very different angles of changes on earth: the causes and effects of languages dying out; an unexpected way to motivate people to do something about the disappearing rain forest; and the causes and effects of melting icebergs in Antarctica.

Setting Goals

In this chapter you will learn:

◈ how cartoons can increase your knowledge of language and culture.

◈ about various ways in which life on earth is rapidly changing.

◈ vocabulary related to the topics discussed.

◈ how to pronounce -s endings.

◈ how to find ways to improve your listening and speaking skills outside of class.

◈ how to anticipate counter (opposing) arguments to present a stronger argument.

Getting Started

LANGUAGE LEARNING STRATEGY

R ead newspaper and magazine cartoons on a regular basis to increase your knowledge of language and culture. Reading newspaper and magazine cartoons will help you learn more about social,
environmental, and political issues in a culture, learn relevant language, and have conversation topics at your disposal.

Apply the Strategy

Look at the following cartoons. With a partner, look for the common thread that runs through all three. What issues are raised in
these cartoons?

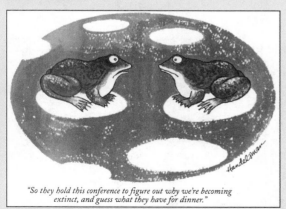

*"So they hold this conference to figure out why we're becoming
extinct, and guess what they have for dinner."*

"I'm starting to get concerned about global warming."

*glade: an open space in the woods or forest

With a partner, make a list of other changes that you think are taking place on the earth. Share your list with your class.

LISTENING 1: DISAPPEARING LANGUAGES

◆ Getting Ready to Listen

> Just as the extinction of any animal species diminishes our world, so does the extinction of any language. Any language is as divine and endless a mystery as a living organism. Should we mourn the loss of a language any less than the loss of a panda or the California condor? Unless we wake up to the problem, we stand to lose up to 95% of our languages in the coming century.
>
> **—MICHAEL KRAUSS**

You are about to listen to an interview on disappearing languages produced by *Living on Earth*, a weekly public radio program that broadcasts news, feature stories, interviews, and commentary on a wide range of topics related to ecological issues.

First, read the following article, which gives some background information that will help you understand the radio interview. After you read, answer the following questions:

- What are the parallels or similarities between the extinction of languages and the extinction of plants and animals?

- How does a language die?

What Causes Language Death?

1   Obvious parallels have been drawn[1] between the extinction of languages and the extinction of plants and animals. In all probability, like the majority of creatures in natural history, the majority of languages in human history have passed from the scene: they have fallen victim to predators,[2] changing environments, or more successful competitors. Moreover, the pace of extinction is clearly accelerating[3] both for languages and for biological species.[4] In the past, despite a few exceptional periods (e.g., the late Mesozoic era, when the dinosaurs died out), the process has proceeded discretely[5] and locally. Today, by contrast, it is proceeding generically[6] and globally. We appear to have entered a period of mass extinctions— a threat to diversity in our natural ecology and also in what might be called our cultural ecology. [It has been estimated] that before

[1]**parallels have been drawn:** similarities have been pointed out
[2]**have fallen victim to predators:** have been hurt by those who harm others for their own benefit
[3]**accelerating:** growing faster
[4]**species:** a type, category, or kind of living thing—for example, a particular species of insect
[5]**discretely:** in individual, separate instances
[6]**generically:** in large groups

industrialism began to affect tropical rain forests, roughly one in a million plants and animals there became extinct each year; today the rate is between one in a thousand and one in a hundred. Instead of individual species facing difficulties in particular habitats,[7] suddenly we are seeing a generalized threat to many species, such as the well-publicized extinction of frogs in diverse environments.

2   Naturally, we do not have similar estimates for the rate of language extinction. Because languages leave no fossil record,[8] there is no way to calculate the rate at which they died out in the past. But the phenomenon of language death is strikingly similar— and causally linked—to the death of biological species. Modern cultures, abetted by[9] new technologies, are encroaching on[10] once-isolated peoples with drastic[11] effects on their way of life and on the environments they inhabit. Destruction of lands and livelihoods;[12] the spread of consumerism, individualism, and other Western values; pressures for assimilation into dominant cultures; and conscious policies of repression directed at indigenous groups[13]—these are among the factors threatening the world's biodiversity as well as its cultural and linguistic diversity.

3   How does a language die? One obvious way is that its speakers can perish through disease or genocide. This was the fate, for example, of most languages spoken by the Arawak peoples of the Caribbean, who disappeared within a generation of their first contact with Christopher Columbus. But such cases are relatively rare. More often language death is the culmination of language shift, resulting from a complex of internal and external pressures that induce[14] a speech community to adopt a language spoken by others. These may include changes in values, rituals, or economic and political life resulting from trade, migration, intermarriage, religious conversion, or military conquest.

Source: From "Endangered Native American Languages: What Is to Be Done, and Why?" by James Crawford, ©1997. Reprinted with permission.

Words and Phrases You Will Hear

Often, seeing words and phrases before you hear them can help your listening comprehension. Take a look at the list on the following page and briefly discuss any unfamiliar items with your teacher.

[7]**habitats:** areas in which a plant or animal normally lives
[8]**fossil record:** remains of ancient animal or plant life preserved in rock
[9]**abetted by:** helped by
[10]**encroaching on:** intruding on
[11]**drastic:** sudden, extreme, and severe
[12]**livelihoods:** ways of earning money to live
[13]**indigenous groups:** native groups
[14]**induce:** force

Places

Kalahari Desert   Tanzania
the Amazonian rain forest

People

the bushmen   Native Americans
the Oro Win   Native Australians

Languages

!Kung   Swahili

Language Sounds

a click sound   a haaaa-type vowel
strident vowels   a trilling of the lips

Foreign Words

!khaaaaow   trrrm trrrm

◆**Vocabulary Building**

You will hear the following sentences in the interview. Try to guess the meanings of the boldface phrases. Use the hints to help you guess.

1. You might expect a language like that, which has all those clicking sounds, **to go easy on** the vowels.

   Hint: If someone starts exercising after a long period of inactivity, a doctor might tell him or her to go easy on the exercise in the beginning.

   to go easy on = _____

2. They use that sound when they have **to coin a new word.**

   Hint: To coin money means to make money from metal.

   to coin a new word = _____

3. We've got to have **a notion** of what is a language and how the human mind creates a language **by taking** all these different sounds **into account.**

   Hint: If you have no idea what someone is talking about, you can say "I haven't the faintest notion of what you mean!"

   a notion = _____

Hint: Although he did poorly on the exam, we should take into account the classes he missed because of his long illness.

by taking into account = _____

4. There are probably now only 20 languages in that region that are really **viable** and able to last for some time.

   Hint: Because of advances in medical technology, a baby born several months prematurely is viable at a much earlier stage than before.

   viable = _____

5. As soon as mothers don't speak to the children in that language, the language will slowly **fade away** as people get older and older.

   Hint: The shapes faded away into the night and could no longer be seen.

   fade away = _____

6. It's part of our whole **tribal being** to be able to speak this language.

   Hint: A tribe is a social group made up of people of the same race, beliefs, customs, and language living in a particular area.

   tribal being = _____

Listen

Listening 1: Disappearing Languages

Listen for the Main Idea

Listen to the interview. Then write one sentence that summarizes the main idea:

_____

_____

_____

Listen and Take Notes

Use the "split-page format" described on page 35 in Chapter 2 to take notes as you listen again to the same material.

- Take out a piece of paper and copy what is written on the following sample page. The underlined headings are included to help you take notes. Copy them before you listen to the tape, leaving plenty of space after each heading so that you will have room to write details. Note: The speaker uses many numerical facts that you will need to put in your notes.

QUESTIONS/IDEAS   NOTES: DISAPPEARING LANGUAGES

Languages Disappearing

The !Kung Language

The Oro Win Language

Why Preserve Rare Languages?

Languages in Trouble

Reasons Rare Languages Fade

Attitude of Speakers of Rare Languages

- As you listen, write only in the Notes column. Indent your notes to show the organization of what you hear. Main points should start farthest to the left. Specific information that comes after each main point should be below and indented a little bit to the right. Also, you can use capital letters and underlining to indicate the most important points.

For note-taking tips regarding abbreviations and signals, see Appendix A.

After You Listen

1. Reread your notes. Add ideas and questions to the left column.

2. Using your notes, fill in the blanks with the correct numbers.

   a. The most common languages are spoken by _____ % of the world's population.

b. More than _____ the world's languages are spoken by fewer than 10,000 people.

c. More than _____ of the world's languages are spoken by _____ people.

d. !Kung is spoken by about _____ people in the Kalahari Desert.

e. !Kung has _____ different ways of beginning a word with a different click sound.

f. Over _____ the words in !Kung begin with a click.

g. There are about _____ languages in the world.

h. Of those languages in the world today, probably _____ won't last another century.

i. We used to have _____ American Indian languages in the United States, but now there are probably only _____ that are really viable.

3. Listen to the interview again and add more details to your notes. Also, correct your answers to #2.

4. Using your notes, answer the following questions orally with a partner:

a. What is unique about the !Kung language?

b. What does Ladefoged find interesting about the Oro Win language?

c. Why does Ladefoged think it is valuable to preserve rare languages?

d. What explanation does Ladefoged give for why the "little languages" slowly fade away?

e. According to Ladefoged, how do people who speak rare languages feel when their languages fade away?

People in the United States often notice a foreign accent, and when they meet you, they may immediately ask where you're from. Don't be offended. Many Americans are interested in the places their own ancestors have come from or where they have traveled (or would like to travel) in different parts of the world. Would someone be likely to ask a near-stranger "Where are you from?" in your native culture?

Talk About It

1. Red Thunder Cloud, the last speaker of the Catawba language, died in 1996. Read the following obituary, which appeared in the *New York Times*, and then discuss the questions that follow.

Red Thunder Cloud, 76, Dies . . .

by David Stout

1   Red Thunder Cloud, a member of the Catawba Nation who was steeped in[1] the history of the American Indians, died Monday in Worcester, Mass. He was the last human link to the ancient language of his people.

2   Thunder Cloud, who was 76, died in St. Vincent's Hospital after a stroke, friends said. Thunder Cloud was also known as Carlos Westez and lived in Northbridge, Mass. He was a story-teller and earned money from selling his own line of teas from herbs that he collected in the woods around his home.

3   "It's always sad when the last living speaker of a language dies," Carl Teeter, emeritus professor of linguistics at Harvard University, said on Friday. "There were once 500 languages in North America. About a hundred are still spoken, and half of them are spoken by older people." Dr. Teeter said the Catawba language, like others, had died off because of prejudice. Not so long ago, he said, Americans who spoke Indian languages "weren't treated too well."

4   Dr. Teeter described Catawba, an oral language with no written form, as related to the Sioux family of languages. He said the similarity indicated that there may have been considerable movement among Indian tribes hundreds of years ago.

5   In the 1940's, Thunder Cloud made a complete recording of all he knew of the Catawba language for the Massachusetts Institute of Technology. About that time, he also recorded some ancient Catawba songs for the Smithsonian Institution. Derek Jordan of Putney, Vt., a friend of Thunder Cloud's, recorded two albums of Catawba songs and legends by Thunder Cloud in 1990.

6   Mr. Jordan said Thunder Cloud had learned Catawba as a boy from his grandfather, Strong Eagle, and from tribal elders. Eventually, there were only two Catawba speakers left: Thunder Cloud and a woman, who died about 40 years ago.

7   Foxx Ayers of Columbia, S.C., a Catawba and friend of Thunder Cloud, recalled on Friday that he resisted his grandmother's efforts to teach him the language because he feared he would be ridiculed. "I wish now that I'd learned," said Ayers, 71.

[1]**steeped in:** thoroughly involved in

8   Mr. Ayers recalled one happy experiment with the language. One day years ago, he was visiting Thunder Cloud, who used to sell pottery made by Mr. Ayer's wife, Sarah, who is also a Catawba. Mr. Ayers's arms were full of pottery when he found his way blocked by Thunder Cloud's dog. The dog responded only to commands in Catawba. So Ayers tried one phrase he had heard Thunder Cloud use (roughly "Swie hay, tanty," or "Move, dog"), and the dog obeyed.

9   Alice Kasakoff, a professor of anthropology at the University of South Carolina, said the conversion[2] of many Catawbas after visits by Mormon missionaries to their enclave[3] in South Carolina may have hastened the decline of the Indian language.

10   Estimates of the number of living Catawbas range from several hundred to more than 1,000. The nation's headquarters is in Rock Hill, S.C.

11   In its scarcity of[4] close relationships, Thunder Cloud's life seemed to foreshadow the passing[5] of the language only he spoke. Mr. Ayers said he recalled that Thunder Cloud was married for a time to a Blackfeet woman, but that the union dissolved.

12   Lenora Pena of Center Falls, R.I., who described herself as Thunder Cloud's closest friend, said he prayed each night in Catawba.

13   Thunder Cloud left no known survivors. Ms. Pena said that Thunder Cloud had a sister but that they had lost track of each other many years ago.

Source: *The New York Times*, January 14, 1996.

- What are some of the important issues that are touched on in the obituary?

- How do you imagine it would feel to be the sole surviving speaker of a language?

- Do you think that survival of a culture is linked to survival of the language spoken by people in that culture? Why or why not?

2. The following charts give a view of the languages that are threatened. Are you surprised by any of the information in the charts?

[2]**conversion:** change of religion
[3]**enclave:** a small area controlled by people who differ in culture, social status, and ethnic background from those in the surrounding area—e.g., a Native American reservation in the United States
[4]**scarcity of:** lack of
[5]**foreshadow the passing:** show in advance the death

MAPPING OUR ENDANGERED[1] TONGUES

Linguists estimate that nearly half the world's
6,500 languages are threatened.

Europe

European languages in danger of disappearing include the Celtic languages of Britain, Ireland, and Brittany in France; several Lappish languages in Scandinavia; various Romani (Gypsy) tongues; and numerous indigenous languages in the former Soviet Union.

Africa

In Africa, multilingualism is the norm rather than the exception. It is common, for example, for many Africans to speak five or six tribal languages in addition to their own mother tongue. Nevertheless, small tribal languages are under continual threat from their larger neighbors. The Khoisan language group, for example, to which the Hottentot and Bushman tongues belong, is almost extinct.[2]

Asia

The most threatened languages in China are located in the Xinjiang and Yunnan provinces. In Southeast Asia, minority languages in Nepal and Malaysia are under threat. In Japan, Ainu, a threatened tongue spoken in Hokkaido, is making a comeback as a result of the efforts of native speakers and a change in official government policy. Relatively few languages are under threat on the Indian subcontinent due to wide-spread multilingualism.

Pacific

Many languages in Papua New Guinea are under threat due to the increasing popularity of two pidgin tongues. In Australia, one of the areas where language extinction has exacted the heaviest toll, few of the surviving 250 or so aboriginal languages are still viable.

Americas

In Arctic North America, many Eskimo and Amerindian languages are threatened. The status of Native American tongues in Canada and the United States is perhaps the worst in the world. In Central and South America, large numbers of languages are moribund,[3] while many of the languages that are still viable have drastically reduced numbers of speakers.

Source: *UNESCO's Atlas of the World's Languages in Danger of Disappearing*

[1]**endangered:** a language is considered endangered when it is no longer spoken by children
[2]**extinct:** a language is considered extinct when there are no speakers left
[3]**moribund:** a language is considered moribund when only a handful of elderly speakers are left

WORLD'S TOP TEN LANGUAGES

First-language speaker estimates given in millions:

1.	Mandarin Chinese	726
2.	English	427
3.	Spanish	266
4.	Hindi	182
5.	Arabic	181
6.	Portuguese	165
7.	Bengali	162
8.	Russian	158
9.	Japanese	124
10.	German	121

Source: *The Cambridge Encyclopedia of Language*

DISTRIBUTION OF THE WORLD'S LANGUAGES

Total number of languages: 6,528

Europe	3%	(209)
Americas	15%	(949)
Africa	31%	(1,995)
Pacific	21%	(1,341)
Asia	31%	(2,034)

Source: *The Cambridge Encyclopedia of Language*

3. In small groups, discuss the following questions:

- Who or what do you think is to blame when a language disappears?

- Do you think that much can be done to save rare languages, especially since many of them have no written form? Or is it inevitable that rare languages will disappear?

- Do you think it is important to try to save rare languages? Why or why not? If you think it is important, what are some concrete steps that can be taken to ensure their survival?

LISTENING 2: EAT CHOCOLATE AND SUPPORT THE ENVIRONMENT!

◆ Getting Ready to Listen

Languages are not the only things disappearing from the earth. Although scientists have been warning us about the disappearing rain forest for years, it has been difficult for conservationists to get all levels of society interested in protecting the rain forest. You will listen to radio commentator Suzanne Elston explain why she thinks that may have changed.

What does this cartoon suggest to you about the rain forest?

"Hard to believe this was all rain forest just fifteen years ago."

◆ Words and Phrases You Will Hear

Often, seeing words and phrases before you hear them can help your listening comprehension. Take a look at the following list and briefly discuss any unfamiliar items with your teacher.

The Environment

acre upon acre of the world's rain forest

a certain plant species

conservationists

environmental issues

the lungs of the planet

large plantations

more than half the species found on earth

vulnerable to pests and disease

clear another strip of rain forest

deforestation

a global shortage

the canopy of the rain forest

International Companies and Organizations

the huge multinational corporations

a global cooperative

development agencies

conservation groups

agricultural experts

corporate concern about the bottom line

◆**Vocabulary Building**

You will hear the following sentences in the radio commentary. Try to guess the meanings of the boldface phrases. Use the hints to help you guess.

1. The impact of their destruction **has never hit home** for most people.

   Hint: For many people, a faraway crisis hits home only when it begins to affect them directly in some way.

   has never hit home = _____

2. Scientists, hoping **to head off** the potential crisis, discovered that cocoa plants prefer to grow under the canopy of the rain forest.

   Hint: Sometimes a government has to take extreme measures in order to head off an economic crisis.

   to head off = _____

3. Development agencies, conservationists, and agricultural groups will work alongside local farmers to create **a sustainable system** of cocoa farming.

   Hint: "To sustain" means to maintain, to keep in existence over a period of time.

   a sustainable system = _____

4. One of the more interesting projects will involve using cocoa plants as part of a reforestation effort **to revitalize** war-torn areas of Vietnam.

   Hint: To "vitalize" means to fill with life, to animate, to make more lively or vigorous.

   to revitalize = _____

Listen

Listening 2: Eat Chocolate and Support the Environment!

Listen for the Main Idea

Listen to the radio commentary. Write one sentence that summarizes the main idea:

_____

_____

_____

Listen for More Information

- Read the following questions.
- Listen to the commentary again.
- After you listen, answer the questions with a partner. Write short answers on the lines.
- Listen again to check your answers and to add more information.

1. Why do we have trouble relating to big environmental issues?

_____

_____

2. Why is there a potential chocolate shortage?

_____

_____

_____

3. How soon will the shortage hit?

_____

_____

4. How do chocolate companies plan to prevent the potential crisis?

_____

_____

_____

 **After You Listen**

1. What do you think is the point of the commentary? What do you think it will take to get people from all levels of society—from

individual citizens to private corporations to the government—interested in saving the rain forest?

2. Do you think saving endangered languages is as important as saving the rain forest? Do you think it is possible to get people from all levels of society—including corporations—interested in saving endangered languages?

Write a one-paragraph summary of the commentary. Refer only to your notes. Be sure to use your own words. Refer to Appendix B for guidelines on paraphrasing and Appendix C for guidelines on summarizing.

- Your first sentence should both introduce the person whose ideas are referred to, Suzanne Elston, and contain the main idea of the commentary. Because many people don't know her, it will be necessary to explain who she is by using an appositive: "Suzanne Elston, *commentator on the public radio program Living on Earth, . . .*"

- In subsequent sentences, include the main points and some of the details. Remember to use language of attribution because you will be giving the ideas of the commentator.

The Sound of It: Pronouncing -*s* Endings

It is very important that you clearly pronounce the final -*s* at the end of present-tense verbs in the third-person singular (such as in *wants*) and the final -*s* on plural nouns (such as in *books*) and possessive nouns (*Brian's*). If you don't pronounce these -*s* sounds clearly, you will be making not just pronunciation mistakes, but also grammatical mistakes.

Look at Laura Knoy's introduction to the radio commentary you heard. All of the final -*s* sounds for present-tense verbs in the third-person singular, possessive nouns, and plural nouns have been underlined. Read the paragraph aloud without saying the -*s* endings. Does it sound strange?

> Language**s**, of course, are not the only thing**s** vanishing from the earth. Acre upon acre of the world'**s** rain forest are lost each day, and along with them a certain plant species is disappearing. For year**s** conservationist**s** have searched for an issue that would motivate all level**s** of society to protect the rain forest. As commentator Suzanne Elston explain**s**, they just may have found one.

- Before you read the paragraph aloud again, read the explanation and rules for pronouncing -*s* endings on the next page.

- After you read the pronunciation rules, read the paragraph aloud again, concentrating on pronouncing all of the -s endings correctly.

Pronouncing the -s Ending

The -s endings can have three sounds: the voiceless /s/, the voiced /z/, or a new syllable, /ɪz/.

To determine which sound to use, you need to know whether the last sound (not letter) of a word is voiced or voiceless. All vowel sounds are voiced.

You can feel whether consonant sounds are voiced or voiceless by holding your hand against your throat and saying the sounds. If you feel a vibration, the sound is voiced.

<table>
<tr><th colspan="5" align="center">Final -s Ending Rules</th></tr>
<tr><th>Final
Sound of
Word</th><th>Pronunciation
of -s Ending</th><th>New
Syllable
Added?</th><th colspan="2" align="center">Examples</th></tr>
<tr><td>voiceless</td><td>/s/</td><td>no</td><td>asks sounds like</td><td>/æsks/</td></tr>
<tr><td>voiced</td><td>/z/</td><td>no</td><td>teachers sounds like</td><td>/ˈti-tʃərz/</td></tr>
<tr><td>s, z, sh, ch, j</td><td>/ɪz/</td><td>yes</td><td>classes sounds like</td><td>/ˈklæ-sɪz/</td></tr>
</table>

TUNING IN: "Melting Icebergs"

In the video clip you are about to watch, you will learn about something else that is changing—the receding glaciers of Antarctica.

© CNN

- What do you already know about this continent?

Vocabulary in the Video

With a partner, try to guess the meanings of the following key words and phrases used in the video clip about Antarctica. If you do not know a word or phrase, try to guess its meaning from context when you watch the video clip.

Words and Phrases	Meanings
dire predictions	
the Antarctic Peninsula	
the global rate of warming	
heat-trapping gases	
Mother Nature	
receding glaciers	
a 500-square-mile chunk of the ice	
winter pack ice	
one of the world's greatest geophysical events	
prime habitat for polar wildlife	
penguins	
one of the world's harshest environments	

> Antarctica is covered with a massive ice sheet that's more than two miles thick in places.
>
> —JOEL ACHENBACH

Watch the Video

Watch the video at least two times. First, just watch. Second, write down some notes in each category on the following page. From this information, you and your group will create four questions to ask other groups.

Increased temperatures at the Antarctica Peninsula
Glaciers around the Larsen Ice Shelf
Effect on the wildlife
Importance (ecological value/impact worldwide)

> The closest Antarctica comes to the extreme tip of South America is about six hundred miles.
>
> **—JOEL ACHENBACH**

◁Talk About It

With your group and using your notes, create four questions. Two should be comprehension questions, and two should ask for students' opinions about the issues concerning the receding glaciers. Write the four questions on one sheet of paper. Then exchange questions with another group. Follow these steps:

- Have a discussion as you and the members of your group answer the other group's questions orally. Choose one student to write short notes on the paper with the questions.

- Combine the two groups. Tell the other group what your group said in answer to their questions. Refer to the notes if necessary.

ACADEMIC POWER STRATEGY

Find ways to improve your listening and speaking skills outside of class. There are many ways you can continue to work on your listening and speaking skills on your own, even after your semester or program ends. For example, most of the listening passages in this book were obtained from public radio station programs, many of which offer audiotapes and transcripts of their broadcasts. Obtaining tapes and transcripts of programs that you find interesting is a great way to continue to learn English outside of the classroom.

(continued on next page)

Apply the Strategy

Find out how to get a tape and transcript of a program you are interested in. Check some of these web sites for current as well as past programs. Find out how to order a tape and a transcript, how much it costs, and how long it will take.

Fresh Air from radio station WHYY in Philadelphia at **www.whyy.org**

On the Media from radio station WNYC in New York City at **www.wnyc.org**

All Things Considered from National Public Radio at **www.npr.org**

Morning Edition from National Public Radio at **www.npr.org**

Talk of the Nation from National Public Radio at **www.npr.org**

Weekend Edition from National Public Radio at **www.npr.org**

Living on Earth produced at Harvard University at **www.loe.org**

PUTTING IT ALL TOGETHER

◆ Public Speaking

Persuasive Speech

So far in this chapter, you have looked at some problems the world faces and have talked about some of the things that can be done about them. Now it is your turn to persuade your classmates that a particular problem or issue is serious and that you can offer some useful solutions.

Think of a problem you have observed or encountered at home, at school, on the job, or in public. Or think of a problem you have read or heard about. Draw on outside sources—articles, books, pamphlets, interviews, and so on—as sources of facts and opinions for this speech.

Prepare a 5–6-minute speech in which you explain the problem and then propose one or more solutions. For your speech, do the following:

- Describe the problem and explain why it is serious.

- Think of reasons why people might not think the problem is serious, state what they are and why you disagree with them.

- Offer one or more effective solutions.

• Address the counterarguments to your solution and explain why your solution is better.

For an explanation of counterarguments, look at the Language Learning Strategy on page 228.

Preparation

1. Choose and research an appropriate problem. Here are some examples of the types of topics that would be appropriate for a persuasive speech:

   a local environmental problem

   the effect of American culture on your native country

   car theft

   computer viruses

   cheating

   vandalism on public transportation

   lack of good public transportation

   homelessness on the streets

   lack of tolerance

   decline in public civility

   violence on TV

   drunk driving accidents

   problems created by cell phones (for example, noise and/or car accidents)

   smoking in public places

2. Prepare your persuasive talk. Do not write your speech out or memorize it. Use notecards to help you remember what you want to say.

3. Practice your speech several times. Concentrate on pronouncing -s endings correctly.

Presentation

1. Present your persuasive speech to your classmates.

2. Evaluate your presentation by using the student self-evaluation form in Appendix G.

LANGUAGE LEARNING STRATEGY

Apply the Strategy

Anticipate counter (opposing) arguments when you want to persuade someone that a course of action that you are proposing is an effective one. Anticipating counterarguments will show that you have thought carefully about the issue and will help make your own argument more persuasive.

Anticipate and counter possible objections to your persuasive speech. First, look at some examples. Suppose that you want to persuade people that we should all care about the fact that languages are disappearing. The following are three possible counterarguments and responses:

Counterargument 1: What does a rare language spoken by only a few thousand people have to do with me? Why should I care?

Response: Some of you might ask, "What does a rare language spoken only by a few thousand people have to do with me?" I would answer that it has a lot to do with you. For example, scientists are now discovering that some of these languages spoken by only a few thousand people contain words for plants that the scientists have never heard of. Often these are plants that have been used for medicinal purposes for centuries by tribes who speak these rare languages. Scientists have discovered new plant species as a result of the research done by linguists on rare languages. This knowledge has potential benefit for all of us, and for this reason, it is important to preserve languages even if they are spoken by only a few thousand people.

Analysis: The speaker states the objection and then answers the objection with a concrete example.

Counterargument 2: If young people aren't interested in learning the language spoken by their elders, it doesn't matter if anyone else cares or not.

Response: Another objection people might have is that "if young people themselves are not interested in learning the language of their elders, it doesn't matter if anyone else cares or not." There is certainly truth to this argument, but I think we can all look back to when we were children and see things we didn't do because they weren't important to us at the time. It's only now that we are older that we wish we had studied harder or spent more time with a grandparent or learned more about our culture. Is it right to let a language die out because children aren't interested in learning it?

I think the key to getting children interested in learning the languages of their elders is to look at what children enjoy doing and find ways for them to do those things while using their native languages. We need to look at how children's lives have changed and create new and different opportunities for them to use their languages in a meaningful way.

Analysis: The speaker first stated the objection, acknowledged it had some validity, and proceeded to explain how the objection could be overcome.

Counterargument 3: As people from small tribes become dispersed, it is inevitable that their languages will be lost.

Response: A third argument that I often hear is that languages will inevitably disappear as the people who speak them no longer live in the same communities, but become dispersed. However, I don't accept that point of view. I can give you the example of the Lakota people, who have created a web site to promote their culture and language. The Lakota tribe recognized that how people communicate and exchange ideas today has shifted radically, and instead of complaining about this change, they have taken advantage of it to help their culture and their language survive.

Analysis: The speaker states the objection and then answers it, again by giving a concrete example.

Language You Can Use: Stating and Countering Objections

Stating the Objection:

Some of you might argue that . . .

Some people might say that . . .

There are those who would ask . . .

Some of you might object to my solution by saying that . . .

Another objection to this proposal might be that . . .

You might wonder why someone would want to take the course of action I am suggesting since . . .

I know that one argument that is often heard is that . . .

Countering the Objection:

I would counter this argument by saying . . .

I would like to point out that . . .

There is some truth to this argument; however, . . .

I can see why this argument might seem appealing, but . . .
At first sight, this might seem to be the case, but in fact . . .
Even if you . . ., what about . . .?
As I've said before, . . .
I don't accept this argument because . . .

Listening Log Report

Bring your Listening Log to class and report on one entry in a small group.

Search the Web

Learn more about endangered languages, endangered biological species, and endangered land by searching the Web. Possible key words: endangered languages, Lakota, endangered species, endangered coastline, flooding coastlines, Antarctica, global warming, receding icebergs, greenhouse effect.

Test-Taking Tip

Reduce test anxiety by being prepared. Before a test, meet with other students to review material covered in class. Talking aloud about what you have studied helps reinforce what you have learned. Studying with others will also give you confidence which will help you succeed.

CHECK YOUR PROGRESS

On a scale of 1 to 5, rate how well you have mastered the goals set at the beginning of the chapter:

1 2 3 4 5   learn how cartoons can increase your knowledge of language and culture.

1 2 3 4 5   learn about various ways in which life on earth is rapidly changing.

1 2 3 4 5   learn vocabulary related to the topics discussed.

1 2 3 4 5   learn how to pronounce -s endings.

1 2 3 4 5   learn how to find ways to improve your listening and speaking skills outside of class.

1 2 3 4 5   learn how to anticipate counter (opposing) arguments to present a stronger argument.

If you have given yourself a 3 or lower on any of these goals:

- visit the *Tapestry* web site for additional practice.
- ask your instructor for extra help.
- review the sections of the chapter that you found difficult.
- work with a partner or study group to further your progress.

APPENDIX A: NOTE TAKING

Here are a few hints for taking notes:

1. Choose a format that is comfortable for you, but make sure that it is easy to see the difference between main ideas and details in your headings:

Some ways to write headings:

- Use capital letters:
  WHY NOTE TAKING IS IMPORTANT

- Underline: <u>Why note taking is important</u>

- Use a box: | Why note taking is important |

- Put the heading in a circle in the center of a page with lines for details extending out:

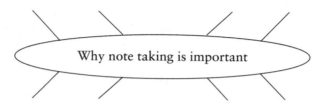

Some ways to write details:

- Indent below heading and use dashes:

  WHY NOTE TAKING IS IMPORTANT
  —we quickly forget what we hear
  —material is easier to remember

- Place in circles around main idea:

- Indent below heading and use bullets:

  | Why note taking is important |

  - we quickly forget what we hear
  - material is easier to remember

we quickly forget what we hear   material is easy to remember

Why note taking is important

2. Don't try to write everything you hear, word for word, as if you were taking dictation.

3. Become aware of when a speaker is using *signal words* that indicate where the lecture is going. (see p. 233)

4. Use *abbreviations* to save time. Some examples follow, but use whatever abbreviations you are familiar with. And when you hear long words, try to make up abbreviations. (see p. 234)

SIGNAL WORDS AND PHRASES

Some Bell Phrases. Also known as "signal words" and "signal phrases," these indicate an important point that should be remembered.

Additive words: These say, "Here's more of the same coming up. It's just as important as what we have already said."
Examples:

also	furthermore
and	in addition
besides	moreover
further	too

Equivalent words: They say, "It does what I have just said, but it does this too."
Examples:

as well as	likewise
at the same	similarly
equally important	time

Amplification words: The author is saying, "I want to be sure that you understand my idea: so here's a specific instance."
Examples:

as	like
for example (e.g.)	specifically
for instance	such as

Alternative words: These point up, "Sometimes there is a choice; other times there isn't."
Examples:

either/or	otherwise
other than	neither/nor

Repetitive words: They say, "I said it once, but I'm going to say it again in case you missed it the first time."
Examples:

again	that is (i.e.)
in other words	to repeat

Contrast-and-change words: "So far I've given you only one side of the story; now let's take a look at the other side."
Examples:

but	on the contrary
conversely	on the other hand
despite	rather than
even though	regardless
however	still
in spite of	though
instead of	whereas
nevertheless	yet
notwithstanding	

Cause-and-effect words: "All this has happened; now I'll tell you why."
Examples:

accordingly	since
because	so
consequently	then
for this reason	therefore
hence	thus

Qualifying words: These say, "Here is what we can expect. These are the conditions we are working under."
Examples:

although	unless
if	whenever
provided that	

Concession words: They say "Okay, we agree on this much."

Examples:

accepting the data	of course
granted that	

Emphasizing words: They say "Wake up and take notice!"

Examples:

above all	more important
indeed	

Order words: The author is saying "You keep your mind on reading; I'll keep the numbers straight."

Examples:

finally	next
first	second
last	then

Time words: "Let's keep the record straight on who said what and especially when."

Examples:

afterward	presently
before	previously
formerly	subsequently
meanwhile	ultimately
now	

Summarizing words: These say "I've said many things so far; let's stop here and pull them together."

Examples:

for these reasons	in conclusion
in brief	to sum up

ABBREVIATIONS

Personal Shorthand. These are some commonly used abbreviations. If you wish, you can tear out or photocopy this list and tape it inside the cover of your binder or notebook.

advantage	*adv*	in order to	*i.o.t.*	regarding	*re*
against	*vs*	individual	*indiv*	should be	*s/b*
and	+	information	*info*	significant	*signif*
and so forth	*etc*	important	*impt*	that is	*i.e.*
association	*assoc*	introduction	*intro*	therefore	∴
because	*bec*	maximum	*max*	with	*w/*
consequently	∴	necessary	*nec*	without	*w/o*
department	*dept*	organization	*org*	with regard to	*w.r.t.*
development	*devmt*	particular	*partic*		
for example	*ex* or *eg*	politics	*pol*		
government	*govt*	psychology	*psych*		

Source: From *Learning Success*, 1st edition, by C. M. Wahlstrom and B. K. Williams. © 1996. Reprinted with permission of Wadsworth Publishing, a division of Thomson Learning. Fax 800-730-2215.

APPENDIX B: PARAPHRASING

There are two ways to report what others have said. One way is to use quotation marks around the exact words. The other way is to paraphrase—that is, to put someone else's ideas into your own words. In both cases, when you quote or paraphrase, it is essential to use *attribution,* which means that you indicate who the speaker is.

Below are examples of quoting and paraphrasing from Chapter 1. Notice the use of attribution in each sentence.

1. **Change the word order.** For example, change from active voice to passive voice (or passive to active):

   Quotation: Lillian Glass says, "*I encourage all of my clients* to read the newspaper. . . ."

   Paraphrase: Lillian Glass's *clients are all encouraged* to read the newspaper.

2. **Change a word from one part of speech to another.**

   Quotation: According to Lillian Glass, "The best way to entice a person to have a conversation with you is by *being sincere and respectful.* . . ."

   Paraphrase: According to Lillian Glass, the best way to get someone to talk to you is by *showing sincerity and respect.*

3. **Use synonyms.**

   Quotation: According to Lillian Glass, "The best way to *entice a person to have a conversation with you* is by being sincere and respectful. . . ."

   Paraphrase: According to Lillian Glass, the best way to *get someone to talk to you* is by showing sincerity and respect.

4. **Use a negative or some other reversal that does not change the meaning.**

   Quotation: Glass asserts that "The best kind of ice breaker is one that's positive."

   Paraphrase: Glass asserts that the best kind of ice breaker isn't negative.

5. **Combine sentences.**

   It can be helpful to combine sentences when you want to paraphrase, especially if the original sentences were short.

   Quotation: Another recommendation that Glass gives is to "have a sense of humor. Everyone enjoys a humorous story or joke."

   Paraphrase: Glass also recommends that people have a sense of humor because everyone likes funny jokes and stories.

6. **Use pronouns to replace names.**

   Quotation: "Dr. Glass has coached many celebrities on their voices, accents, and dialects."

   Paraphrase: *She* has taught many celebrities how to use their voices, accents, and dialects.

(adapted from *Improving the Grammar of Written English: The Handbook* by Patricia Byrd and Beverly Benson. Wadsworth Publishing Company, Inc., 1989.)

APPENDIX C: SUMMARIZING

1. What is a summary?

A summary is an oral or written explanation of something you heard, saw, or read. You can summarize a lecture that you heard or a movie you saw. You can also summarize a newspaper article or a reading from a book. A summary is always shorter than the original material.

2. Why is it important to learn how to write a summary?

You need to learn how to tell other people the main idea of what you heard, saw, or read. If people ask you what a movie was about, you first tell them the main idea of the story. If they are interested, you might give them a few details. Telling everything about a movie isn't summarizing.

3. What should I put in a summary?

Remember that you need to put the main idea first. You should add details if you think the people who listen to or read your summary won't understand the main idea without more explanation.

Also, consider what you are asked to do. If your teacher asks for a one-sentence summary, give only the main idea. If your teacher asks for a brief summary, write the main idea plus a few details. If your teacher asks for a detailed summary, include some, but not all the details.

Sometimes you will be asked to write a summary and then give your opinion. In this case, be sure to put your opinion in a separate paragraph.

4. What should I put in the first sentence?

State the main idea in the first sentence. Here are some suggestions for ways to start:

- According to Lillian Glass, . . .
- In Lillian Glass's opinion, . . .
- In the listening passage, Lillian Glass discusses/discussed . . .
- The listening passage is/was about . . .

If you know the title of the source, use it in the first sentence between quotation marks. Write, for example:

- The listening passage, "How to Be a Good Conversationalist," is/was about . . .
- In her column, "So, What's New with You?," Adair Lara talks about . . .

Note: You can use either simple present or simple past tense.

5. What should I *not* put in a summary?

Don't express your own opinion, and don't add information that was not in what you heard or read.

6. Should I use the exact words that I heard? Can I copy from what I read?

No. You should try to use your own words (see Appendix B for tips on paraphrasing). If you must copy, don't copy too much, and be sure to put what you copy between quotation marks.

APPENDIX D: LISTENING LOGS

1. What is a listening log?

A listening log is like a journal. It is a small book or section of your notebook in which you write information and your thoughts about what you listened to on TV or the radio. At least twice every week, you will watch or listen to programs and take notes. You will put your notes into your log and then write a short summary of what you saw and heard. After that, you will write your reaction to the program in a short paragraph.

2. In more detail, what should go into my log?

Twice each week, for each program you watch or listen to, write the following:

- The name of the program you watched or listened to
- The date of broadcast
- Your notes, in list form
- A short summary in your own words— no more than one paragraph. Don't try to explain everything that you saw or heard. Just give the main idea and a few details.
- Your personal opinion of the program in a separate paragraph

3. Why should we keep listening logs?

Logs are useful for a number of reasons:

- You may be unaware of good programs to watch on TV or listen to on the radio in English. Keeping a listening log encourages you to search them out and listen to them regularly.
- Listening outside of class helps you to learn English and understand American culture. As you know, it is not enough to speak English only in class.
- You practice the important skills of note taking, summarizing, and writing down your re-actions. Then, in class, you have opportunities to express your ideas orally in a small group.

4. How often should I turn in my log?

Your teacher will decide. Perhaps you will need to turn it in every two or three weeks.

5. How many entries should be in my log each time I turn it in?

Each week you should write two entries. If your teacher collects the log every two weeks, your log will contain four entries each time (and perhaps more if you want extra credit).

6. Are logs graded?

Your teacher may collect the first logs at the end of the first week to see if everyone understands what to do, and this log may not be graded. Subsequent logs, collected every two or three weeks, often receive letter grades, but your teacher will make the decision.

7. How are logs graded?

Again, that will be your teacher's decision. However, the following are often considered in log grades:

- Whether or not you have made at least two entries per week
- Whether or not you have three sections per entry—notes, summary, reaction
- The quality of these three sections

8. Is it OK to watch closed-captioned TV?

Yes, it's a great idea. For those of you who don't know, closed-captioning prints the spoken words in a TV program along the bottom of the TV screen. This captioning was originally intended for the deaf, but it was also found to be helpful to people learning a language. All new TVs sold in the United States after 1994 can receive closed-captioned programs.

Another advantage would be having access to a VCR. You might tape a few minutes of a TV program and then play it back over and over. With each replay, your comprehension will increase.

9. How can I write about a news program that has a lot of stories?

You should summarize and react to only one or two of the news stories, not all. If you watch a one-hour news-magazine show that contains three stories, write about only one.

10. **What should I do if I don't understand what I'm listening to?**

You should write a note to your teacher in your log that you didn't understand a particular program. Then try to find something else to listen to.

11. **Can I see an example of a log entry?**

Yes. Here's one written by a student who listened to a program on National Public Radio:

NPR
April 27, 1993, 5:30–6:00 p.m.
Denmark's child care system

Notes:
Careers and Motherhood:
• Denmark's second largest city
• nursery—elementary school
• rich—pay one-third of operating cost
• poor—pay nothing

Summary:
Denmark's second largest city has a wonderful child care system. Mothers who juggle careers and motherhood really love this system. The program is subsidized by the ministry policies. These child-care centers are no different from regular kindergartens. They take care of children from the age of three months, and will even care for elementary schoolers after school. The only difference is that better-off families pay one third of operating cost and less well-off families pay nothing.

Personal Reaction:
Many women have to struggle to keep their jobs while raising children at the same time. The government or individual communities in the U.S. should develop a program like the one in Denmark. This would help reduce the hardship of balancing working with parenting.

12. **What specific TV programs should I watch?**

Programs and schedules can change a great deal, but here are some shows that have been on TV in the United States for a long time. Some of the shows indicated can be seen in reruns only. If you are in the United States, your class can be divided into groups that find out the day, time, and channel of each show and then report the schedule to the whole class. If you are not in the United States, if possible, make a list of TV shows that are broadcast in English that you might want to watch.

TYPE OF SHOW	DAY AND TIME	CHANNEL
NEWS		
Lehrer Newshour		
NBC News		
CBS News		
ABC News		
Nightline		
Washington Week in Review		
CNN		
Other:		
NEWS MAGAZINE SHOWS (SHORT DOCUMENTARIES)		
60 Minutes		
20/20		
Dateline		
Other:		
SUNDAY MORNING NEWS SHOWS		
Sunday Morning		
Meet the Press		
Face the Nation		
Other:		

TYPE OF SHOW	DAY AND TIME	CHANNEL

TALK SHOWS

Oprah Winfrey

Other:

LATE-NIGHT SHOWS

Tonight Show

Late Show with
David Letterman

Saturday Night Live

Other:

COMEDIES

Seinfeld

The Simpsons

Roseanne

Other:

DRAMAS

ER

The Practice

Other:

13. **What radio programs should I listen to?**

If you prefer to listen to noncommercial radio, then you would probably like National Public Radio (NPR). Ask someone in your area to tell you the number on the radio dial for NPR. In some areas, there may be more than one local station that carries NPR broadcasts.

APPENDIX E: GUEST SPEAKERS

Before the Visit

1. Make a list of people in your school or community who can speak on a topic related to the chapter that you are working on. Choose the person that most students agree they would like to invite to speak.

2. Contact the possible speaker and invite him or her to come and speak to the class. (In most situations, your teacher would probably do this.) If the speaker accepts, ask him or her to send a handout or other material before the visit, if possible, so the class can become familiar with the vocabulary related to the topic of the speech.

3. Once the visit has been arranged, decide as a class on a master list of questions you would like to ask. Send this list to the speaker. (Guest speakers can get nervous too, and knowing ahead of time what the audience is interested in will make your guest more comfortable.)

4. Choose a student to contact the speaker and get information for a one-minute *speech of introduction*. The student should find out where the speaker is from, what job he or she has, and so on, and then should prepare easy-to-read notes on an index card. The student "introducer" should include some of the following phrases in the speech of introduction:

   - I would like to introduce our guest speaker,

     _____.

   - I am very pleased to introduce

     _____.

   - _____ is originally from

     _____.

   - _____ is currently

     _____ .

   - _____ is going to speak

     to us about _____.

   - Everyone, please welcome

     _____.

During the Visit

5. The designated student should introduce the guest to the class.

6. Everyone should use active listening skills (nodding, eye contact, etc.) and take notes as they listen to the speaker's presentation. It is possible that the speaker will ask the class comprehension questions to make sure that everyone is following what is being said.

7. During the question-and-answer session that follows the presentation, students should refer to the list of questions that they prepared ahead of time. They should also feel free to come up with new questions and comments. Questions can be related to the content of the presentation, or they can be used to ask for clarification.

After the Visit

8. The class should do the following:

   - Discuss how well they understood the presentation and what aspects of the speaker's style increased or decreased their comprehension.
   - Write a summary of and reaction to the main points that were covered.

9. One student should send the visitor a thank-you note on behalf of the entire class.

APPENDIX F: INFORMAL PANEL DISCUSSIONS

In a regular informal panel discussion, participants provide information to an audience on a particular topic. When a topic is controversial, the discussion resembles a debate, with participants taking sides or positions. Their discussion is guided by an impartial moderator, who makes sure that everyone has a chance to speak and that the discussion stays on target. This is different from a formal debate, in which each participant speaks for a specified amount of time and there is less spontaneous give-and-take of opinion.

In the informal debate or panel discussion, participants may discuss a controversial subject. Typically, those who have the same position sit together on one side of the moderator and face an audience, as shown below:

Those in favor of something	MODERATOR	Those against something

A U D I E N C E

Participants, who express their own opinions or take on special roles, often interrupt each other, which makes it necessary for the moderator to "control traffic." These discussions can become very exciting.

Following a panel discussion, the moderator may invite the audience to ask questions and make comments to the panel members.

The suggested procedure for an informal panel discussion is as follows:

Preparation

1. Each group meets separately to prepare their arguments. They brainstorm their points and make a list, and they also anticipate the points they think the other side will make. The number of panel discussions that go on at the same time will vary according to the size of the class.

2. The moderator plans the introduction. It is helpful for the moderator to think of his or her role as one similar to a TV host who gives background information about the guests and introduces them. The moderator should consult with the teacher about the best way to introduce the subject of the discussion. Once the moderator is ready, if the groups are still preparing, the moderator should visit the groups to get an idea of the points they will raise. This will make it easier for the moderator to prepare some questions in advance. The moderator should always keep in mind that she or he should not express personal opinions in the discussion.

3. If it is possible, arrangements should be made to videotape the discussion.

Discussion

1. The moderator welcomes the audience, gives the introduction, and then introduces the panel members. (They could wear name tags or have signs on their desks that indicate their names or roles.)

2. The moderator then poses a question to the last panel member who was introduced.

3. The moderator "controls traffic," giving each panel member a chance to complete his or her thought before the next panel member begins speaking. When there is a silence, the moderator breaks in to ask prepared, specific questions to keep the discussion going.

4. The moderator clarifies, summarizes, restates, or paraphrases arguments when necessary. To do this, he or she will have to try to be alert to signs of possible misunderstanding or lack of comprehension on the part of the audience or panel members.

5. The moderator also tries to keep the discussion coherent. That is, if a speaker brings up a point for discussion and another speaker makes an unrelated remark, the moderator should interrupt and get the discussion back on track.

6. At the end of the allotted time, the moderator summarizes the main points of the discussion. The moderator then asks for questions and/or comments from the audience and continues to "control traffic."

USEFUL PHRASES IN A PANEL DISCUSSION

MODERATOR	PANEL MEMBERS

To introduce a speaker and control traffic, say:

I'd like to introduce . . .

Let's start with . . .

First _____ will speak, and then _____

Please don't speak out of turn!

I think _____ has a question.

Now our panel will take questions from the audience.

Sorry to cut you off, but . . .

To restate, say:

If I understand, your idea is that . . .

So you're saying . . .

In other words, you believe that . . .

Then ask:

Is that right?

Is that what you mean?

To reflect, say:

So your opinion is that . . .

So you feel that . . .

You thought it was . . .

To summarize, say:

In summary, then, you think . . .

These, then, are the ideas that you have expressed:

To clarify, ask:

Who? What? Where? When?

Why? How? How much/many?

To "get the floor," say:

Excuse me for interrupting, but . . .

That's true, but . . .

Yes, but . . .

I'd like to make a point here.

I'd like to ask a question.

I have a question for . . .

I'd like to comment on that.

To express total agreement, say:

Exactly.

That makes sense to me.

That's how I feel about it, too.

To express partial agreement, say:

Yes, but . . .

Yes, but on the other hand, . . .

That may be true, but . . .

To express total disagreement, say:

I don't agree.

I disagree with . . .

I don't see it that way.

On the contrary, . . .

To express your opinion, say:

As I see it, . . .

From my point of view, . . .

I (firmly/strongly) believe, think, feel . . .

In my opinion, . . .

USEFUL PHRASES IN A PANEL DISCUSSION

MODERATOR	PANEL MEMBERS

MODERATOR

To get back onto the topic, say:

We've gotten off on a tangent. Let's get back on topic.

That's not related to _____. We need to talk about _____.

To respond to an irrelevant remark, say:

That doesn't relate to what _____ just said.

PANEL MEMBERS

If you don't understand what you've heard, say:

I'm sorry. I didn't catch that.

I'm sorry. I didn't get the part about . . .

Could you please repeat . . .

I'm sorry. I'm not following you.

I'm sorry, but I'm lost.

I didn't understand your question. Could you please rephrase it?

To stall (give yourself time), say:

That's a good/interesting/difficult question. Let me think about it.

To check for comprehension, say:

Are you following me?

Do you know what I mean?

Does this make sense?

APPENDIX G: ORAL PRESENTATION FEEDBACK FORMS

SPEECH EVALUATION BY TEACHER

NAME OF SPEAKER: _____   **GRADE:** _____

	Strongly Disagree				Strongly Agree
1. The main idea was clearly stated.	1	2	3	4	5
2. Enough details were given to clarify the main idea.	1	2	3	4	5
3. The speech was well organized.	1	2	3	4	5
4. The speech was well prepared.	1	2	3	4	5

The Speaker:

5. showed interest in the topic.	1	2	3	4	5
6. glanced at brief notes and didn't read a written speech.	1	2	3	4	5
7. spoke clearly, at a moderate speed.	1	2	3	4	5
8. spoke in a voice that was neither too loud nor too soft.	1	2	3	4	5
9. recognized when it was necessary to define words and/or give an example.	1	2	3	4	5
10. used visual aids as necessary.	1	2	3	4	5
11. used eye contact effectively—that is, looked at people in all parts of the room.	1	2	3	4	5
12. used humor and smiled when appropriate.	1	2	3	4	5

Pronunciation Notes   **Grammar/Vocabulary Notes**

Comments:

PEER EVALUATION

NAME OF SPEAKER: _____ **NAME OF PEER EVALUATOR:** _____

Note: Each speech should have at least two peer evaluators.

	Strongly Disagree				Strongly Agree
1. The main idea was clearly stated.	1	2	3	4	5
2. Enough details were given to clarify the main idea.	1	2	3	4	5
3. The speech was well organized.	1	2	3	4	5
4. The speech was well prepared.	1	2	3	4	5

The Speaker:

5. showed interest in the topic.	1	2	3	4	5
6. glanced at brief notes and didn't read a written speech.	1	2	3	4	5
7. spoke clearly, at a moderate speed.	1	2	3	4	5
8. spoke in a voice that was neither too loud nor too soft.	1	2	3	4	5
9. recognized when it was necessary to define words and/or give an example.	1	2	3	4	5
10. used visual aids as necessary.	1	2	3	4	5
11. used eye contact effectively—that is, looked at people in all parts of the room.	1	2	3	4	5
12. used humor and smiled when appropriate.	1	2	3	4	5

I recommend that next time you

One thing very good about your speech was

SELF-EVALUATION

NAME: _____   TOPIC: _____

Note: Do this evaluation after watching the videotape of your speech, if possible.

	Strongly Disagree				Strongly Agree
1. The main idea was clearly stated.	1	2	3	4	5
2. I gave enough details to clarify the main idea.	1	2	3	4	5
3. My speech was well organized.	1	2	3	4	5
4. My speech was well prepared.	1	2	3	4	5
5. I showed interest in the topic.	1	2	3	4	5
6. I glanced at brief notes and didn't read a written speech.	1	2	3	4	5
7. I spoke clearly, at a moderate speed.	1	2	3	4	5
8. I spoke in a voice that was neither too loud nor too soft.	1	2	3	4	5
9. I recognized when it was necessary to define words and/or give an example.	1	2	3	4	5
10. I used visual aids as necessary.	1	2	3	4	5
11. I used eye contact effectively. That is, I looked at people in all parts of the room.	1	2	3	4	5
12. I used humor and smiled when appropriate.	1	2	3	4	5

If I could make this speech again, I would

What I especially liked about my speech was

Additional comments:

APPENDIX H: LEARNING STYLES SURVEY— HOW DO YOU LEARN BEST?

There are 12 incomplete sentences and 3 choices for completing each. Circle the answer that best corresponds to your style, as follows:

3 = the choice that is *most* like you.

2 = your second choice.

1 = the choice that is *least* like you.

1. When I want to learn something new, I usually . . .
   a. want someone to explain it to me. 1 2 3
   b. want to read about it in a book or magazine. 1 2 3
   c. want to try it out, take notes, or make a model of it. 1 2 3

2. At a party, most of the time I like to . . .
   a. listen and talk to two or three people at once. 1 2 3
   b. see how everyone looks and watch the people. 1 2 3
   c. dance, play games, or take part in some activities. 1 2 3

3. If I were helping with a musical show, I would most likely . . .
   a. write the music, sing the songs, or play the accompaniment. 1 2 3
   b. design the costumes, paint the scenery, or work the lighting effects. 1 2 3
   c. make the costumes, build the sets, or take an acting role. 1 2 3

4. When I am angry, my first reaction is to . . .
   a. tell people off, laugh, joke, or talk it over with someone. 1 2 3
   b. blame myself or someone else, daydream about taking revenge, or keep it inside. 1 2 3
   c. make a fist or tense my muscles, take it out on something else, or hit or throw things. 1 2 3

5. A good experience I would like to have is . . .
   a. hearing the thunderous applause for my speech or music. 1 2 3
   b. photographing the prize picture of an exciting newspaper story. 1 2 3
   c. achieving the fame of being first in a physical activity such as dancing, acting, surfing, or a sports event. 1 2 3

6. I prefer a teacher to . . .
   a. use the lecture method, with informative explanations and discussions. 1 2 3
   b. write on the chalkboard and use visual aids and assigned readings. 1 2 3
   c. use posters and models and have some activities in class. 1 2 3

7. I know that I talk with . . .
   a. different tones of voice. 1 2 3
   b. my eyes and facial expressions. 1 2 3
   c. my hands and gestures. 1 2 3

8. If I had to remember an event so I could record it later, I would choose to . . .
   a. tell it aloud to someone, or hear an audiotape recording or a song about it. 1 2 3
   b. see pictures of it or read a description. 1 2 3
   c. replay it in some practice rehearsal, using movements such as dance, play acting, or drill. 1 2 3

9. When I cook something new, I like to . . .
   a. have someone tell me the directions. 1 2 3
   b. read the recipe. 1 2 3
   c. use my pots and dishes, stir often, and taste-test. 1 2 3

10. My emotions can often be interpreted from my . . .
    a. voice quality. 1 2 3
    b. facial expression. 1 2 3
    c. general body tone. 1 2 3

11. When driving, I . . .
    a. turn on the radio as soon as I enter the car. 1 2 3
    b. like quiet so I can concentrate. 1 2 3
    c. shift my body position frequently to avoid getting tired. 1 2 3

12. In my free time, I like to . . .
    a. listen to the radio, talk on the telephone, or attend a musical event. 1 2 3
    b. go to the movies, watch TV, or read a magazine or book. 1 2 3
    c. get some exercise, go for a walk, play games, or make things. 1 2 3

SCORING

Add up the points for all the "a" answers, then all the "b" answers, then all the "c" answers.

Total points for all "a" answers: _____
Total points for all "b" answers: _____
Total points for all "c" answers: _____

Interpretation

- If "a" has the highest score, that indicates your learning style preference is principally *auditory.*

- If "b" has the highest score, your learning style is principally *visual.*

- If "c" has the highest score, your learning style is principally *kinesthetic.*

- If all scores are reasonably equal, that indicates your learning style preference is *mixed.*

The Four Learning Styles: Which Fits You?

People have four ways in which they favor learning new material: *auditory, visual, kinesthetic,* and *mixed modality.* Let's consider these.

Auditory Learning Style

Auditory has to do with listening and also speaking. Auditory learners use their voices and their ears as the primary means of learning. They recall what they hear and what they themselves express verbally.

   "When something is hard to understand, they want to talk it through," write professors Adele Ducharme and Luck Watford of Valdosta State University in Georgia. "When they're excited and enthusiastic about learning, they want to verbally express their response. . . . These learners love class discussion, they grow by working and talking with others, and they appreciate a teacher taking time to explain something to them."

   If you're this type of person, it's important to know that such learners are easily distracted by sounds. Thus, it's a good idea that they *not* listen to the radio while studying, because they attend to all the sounds around them. However, an effective study technique for this type of learner, is to repeat something aloud several times because that helps them memorize it. These types of learners may do well in learning foreign languages, music, and other subjects that depend on a strong auditory sense.

Visual Learning Styles

Visual, of course, refers to the sense of sight. Visual learners like to see pictures of things described or words written down. "They will seek out illustrations, diagrams, and charts to help them understand and remember information," say Ducharme and Watford. "They appreciate being able to follow what a teacher is presenting with material written on an overhead transparency or in a handout." For visual learners, an effective technique for reviewing and studying material is to read over their notes and recopy and reorganize information in outline form.

Kinesthetic Learning Style

Kinesthetic has to do with the sense of touch and of physical manipulation. Kinesthetic learners learn best when they touch and are physically involved in what they are studying. These are the kind of people who fidget when they have to sit still and who express enthusiasm by jumping up and down. "These learners want to act out a situation, to make a product, to do a project, and in general to be busy with their learning," say Ducharme and Watford. "They find that when they physically do something, they understand it and they remember it."

Mixed-Modality Learning Style

Modality means "style." As you might guess, mixed-modality learners are able to function in any three of these learning styles or "modalities"—auditory, visual, and kinesthetic. Clearly, these people are at an advantage because they can handle information in whatever way it is presented to them.

Source: From *Learning Success,* 1st edition, by C. M. Wahlstrom and B. K. Williams. © 1996. Reprinted with permission of Wadsworth Publishing, a division of Thomson Learning. Fax 800-730-2215.

TRANSCRIPTS
CHAPTER 1: SMALL TALK—NOT DEEP, BUT IMPORTANT

Listening (5 min.), Part I, page 6:
How to Be a Good Conversationalist

Have you ever wished you were better at making conversation? A great conversationalist is someone who connects with people and makes them feel important. When they talk to you, they make you feel like you're the only person in the room.

Becoming a good conversationalist requires knowing three things: first, how to start a conversation; second, how to keep it going; and third, how to end it.

Starting a conversation usually means coming up with an opening line or ice breaker. The best kind of ice breaker is one that's positive. The last thing people want to hear from a stranger is how noisy the party is, how awful the food is, or how ugly the people are dressed.

A compliment is always a good ice breaker and will usually be appreciated. Any news event is a good ice breaker. I encourage all of my clients to read the newspaper because it's so important to know what's going on in the world. The fact is, any opening line will do, as long as it's not negative, and as long as it's not a line. The best way to entice a person to have a conversation with you is by being sincere and respectful, and letting them know that you are interested in talking to them.

Part II, page 6:

Once you've got a conversation going, the best way to keep it going is by asking the other person questions that don't require just a *yes* or *no* answer or questions which show genuine interest on your part. For example, if someone says, "I'm from Miami," you may respond with, "Oh, I've been to Miami!" and continue with, "How long have you lived there?" Then, "I was born there, and I've lived there all my life." You might say, "I've never met anyone who is a Florida native. Is your family from Miami as well?"

You keep asking questions based on the last thing a person says. This is called the "elaboration technique." Choose questions that will get the other person to elaborate on what they're saying. Ask questions similar to those a reporter might ask to draw a person out: who, what, when, where, and why questions.

Once you hit on something you find interesting, keep asking questions in order to get the person to elaborate about the topic as much as possible. A good conversationalist elaborates on the experiences they've had. Instead of saying the party was fun, tell why it was fun. Describe why you had a good time—who was there, what happened, where it was, and how people arranged the party. Go into detail. Description is the best form of communication because it keeps people's interest up and stimulates them. Use words to create images and paint pictures so that the other person can get a visual as well as an auditory image of what you're describing to them. If you use the description effectively, you can make the person feel as though they were actually there.

In order to keep a conversation going, there are seven tips that can help you be an excellent communicator:

1. Be aware of your own body and facial language. Make good facial contact when you speak, and be physically expressive without being excessive.
2. Don't gossip. You run the risk of offending the person you're talking to. It also makes you look small.
3. Cultivate a wide range of topics.
4. Have a sense of humor. Everyone enjoys a humorous story or joke. Sexual and ethnic humor, however, are not worth the effects that the jokes may have on your total image. People may be offended, which may in turn reflect poor judgment on your part and may encourage them to think less of you.
5. Don't interrupt. People hate being interrupted. Fight the impulse to interrupt and give the person you're talking to the time they need to complete what they're saying to you.
6. Be enthusiastic and upbeat. Don't be afraid to show enthusiasm. It allows the other person to feel that you're interested in what they're saying to you.

7. Be flexible in your point of view. Try to be as open as possible, and try to see things from the other person's point of view.

Part III, page 6:

If you started a conversation with another person, and you're having difficulty ending it, there are several signals you can send to the other person that will bring the conversation to its close without hurting anyone's feelings. Breaking eye contact is a discreet signal that the conversation is about to end.

Another way to signal is to use transition words like *well,* or *at any rate.* You may want to recap all that was said. Whatever you do, don't lie to the other person. If you're not interested in talking to them again, don't mention the possibility of a future meeting just to be polite. That's hypocritical. Instead, you may want to say, "Nice meeting you." And then, leave.

Finally, be sure to give the other person a good, firm handshake. The final impression you make can be just as important as the initial one you made.

CHAPTER 2: HIGH-TECH COMMUNICATION— A CURSE OR A BLESSING?

Listening (8 min.), Part I, page 29: Miss Manners® on Cell Phones

Terry Gross: This is *Fresh Air.* I'm Terry Gross. When it comes to communicating long distance, all the rules of the game have changed. Beepers ring in movie theaters, people carry on heated phone conversations at restaurant tables, officemates read your personal messages that have been faxed to you, while you're being dissed in cyberspace. But we don't need to be faced with high-tech anarchy. Miss Manners is on the case. Miss Manners is the persona of Judith Martin, who has spent the past few decades updating the rules of etiquette to keep pace with a constantly changing world. Martin's new book is called *Miss Manners' Basic Training: Communication.*

Terry Gross: Let's talk about cellular phones. And these are cropping up everywhere now. I've been in the position, I'm sure you have too, of being in a restaurant where the person next to you is carrying on a conversation with their telephone, and one of the first few times I saw that, it was so odd to me. It's becoming more, just more routine. But what do you think about that, sitting alone in a restaurant, talking on the phone to somebody. Does that . . . you're not being rude to your friend if they're not with you.

Miss Manners: That's right. And so why are you paying attention to the person at the next table instead of to your own guest or your own food or your own telephone perhaps? Telephones are disturbing when people scream into them, in which case the disturbance is talking too loudly, not being on the telephone. There are two mistaken notions about the cellular phone. One is that when there is a new piece of equipment, this is hardly new, but it's still something of a novelty, that there are no etiquette rules. That technology is moving faster than etiquette. No, it's not. I'm keeping up. And in this case it's a very simple step because what is rude without a cord . . . with a cord . . . would also be rude without a cord. The cellular telephone can properly be used when a telephone with a very long cord could be used. Telephones are plugged into restaurant tables for people eating by themselves, and as long as they are not noisy, I don't see anything wrong with it. It would be hideously wrong if there were someone else at the table. Obviously, at least it's obvious to me, a cellular telephone does not belong in a concert hall, or a church, or at a dinner party any more than one could make a telephone call, if that had been possible, that would disturb other people at such an event with a regular phone.

Part II, page 33: Miss Manners® on E-mail Etiquette

Terry Gross: I don't know how much time Miss Manners spends in cyberspace, but what are some of the cyberspace etiquette questions that are coming up now?

Miss Manners: E-mail is a fascinating situation in connection with etiquette because for the first time, we have a community that has none of the safeguards, however slight, that ordinary community life has. You can't read someone's body language. You don't know if you've got them by the right name, you certainly don't know people they know and so on. You are dealing not only with strangers, but strangers you can't see and probably never will. And it depends all the more strongly on etiquette. Of all the people in the society who have been going around mindlessly saying, "Oh, etiquette is an old-fashioned thing. We don't need it anymore," none of those are people who spend any time in cyberspace. They're very etiquette-aware, and always writing etiquette rules because the activities that they enjoy in cyberspace can be totally ruined by bad manners. There's an example in the paper today of the Maryland state government had a bulletin board for citizens to make their comments and people were putting obscene comments on it, and they've had to shut it down. The activity is not possible if people are going to be blatantly rude on it. Not only obscenity, but hogging all the time, or trying to sell things to people in a social setting, and so on. And the etiquette rules are multiplying in cyberspace. It's a very exciting frontier of etiquette.

Terry Gross: Do you use e-mail a lot?

Miss Manners: Yes.

Terry Gross: I wonder when you're using e-mail if you use some of the polite formalities that we use in letter writing. Do you write a salutation, "Dear So and So," and a close, you know, "Fondly," "Sincerely," "Thanks"?

Miss Manners: It's not the same as a letter. It's part way between a letter and a telephone call. Really sort of more like a postcard. In more respects than one, in the sense that it's not really private, and don't count on its being. The essential ingredients of form for e-mail are the address, of course, proper identification, and identification of the sub-

ject matter so that you give people a sense of the priority they need to give it. So that is . . . that is key, the line . . . identifying line, with e-mail. I do occasionally stick to the "Dear So and So's," but that's because I'm a sweet little old-fashioned lady who's fond of old forms that are appropriate for letters, but are not necessary on e-mail.

Terry Gross: It is so easy to respond to e-mail.

Miss Manners: It's too easy. That's the problem.

Terry Gross: I'm wondering if you think all messages that are received should be acknowledged, even when there's not much to say except "Got the message." Is it necessary to say that?

Miss Manners: No. This is not like a social letter where you have to write back if you're going to have a correspondence. People will fire off a joke that they heard or pass on a little bit of something quickly, and it does not have to be answered immediately. I thought you were referring to what is a very interesting aspect of this. The ease with which you can send e-mail removes that safety catch that people used to have before they fired off something that was highly emotional, whether it was anger or passion or whatever. And so I have a rule there, that the more emotional the message, the more cumbersome the method by which you have to send it.

Terry Gross: That's probably a really good rule. So that means not the phone, not the fax. . . .

Miss Manners: Exactly. You know how it is. You pick up a telephone, you say something, and you regret it. Well, it's even worse with e-mail. You type something out quickly, and your little itchy finger goes over the send button, and then the whole hand goes over the mouth—"What have I done?" That moment, where you had to actually sit down and write it and then go out and mail it, was a wonderful safety catch, not enough of one, of course, but a good one.

CHAPTER 3: HUMOR—CAN LAUGHTER BE THE BEST MEDICINE?

Listening 1 (4 min.), page 55:
Laughter Makes You Healthier

Scott Simon, Host: There has been much anecdotal evidence in recent years that laughter is in-

deed good medicine. But at a conference in Orlando this week of the American Association of Therapeutic Humor, doctors have begun to quantify that perception, exchanging scientific studies that show the human immune system strengthens as we laugh and just have a good time. One of the leading researchers in this field of humor and health is Dr. Lee Berk of the Loma Linda School of Medicine in Loma Linda, California. Dr. Berk joins us. Thanks for being with us.

Dr. Lee Berk, Loma Linda School Of Medicine: A pleasure to be here.

Simon: Let me guess, do you watch old tapes of *The Honeymooners* by way of research?

Berk: Oh, I tell you I watch everything. I sit down and watch cartoons with my kids before we go to school.

Simon: Well, tell us something about what is the scientific evidence. Can you actually point to something?

Berk: Yeah, and I have in our body a type of immune cell called natural killer cells and this is probably one of the most startling things that we didn't expect to find, but it was—it just blew us out of the water. Natural killer cells are a special type of cell that go after virally infected cells and they go after tumor cells. And I'm not saying this is a panacea, if it cures one from cancer, but the point is that during laughter and afterwards we saw increases in the ability of those natural killer cells to kill certain types of tumor cells. That was incredible. So we took a next step further to say—were there certain components of the immune system that were increased? That helped these natural killer cells and other immune cells to turn on? And we have just presented data showing that a type of cytokine, one of the hormones of the immune system, if you please, actually increases to kick the natural killer cell into gear and increase its activity and its ability to kill virally infected cells and other tumor cells.

Simon: How long in the system does some of these advantages seem to last?

Berk: For a number of the components that we measured, particularly when we looked at immunoglobulens or antibodies, we saw their increases that would stay all the way from the day of the experiment—and we did numerous experiments up through the next morning. So that there is quite a residual effect.

Simon: I think a lot of us, Dr. Berk, first became aware of this in any serious way reading the works of Norman Cousins, the late editor and writer

who, of course, had lympthoma and was convinced that laughter forestalled his death and actually had the physical effect that you are describing.

Berk: Norman Cousins was a uh, a great friend of mine, in fact, um, Mr. cousins uh, supported our research financially for many, many years. And a very good friend of his was Allen Funt from *Candid Camera* and Allen Funt used to send Norman Cousins, uh, videos on a regular basis and Norman used to tell me the only way he would get pain-free sleep is he would watch ten to 20 minutes of the *Candid Camera* tapes and then he would get two to four hours of pain-free sleep and this seemed to be the only thing that had worked for him. The question in Norman Cousins' mind was, there must be some sort of physiology here to make this happen. And indeed he came up with a very good statement, he said "beliefs are biology." That is, there has to be physiological changes to the way one thinks or believes. It's more than a diversion. It is actually—it is not alternative medicine. There is actual physiological changes associated with the positive emotional states related to a mirthful laughter.

Simon: Well, doctor thank you very much for speaking with us.

Berk: My pleasure.

Simon: From the Loma Linda School of Medicine in California, Dr. Lee Berk.

Listening 2 (2 min., 45 sec.), page 60: Laugh Sessions

Scott Simon, Host: The latest national enthusiasm in the world's largest democracy may be laughter. Each morning, thousands of people gather throughout India to giggle their way into a new day. But this is not laughter for entertainment so much as laughter for daily exercise.

Madan Kataria is India's godfather of the guffaw, if you please. He's a medical doctor who began this trend a few years back and joins us from Bombay.

Dr. Kataria, thanks for being with us.

Dr. Madan Kataria, Bombay Physician: Thank you.

Simon: And do people laugh at anything like a joke?

Kataria: Initially, we started with jokes. But the jokes didn't really work, because nobody has enough stock of jokes to last 30 days in a month or 365 days in year.

[LAUGHTER]

This exercise is a new technique. What we developed was based on yoga. You know we giggle and have deep-breathing exercises and then start with "ho-ho ha-ha" exercises. That is what—this is something similar to some two-three yogic exercises.

Simon: I understand that that you have categorized laughs. If you could tell us what kind of laughs there are.

Kataria: You know, like one is a hearty laugh. We start with "ho-ho ha-ha ho-ho ha-ha". . .

[LAUGHTER]

And then a variety called pigeon laugh. So keep your mouth shut and laugh like "hmm-hmm-hmm-hmm-hmm." This was over a period of time we developed the different techniques. Now we have more than 20, 30 laughters.

We have a swinging laugh, you know?

Simon: Swinging laugh is what?

Kataria: "Bhhhhhhhhhhhh-ha-ha-ha-ha."

You know, imagine about a group of 100, and, you know like 90, 80 people doing all that together. Even it you take it as a laughter exercise also, it's good for you. You feel so good, so nice. It's like a meditation. You cut off your mind from your physical parts, you know something.

Simon: Yeah. You know, Dr. Kataria, you have talked a lot about yogic principles.

Kataria: Yeah.

Simon: I'm wondering if you've heard the one about the yogi master who says to the hot dog vendor, "make me one with everything."

Kataria: I see.

Simon: Is that an example of the silent laugh?

Kataria: Actually, I'm not very good at telling jokes.

Simon: Well, doctor, it's been—it's been a hoot talking to you, sir.

Kataria: Thank you very much. Why don't you laugh with me right now?

Simon: OK, sure. What kind do we do?

Kataria: Let's have a big laugh.

Simon: I'll try.

[LAUGHTER]

Simon: I can't believe it. Actually, you know it works. I can't believe it.

[LAUGHTER]

Kataria: Thank you . . .

Simon: No, thank you.

Kataria: . . . very much.

Simon: Thank you, doctor. Madan Kataria, the laugh doctor, if you please, from his home in Bombay–Mumbai as it's known now.

CHAPTER 4: ACADEMIC DISHONESTY— HOW COMMON IS CHEATING?

Listening (11 min.), Part I, page 77: Academic Dishonesty in Higher Education

Put away your radios now. Don't speak to others. You may not leave the room for the next three hours, and no one may come in and approach you. All books and notes and items you are carrying should be set aside, out of reach. That way, we will know that you are not cheating.

These are the instructions for the college entrance exam, and although that last explanation for the procedure is seldom included, it is the reason for them. And it's an increasing concern. Educators say cheating is rampant these days, and all of our electronic miracle tools only seem to make things worse. We'll ask you for the answers this hour on *Talk of the Nation*.

Part II, page 78:

A pop quiz now. At top American universities, studies indicate that cheating on tests is practiced by:

    (a)   a quarter of the student body
    (b)   half
    (c)   um, well, say, a third for (c)
and (d)   two-thirds

The mere fact that such studies are under way tells us of the level of concern about cheating and the answer to the question (d), two-thirds admit to cheating, shows that the concern is well-founded. Teachers, administrators, test developers, and students find increasing instances of stealing answers from others, and of copying research papers. And of groups of students joining together to share information in ways that they shouldn't.

At MIT two years ago, charges of cheating were brought against seventy-three students involved with just one assignment in one class. It's the worst known instance in the school's history.

And it's happening elsewhere in this country and abroad, too. An article on the Reuters newswire last year told of an epidemic of cheating in India. There, the report said, some students carried knives to threaten the exam watchers who were supposed to prevent cheating. We haven't heard of instances like that in this country, but the situation is appalling for many educators and students.

Others, however, see opportunity. A senior at Rutgers this year, the state university of New Jersey, published an eighty-six-page book with the title *Cheating 101*. This is not an exposé. It's a how-to guide for would-be cheaters. And traveling around by car, the student author managed to sell many thousands of copies of his self-published work.

Part III, page 82:

Alec: All is not lost at Rutgers, however. It's also the academic home of Donald McCabe, an associate professor of busine*th* ethi . . . business ethics at the Graduate School of Management there. He joins us from the studios of member station WNYC in New York. Hello.

McCabe: Hello, Alec.

Alec: I understand you are attempting to found an institute of academic integrity to counter this sort of thing.

McCabe: That's correct. Not only to counter it, but to instill some positive values, not to just work against negative ones. Fortunately, I'm doing this with a group of colleagues from across the country, including two you'll have on the show later today, I understand.

Alec: Well, also with us by phone now is Sally Cole. She is judicial affairs officer at Stanford University in Palo Alto, California. Hello, Sally Cole.

Cole: Hello.

Alec: Ms. Cole, what is cheating these days? Can you define it?

Cole: Oh, I think any individual probably has their own definition of what constitutes cheating. The study that Don McCabe did, uh, asked a variety of questions about individual student behavior, and the students who were participating in the surveys, including Stanford students, were asked to indicate if they had ever engaged in any of the following list of activities, each of which, um, was dishonest and therefore a form of cheating, though they certainly ranged widely in severity from padding a few items on a bibliography, which is dishonest, I'm not, I'm not implying that it's not, to purchasing a term paper from a paper factory and submitting it with one's own name on it.

Alec: That's . . . that's when you hand in a research paper that someone else has written and you—you paid fifty bucks or something for it.

Cole: Yeah, exactly.

Alec: Uh, Don McCabe—uh, your—your definitions of cheating these days?

McCabe: I think I would generally agree with what Sally said with possibly one qualification. Uh, I've become convinced after looking at the responses of the over six thousand students that responded to my survey that students have a somewhat different perspective on what constitutes explicit cheating versus standards that, you know, "I went to school in the sixties," and certainly I think those standards have changed. And I think partially that results from changes that have occurred in the academic process, and some of the things that Sally or I might personally think are wrong, I think there's a lot of students out there today who do not.

Alec: Are you saying that it's all right to buy a research paper from someone?

McCabe: No, that's an extreme I would never agree with. Certainly, explicit test cheating is an extreme I would not agree with. But there are many students out there, according to the results I found, that are cheating because everybody else is. It's a very standard justification, and as Sally said, that doesn't make it right. But I think I can appreciate more now that I've done the survey than I did before that students today, with all the pressures that graduate schools put on their GPAs and, you know, for admissions standards, feel it very difficult to sit in a class when they see other students cheating in a given course, and not cheat themselves to kind of stay even and stay in competition for those cherished places in graduate school.

Alec: Sally Cole, let me ask you . . . is it cheating to buy research services, not a finished paper, but um, say, very good notes?

Cole: Oh, I think frequently on campuses you can purchase very good notes from, um, student government—you know, a committee, or an agency of the student government that is paid to go into a lecture class and take very good notes and then sell those notes to students, who for whatever reason, don't want to take their own notes.

Alec: Do you think that's cheating?

Cole: Uh, not unless it's explicitly prohibited to use those notes in some way by the instructor in an—in an individual class. A lot of these, um, issues of what constitutes cheating depends, some of it anyway, especially rules concerning collaboration, it will depend on what the instructor's guidelines are in a particular course in question. And those guidelines can change all the way from an expectation that individual students will not consult with anybody about the assignment, will not share notes or any other materials, will do entirely individual work, all the way to the other extreme where collaborative work is not only encouraged, it's expected, and sometimes even, um, group grades are given rather than individual grades.

Alec: But in terms of, uh, in terms of classic cheating, how widespread do you think it is at Stanford?

Cole: What do you mean by "classic cheating"?

Alec: Well, that's a good question, isn't it, the one I asked you. I mean, uh, taking someone else's answers on a test or uh, copying a paper from another student, buying a paper somewhere.

Cole: Well, if the Stanford responses to the survey that Don McCabe did on our campus, um, a year and a half ago, are valid indicators, virtually nobody buys a paper and—and submits that. Um, there is some extent of, let me see—what've we got?—copying from another student during a test.

In the sample of seniors who responded to the survey, the way the question was put, it was, "Since coming to Stanford, have you ever copied from another student during a test?" And, um, so for most students, if they enrolled as freshmen, that would be a four-year period that they would be, um, um, answering. And the statistic that the Stanford respondents presented was 86% saying never, 9% saying once, 4% saying a few times, and zero saying many times. And then the responses vary widely depending on the particular item that you're referring to. Which gets us back to where we were before of what's classic cheating.

Alec: Yeah.

Cole: In a—in a study that was done here a decade earlier, um, students provide a lot of open-ended responses to questions, sort of asking how they feel about these issues and what their attitudes are. And one student gives an example of the kind of thing we're talking about when, it was a sophomore, uh, with an undeclared major who said, "Conferring with other students on take-home material" is a problem because it's hard to see what's wrong with it. So that by a—an instructor's definition, it may be a form of cheating for students to talk to each other on a homework assignment, and what this student is saying is, it's hard to feel that you're really doing something bad when you do that because it helps you to learn. But I think some of what is at issue is having—having rules that are both clearly stated and rules that make sense given what it is the instructor and students are trying to accomplish in a particular class.

Alec: Don McCabe—the extent of cheating at Rutgers, where, as they say, you've got a guy who wrote the book.

McCabe: I really can't tell you the extent of cheating at Rutgers. My survey was done at a total of thirty-one schools, and Rutgers was not one of them, so I can't tell you specifically. At Rutgers, I have reason to believe based on some research that's been done by one of my colleagues at Rutgers, that we're no different than anybody else. But this overall kind of two-thirds rate—uh, two out of three admitting to at least one incident of some form of cheating, uh, is at the extreme. I have to agree with Sally, though, that when you look at forms that I think we—forms of cheating—that we would all agree are very explicit, and you look at people who admit to multiple offenses in a sense, uh, I found, for example, that one in eight students responding to my survey admitted to more than three incidents of explicit test cheating. I personally think, even at a level of one in eight, that still is a substantial problem that we need to deal with.

CHAPTER 5: EXPORTING AMERICAN CULTURE— MCDONALDIZATION OF THE WORLD?

Listening (10 min.), Part I, page 101: Exporting American Culture

Brian Lehrer: We're back with *On the Media*. I'm Brian Lehrer. Ahhh, Paris. You're walking along the Seine. You look up and there's a guy in a beret eating—no, not a baguette—a Big Mac, and Mon Dieu! Under his arm he carries not a copy of Sartre's *Being and Nothingness* but videos of *The X-Files* and the latest Disney flick. Where's that French culture you long to soak up? Well, I might be exaggerating, but the issue of American cultural dominance is a big worry to many nations, and it was the subject of a recent conference in Canada, where culture ministers from 19 countries grappled with the issue. The U.S. was not, however, invited. Does the sun never set on the U.S. media empire? Joining us from his home in Paris is Alain Modoux, Director of the Division of Free Expression and Democracy at UNESCO, that's the United Nations Educational, Scientific and Cultural Organization, and from the NPR studio in Los Angeles, Ambassador Derek Shearer, U.S. Ambassador to Finland from 1994 to 1997. Thanks to both of you for joining us.

Lehrer: Alain Modoux, how big a problem is U.S. cultural hegemony in your opinion?

Modoux: Well, I think that, uh, all around the world there is a great concern about the, the power and the dominant position of the Am—the so-called American culture. I'm not sure this is really American culture. I would call it industrial culture born in the States and developed mainly by American companies. But I think the American culture, the true American culture, is something different.

Lehrer: Well, Ambassador Shearer, how pervasive is this American culture, or perhaps industrial culture born in America, in your opinion?

Shearer: Well, I think what we have is a, a world culture, and there are aspects of American culture which predominate in certain sectors, like big movies out of Hollywood. But the phenomenon we're now in after the Cold War is we have a global economy, and it means not only American products but French products or Italian like Benetton or German cars like VW can reach everybody in the world.

Lehrer: Well, you say world culture, but if an American can forget he's in Europe because he has Disney films playing in theaters and everything from *Baywatch* to CNN on television, why is that world culture not really American industrial culture, as Monsieur Modoux put it?

Shearer: Well, Hollywood is open to the world. One of the unique things about Hollywood and it's very American, which is anybody can come here. And if you have a certain level of talent like Ingmar Bergman or Alfred Hitchcock or Cary Grant or now the directors who are coming from New Zealand or China or the French actress Juliette, uh, Binoche, uh, you can make it in Hollywood. The other interesting thing is that America is open to cultural products from all over the world. Because we're an immigrant nation. And then sometimes we reprocess them and they go out to the world in rock and roll or in music or in dress. But I think that's a very good thing, and I view it as not so much as American cultural hegemony but a kind of democratization of culture around the world.

Lehrer: Democratization of culture, Alain Modoux?

Modoux: Well, uh, here again I think it's a mass culture. Now to say that it's democratization, maybe the word is not the right one, but it's a mass culture, and it's true, it's very popular. I'm traveling myself all around the world and it's true in Beijing, in Cairo, in Rio, in Paris, you can hear everywhere Anglo-Saxon music, you can see, uh, all the youngsters dressed the same way, uh, T-shirts, basketball shoes. . . .

Part II, page 104:

Lehrer: What's the thread from that? Is it that you think all the other countries are losing their own cultural identities?

Modoux: Well, I think that we have to, to make sure that the problem is not so much the dominance of the, this industrialized culture coming from America. The problem is that every country has also to, to make sure that they invest in their own culture. And this is a problem with the movies. Certainly if you take Hollywood movies, they are very, very successful here in France, and I, it's the same in most of the European countries. But a problem is, that of course, to make a movie costs a lot of money. It's true that America has a fantastic, uh, demographic bastion or—so they can, they can pay the film by their own public. The problem is for the small countries in Europe and other parts of the world to invest so that you make sure that the place you have a local production. But of course, the problem with language is also something very important.

Lehrer: A fair concern, Ambassador Shearer?

Shearer: Oh, certainly, but I think, uh, the wrong response is to try and close off your country to world culture or American culture. And the more interesting response is to think about how you meet this challenge and—for example, in France, there's a company called Gaumont which has started to make world-class movies but using English as the language. They made *The Fifth Element,* which was directed by Luc Besson and starred Bruce Willis, and now they're going to make the Jeanne d'Arc story but in English, for the world market. So it's an interesting approach, which is they're going to meet the challenge head-on. Uh, you have a French heroine, Jeanne d'Arc, but you make it in English so that you reach the world market. I think that's the right approach. I think the other thing that's interesting is that there are smaller countries that make excellent movies. I mean, *The Full Monty*'s a classic example but there's been a revival of the Irish film industry and great movies made by that country. Um, Australia's made some wonderful movies, and even Japan, that of course gave us *Godzilla* and made a lot of classics, uh, in the older days with Kurosawa, has made some; the movie I loved best last year was called *Shall We Dance?,* which was a Japanese movie.

Modoux: I agree with you, Mr. Ambassador, but what is very important you are pointing out that, the, the language is the, uh, the key question. And this is a problem. Is the culture or the survival of culture possible if you have every time to produce in another language which is not the national language, and probably this is the key question. Of course, I myself am from a multilinguist, multilanguage country. I'm totally in favor of people speaking three, four, five languages, no question to avoid English. But a problem is if you have to go to the world and the only way is to use English, of course this is a real problem for the other languages.

Shearer: Well, I was going to say that I don't think it's the only way, but I do think it's an interesting question to what extent English, which of course doesn't belong to America but comes from that small little theme park island called Great Britain, uh, you know, and gives us Shakespeare in English, that goes around the world. Some people have Shakespeare in English; sometimes they translate it into Hindi or into French or into Russian. Uh, so English itself is not American dominance. And it is an interesting question whether it's a good or bad thing that we have a global language or whether we will in the future. We certainly do in the Internet, for example.

Modoux: I must say something. I was a few months ago in, in Asia and we had a discussion on exactly the same theme, and there was somebody from Pakistan complaining about the Indian cultural imperialism. And I was also with students, Arab students complaining about the Egyptian cultural imperialism. So it meant that apart from the dominant position of the, of the Am—of America regarding the world, you have very, very important power at the regional level, like India in Asia, like Brazil and Mexico in Latin America, like uh, Egypt in, uh, the Middle East, or Hong Kong in the Far East. And because all these countries can use a language which is spoken by many countries, I think this is the fundamental point. They can distribute their films thanks to the common language.

Part III, page 106:

Lehrer: Well, I know that one of the recommendations that came out of the Canadian conference was a global competitor to CNN because it's seen as a dominant information source generated in the United States. Do you think that's . . .

Modoux: No.

Lehrer: . . . necessary?

Modoux: Here again, personally I can tell you here in Europe people are watching CNN only when you have a big crisis but otherwi—where CNN until now was better organized than other networks, but the normal time people are not watching CNN. If they are at home. When you are traveling, of course, if you go to Thailand you don't understand Thai or if you go to Russia you don't understand Russian and you have CNN on, on the TV set at the hotel. Of course there is a chance to learn a bit about the world watching CNN, but this is because CNN again is better organized than the others. I am not criticizing the Americans. Myself, I don't want to criticize those who are better organized. And for instance I, personally, I think that the French channels are bad, are very badly organized at the world level. I, I can't find a good program in French when I go around the world.

Shearer: Where the BBC, for example, is a competitor with CNN.

Modoux: Exactly.

Lehrer: Well, we're, we're using the word *culture* but mostly speaking of entertainment industry product. Is part . . .

Modoux: You're right.

Lehrer: . . . of this debate what defines a nation's culture versus what is merely entertainment? Ambassador Shearer?

Shearer: Yeah, I think there's too much focus on movies. As I say, I can defend Hollywood movies and also I gave you examples of small countries that make good movies, but where I just served in Finland, this is a small country of 5 million people, but they have an incredibly strong local culture.

The best composers in the world, uh, are Finnish, and in fact, uh, the head of the L.A. Philharmonic, Esa-Pekka Salonen, is a Finn. Some of the best architects in the world are Finns; some of the best designers of, of furniture and plateware are Finns. So you have a small country that produces incredible amounts of culture broadly defined, and they compete in the world market, and, you know, they watch *Baywatch* and, uh, *Star Trek* and things like that on television, but they also have their own local programming. And so I think part of this new world economy is how a small country can develop its strengths, its market niches, and part of the answer is you have to have a strong local civil society, a good education. It's not simply a culture minister, you know, passing a law.

Lehrer: So what's the United Nations Cultural Organization doing about this, Alain Modoux?

Modoux: Well, uh, I think that, uh, Mr. Ambassador is right regarding a country like Finland. Instead of being on the defensive, they are, they are, they have a policy which is open to the rest of the world. And the problem is for those countries where in particular you have censorship, let's be clear, too. Most of the countries who are complaining about the influence of other countries are themselves closed to other countries. They censor their own programs, their own people. I think that the free flow of information, the free flow of ideas, or image and pictures. If you don't respect this free flow, of course, uh, you, uh, you can't participate in the world, in the world venture.

Lehrer: This is a discussion that's going to take place for some time, I think, in the era of globalization juxtaposing free trade and cultural values. Alain Modoux and Ambassador Derek Shearer, thank you very much.

Shearer: Thank you, Brian.

Modoux: Thank you.

CHAPTER 6: MEDICAL ETHICS—SHOULD DOCTORS EVER LIE?

Listening 1, Part I, page 124:
Placebos—How Effective Are They?

Today I want to talk about placebos and some of the things that scientists have learned recently about the factors that influence a placebo's effectiveness. First, let's look at the origin of the word *placebo*. It comes from the Latin verb for "I shall please," and in the classical sense, a placebo is an imitation medicine that a doctor gives to calm an anxious patient, or to placate a persistent one who is perhaps demanding pills the doctor is reluctant to give. By imitation medicine, I mean that it's so-called medicine; it has no pharmacological substances in it. In other words, it isn't really medicine—the patient just thinks it is. So if a doctor gives a patient sugar pills instead of painkillers but the patient thinks he or she's receiving painkillers, this would be an example of a placebo.

Maybe you wonder why a doctor would even give a placebo. Well, it has to do with the power of a patient's belief that he or she will get well. Doctors know that often, even more than the actual prescription, it's the prescription slip—the piece of paper with the magic writing on it—that is the vital ingredient that helps patients get rid of whatever is ailing them. It serves as a kind of promise from the doctor that the patient will get well. It isn't the drug itself that's so necessary—it's the belief in recovery that's so important. And so a doctor may prescribe a placebo in cases where reassurance for the patient is far more useful than some name-brand pill taken 3 times a day. In fact, studies show that up to 90% of patients who seek medical help are suffering from self-limiting disorders that are well within the range of the body's own power to heal. The best physicians know how to distinguish effectively between patients who truly need serious medical intervention and those who don't. For the latter, a doctor may choose to prescribe a placebo both because the patient feels more comfortable with a prescription in his or her hand and because the doctor knows that the placebo can actually serve a therapeutic purpose.

Part II, page 124:

Strange as it may sound, placebos have even been known to work in fighting serious illnesses. There's an interesting story that illustrates the power of a patient's belief in recovery. The story takes place back in 1957, I believe in California. But that's not important. Anyway, there was a man, I'll call him "Mr. Smith," who was found to have cancer, and who was given only a few days to live. He was hospitalized with tumors the size of oranges, and during this time he heard that scientists had discovered a horse serum that appeared to be effective against cancer—serum, by the way, is the watery part of an animal's blood, and it's often used in immunizations against disease.

So Mr. Smith begged to receive it, and finally his doctor agreed and gave him an injection of the horse serum. To everyone's surprise, two days later Mr. Smith's tumors had disappeared, and instead of being on his deathbed, he was up joking with the nurses.

Well, two months later, Mr. Smith just happened to read medical reports that the horse serum was a fake remedy, and immediately he suffered a relapse and the tumors reappeared. His doctor told Mr. Smith not to believe everything he read in the papers, and then the doctor injected Smith with what the doctor said was a new super-refined double-strength version of the drug. In fact, it wasn't—it was just water this time, but amazingly the tumors melted away again. Mr. Smith was quite healthy for another two months, until he read another report stating that evidence showed that the horse serum was totally worthless. Mr. Smith died two days later.

Clearly, Mr. Smith's beliefs about the usefulness of the horse serum played an important role in his initial recovery and later death. This may seem to you to be one of those strange tales that medicine can't explain. But it isn't, really. You see, more and more studies are showing that placebos can work wonders, that a patient's belief that he or she will benefit from a treatment can be an important factor in a cure. Some of these studies have even shown that although some people respond more strongly to placebos than others do, it seems that everyone responds at some time or another.

Part III, page 124:

What accounts for the effectiveness of a placebo? We don't know for sure, but in addition to the patient's belief that the cure will work, another factor that seems to play an important role is the quality of a patient's relationship with a doctor. The doctor's attitude toward the patient, his ability to convince the patient he is not being taken lightly, his success in gaining the full confidence of the patient—these are important factors in maximizing the effect of a placebo. The more enthusiastic the physician is about the treatment, the more likely it is that the treatment will work.

Let me give you an example that illustrates the doctor's role in making a placebo work. There was a study done in which patients with identical symptoms—they all had bleeding ulcers—were divided into two groups. The members of one group were told that they were being given a new experimental drug and that this drug had been shown to be effective and would definitely provide relief. Patients in the second group were told that they were being given a new experimental drug, but they were also told that it wasn't clear whether the drug would help or not but that it was worth a try. Now both groups were, in fact, receiving a placebo. What were the results? Well, the first group of patients—the ones who had been told the drug was effective—did considerably better. Seventy percent of them felt relief from their ulcers. Only 25% of the second group reported improvement. So it appears that the doctor really is an agent for optimism and hope and a great inducer of beliefs. The doctor's attitude can have a major influence on the patient's attitude. There are many studies that show similar results.

So what can we conclude? There is a lot we still don't know about how and why placebos work, but clearly the patient's beliefs and the physician's attitude both seem to play a key role in the effectiveness of placebos.

Listening 2 (6 min.), Part I, page 130: Should Doctors Ever Lie?

Announcer: *Trust* was a word that was used early and often during the campaign, and when it comes to politicians, people really must think about whether they can trust their representatives to represent them. But when it comes to the relationship between a patient and doctor, the word *trust* should be a given. Doctors are, after all, supposed to do what's best for us, and this involves telling the truth. However, *on occasion*, a doctor must choose between being truthful and acting in the patient's best interests. We asked our medical commentators, Drs. Michael Wilkes and Miriam Shuchman, to join us with their opinions on this subject. Good morning to both of you.

Both: Good morning, Liane.

Liane: Miriam, when might a doctor choose not to tell a patient the truth?

Miriam: Well, Liane, there are actually several situations when a doctor might be tempted to deceive a patient. It used to be that if a patient was diagnosed with a serious form of cancer, the

doctor wouldn't even tell them. That wouldn't happen anymore, uh, but the doctor might be tempted *to paint a more optimistic picture* than is really the case, so if this was a cancer where the patient has six months to live, the doctor might not tell them that. They might just tell them that it's very serious.

Michael: My worry, though, is that doctors might also *paint a more rosy picture* in order to convince a patient to undergo a more aggressive treatment, say, say, *chemotherapy*, a treatment that they might not under—or choose to undergo if they had more information. To, to me, uh, there really is no distinction between withholding information from a person and *outright* lying. In both cases, the doctor is being *paternalistic*. He's deciding what information the patient needs to know.

Miriam: I think that as doctors, though, we're always in the position of deciding what information to give a patient. We don't want to overburden them with too many details that could just be frightening and not useful. But we want them to have the information that's really important for making decisions.

Michael: Yeah, but can you ever really know what a patient thinks is important? Every piece of information that a doctor gives a patient is filtered through the doctor's *filter*, a filter that includes cultural *bias*, religious bias, economic bias, and their own personal values. And there's some very compelling data that sick people really want very much more information about their condition than they're currently being told.

Part II, page 130:

Liane: Michael, have you ever been *tempted* to be less than perfectly honest with a patient?

Michael: Absolutely. There's always that temptation, Liane. Telling the truth in medicine is one of the most difficult things to do. The, uh, there is an issue that came up recently when another physician suggested that I prescribe a placebo, or sugar pill that had no biologic effects for a patient. A 70-year-old man had just moved to town, and he came to see me to get a refill of a prescription for a sleeping pill that he'd been given for a long time. In fact, it turned out he's been taking the pill every night since his wife died several years ago.

As I spoke with him, it became clear to me that he recognized that he was addicted to the sleeping medicine. In fact, he said he wanted to stop, but every time he tried to stop taking the medicine, he couldn't sleep and *ended up* taking a sleeping pill. Now, a doctor at the hospital suggested that I use a placebo. He said that he'd had great luck using this kind of placebo for exactly these types of addictions. The problem was that there was no way that I could use the placebo without deceiving the patient. So the issue here for me was whether doctors are justified in telling these little *white lies* in order to benefit the patient.

Liane: Miriam, as an ethics specialist, what do you say? What does medical ethics tell us is right in this situation?

Miriam: Well, I think the conflict for the doctor here is that he's really seeing two duties. One is not to lie to a patient, and the other is, uh, to always do what's beneficial for the patient, not to do harm. So, in this case, the doctor who suggested the placebo may think that it's most beneficial to prescribe the placebo, it won't have any side effects, uh, and, the little white lie he thinks is not as important.

Liane: So, should people be concerned that, uh, when they go to their doctor that the doctor might be prescribing a placebo?

Miriam: Absolutely not. First of all, the use of placebos in clinical practice is very rare. They're mostly used in research where people are told they're going to be receiving a placebo. And second, there are doctrines and policies around this. It's called informed consent, and what it means is that before a patient can agree to a given treatment or procedure, the doctor is obliged to in-form them about the risks and benefits of that treatment, and most doctors are aware of that.

Michael: You know, it's probably worth mentioning here that experts feel that about 30% of the medicine that we currently prescribe really have no biologic activity. They work through the power of suggestion. Um, cough medicines are a great example of this sort of drug. Now that doesn't mean that cough medicines don't work. What I'm trying to suggest is that they work through an effect on the mind rather than on the body, say, on the diaphragm or in the lung tissue or muscles themselves. Anyway, I feel there are too many times when doctors aren't being truthful with patients because they feel they know what's best for the patient.

Liane: We talked about placebos, but what about lying? How often do doctors lie to their patients?

Miriam: Liane, I can't give you a statistic on that, but I don't think it happens very often. Doctors don't in—intentionally mislead their patients. But what does happen is that patients aren't given the information they really need to make decisions. Doctors don't give them the chance to ask the questions that would get them that information.

Liane: Michael, what happened to the man who was hooked on the sleeping pill?

Michael: Liane, we talked about it for a long time at the hospital. The bottom line was I, uh, I chose not to use a placebo. The downside of that decision is that the man is still addicted to the medicine although I'm slowly weaning him off by using some behavior modification techniques.

Liane: *Weekend Edition* medical commentators Drs. Michael Wilkes and Miriam Shuchman.

CHAPTER 7: THE TIME BIND— ARE TWENTY-FOUR HOURS A DAY ENOUGH?

Listening (7 min.), Part I, page 145: The Time Bind

Host Terry Gross: This is *Fresh Air*. I'm Terry Gross.
The most common complaint I hear is this: there doesn't seem to be enough time for work and a life outside work. This is a particularly frustrating predicament for working parents, who feel they're damaging their children by not spending enough time with them.

Newsweek and *U.S. News & World Report* both had cover stories on the subject this month. Each refers to a new book by my guest, Arlie Hochschild, called *The Time Bind*. Hochschild did a study of employees at a Fortune 500 company known for its family-friendly policies. She keeps the company anonymous, referring to it only as "Amerco."

It's an old cliché that men often seek refuge at work from the demands of the wife and children at home. Hochschild reports that's still true. What's changed is that now many mothers are also seeking refuge at work from the demands of family life.

Part II, page 146:

Arlie Hochschild, Professor of Sociology, Author, *The Time Bind: When Work Becomes Home & Home Becomes Work:* Well, let me say it first that they didn't think they wanted to get out of the house, that, in fact, women are—felt like they were just getting through the day.

You know, it's not something they were thinking about, but when you ask them: where is it you feel appreciated? Where is it you feel really seen for your contribution? Where is it you feel good at what you're doing? And where are your friends and your social supports? They would often answer: at work.

It's as if the village had gone to work, and when you asked them what it was like being at home, they would often say there's a lot to do. One woman, for example, said: "I come home and put the key in the door and one child hasn't talked to anybody all day." Another—the baby isn't in bed. The dishes are in the sink, and her husband just kind of felt like he was babysitting. He was waiting for her to come home, and as soon as she was home, it was all her job.

And she didn't feel appreciated. She didn't feel valued. There weren't any recognition ceremonies for her at home. So it wasn't something people were intending.

It wasn't something that people were really conscious of, wasn't a sort of a way of seeing family and home life that I think we've been aware of before. But this was a theme, that home had become a kind of a workplace, and for some of the people some of the time, work had become a little bit of a home.

Gross: What were some of the things about work that made it seem more like home? And also, what were some of the things about work that made some people feel like they got more rewards? That work was the place where they felt

more self-confident? That work was the place where they had an affirming network of people?

Hochschild: Well, this depends a lot on the workplace. It's not every workplace that's heaven. But it also depends whether you're a manager, a clerical worker, a production line worker.

But among managers, at a lot of Fortune 500 companies, there are new motivational programs—the total quality program, for example, that talks about valuing the individual and, you know, delighting the internal customer, and so on. And there are a lot of recognition ceremonies and teams—you work in teams.

So that the company actually thinks a lot about trying to make workers feel good—you know, gyms at work. As I see, this is kind of an elite picture, but it created a kind of a managed atmosphere that—kind of managed cheer—that was a relief to a lot of people.

And even if people didn't like their—the content of their jobs—they had kind of lousy production-level jobs—their pals were there. Their flirtations were there. Their friends were often there to talk in the break room with— have a beer after work with.

Gross: An interesting point you make is there were so many marriages breaking up. It even seems that you can get your pink slip at home. Home doesn't . . .

Hochschild: Yeah.

Gross: . . . mean security in the way that it once did.

Hochschild: Yeah, it's quite right that for a lot of the workers at this company, they've been working at Amerco, the company I was studying, for 10, 15 years, but they were on their second or third relationship or marriage. So they were getting their pink slips at home.

Gross: Let's look more specifically at the company that you studied that you based your conclusions on. It's a Fortune 500 company that you gave a pseudonym to protect their identity.

Hochschild: Right.

Gross: Tell us something about the company and the policies—the work/home balance policies— that they initiated which you studied.

Hochschild: Well, the reason I went to Amerco was because of these policies. It was a vanguard family-friendly company that offered paternity leave; it offered part-time work with benefits, and either temporary or permanent—offered job sharing; two people could share one job; three people could share two. It offered flex-time. You could come early and leave early, or come late and leave late. It offered flex-place—you could work from home part of the time or all of the time.

So those were the policies that were on the books, and one of the big surprises and para-doxes was to realize that a lot of the families that I interviewed were working very long hours, and needed time at home. And these were people with strong family values, who wanted some balance in their life—were somehow shy about coming forward for these policies.

And so that was kind of—what I didn't expect to find going in, but got haunted by and interested by coming out. You know, why—what was the obstacle in the way of achieving some kind of bal-ance between work and family? Now, why—why was this not working out in a company that seemed to promise good news on this score?

Gross: Do you think sometimes that although some companies will put policies into place that make it seem like you can work more at home or take more flexible hours—that the company might also at the same time really underestimate what it takes to do your job in an adequate way, and so in a way, they might be paying lip service to flexi-bility, but still requiring you to work really hard and really long hours?

Hochschild: I think you're completely right about that. For a lot of companies, family-friendly poli-cies are a fig leaf on top of a highly-workaholic culture from which the company gets a lot of benefit.

CHAPTER 8: MARKETING TECHNIQUES— ARE WE REALLY INFLUENCED?

Listening 1, page 165:
Store Design and Consumer Behavior

"Retailers can have absolute control over the re-sponse of their customers," claims Joseph Weishar, author of *Design for Effective Selling Space*. He says that shoppers move in predictable patterns and they respond predictably to light and color stimuli. This suggests that the right store design can turn a browser into a buyer. If you can get the customer to see what you want them to see, they will probably buy what you want to sell them.

More and more retailers are buying his theory. Renovation, remodeling, and attention to store de-sign are on the rise. A survey of retailers by the In-ternational Mass Retail Association found that 60 percent were boosting plans for renovating stores and building stores based on new designs. Among full-price specialty stores, 80 percent had hired store design consultants.

Sears is spending $4 billion to upgrade its stores, and Kmart is spending $2.3 billion for store improvement. JCPenney has been spending more than $500 million a year on redesigning its stores.

Benetton is redoing its 200 U.S. locations, spending $400,000 per store.

Cosmetic changes? Not at all. According to Weishar, there is a science to store design. For ex-ample, did you know, as store designers do, that customers walk into a store and turn right 80 per-cent of the time? As a result, whatever you en-counter to the right of the entrance is what the retailer most wants you to buy that day. Did you know that wide aisles will persuade you to pay higher prices and that fluorescent lights flash the words "good value" through your brain?

Weishar cites luxury retailer Bergdorf Goodman as an example of his wide aisles-equal-high-prices theory: Bergdorf Goodman has less merchandise per cubic foot than any large specialty store in New York, yet it reports one of the highest sales per square foot in the country—as high as $2,000 per square foot. The spacious look ignites thoughts of exclusivity and helps persuade customers to buy the high-priced goods.

Other high-profile success stories include The Gap and Disney stores. The Gap has designed a perfect store for its merchandise, according to

Weishar. The table at the front of the store is angled so that it appears as a diamond shape. That is intentional. The angle guides the customer to the right, straight into a collection of newly arrived, full-priced clothing.

Creators of the Disney stores say that they are designed to communicate the fun and excitement of the theme parks and famous characters. They also have another purpose: to get customers to walk to the back wall. That's the goal of every boutique and department, says Weishar. Chances are good that when you get to the wall, you won't walk back out along the route you came in on. And if you go back by another route, you'll pass more merchandise. Disney stores run a huge video screen at the back of every store. The full-screen animation with familiar songs lures customers back—often dragged by their kids. By the time you walk all the way in and all the way out, your chances of avoiding a purchase are slim. A Disney store does three times the business of its average mall competition.

Listening 2 (2 min., 45 sec.), page 171: How do Smells Influence Our Behavior?

Neal Conan: Bakers figured out a long time ago that venting their ovens onto the sidewalk will lure in drooling customers. This week, researchers in Chicago released a study suggesting that the right smell can actually change the way we feel and even persuade us to take more risks with our money. Dr. Alan Hirsch is the neurologic director of the Smell and Taste Treatment and Research Foundation in Chicago, and he joins us from our Chicago bureau. Dr. Hirsch, the study you did involved odorizing a Las Vegas casino. Two banks of slot machines were treated with different smells, a third area was left untreated as a control, so what happened?

Alan Hirsch: Well, what we found was, in the presence of a pleasant odor, there was an increased amount of money people placed in slot machines. The increase was of 45.11%, which was highly significant because when we looked at the control area where there was no odor, there was only a two percent change compared to the weekends before and the weekends after.

Neal Conan: In this particular odor, I mean, what does it smell like?

Alan Hirsch: That's a very good question, and I don't know the answer for you. Unlike smelling something and saying oh gee, this smells like bananas or this smells like baked goods or whatever, it had multiple different odorants so that it was very hard to distinguish any high note. I think that the most accurate description was, is that uniformly people described it as being pleasant. So it's very clear—we're just at the tip of the iceberg of understanding smells and how it impacts upon us.

Neal Conan: You think this does have other applications.

Alan Hirsch: Oh, by all means. One thing that we can see is that if this odor is having an impact on leisure time activity in terms of leisure time gambling, then possibly the same odor will have an impact on other leisure time activity. For instance, in the year 2010 when you wake up, you may wake up to a smell that makes you more awake and alert, and then you'll go off to the health club and you'll exercise in the presence of a smell that tends to increase your muscle strength, and then you'll go to work and work where there are smells that are increasing your efficiency, and then you'll go home and and you relax to a smell that makes you more relaxed, and then you either go to bed with a smell that makes you more aroused or makes you more sleepy, depending upon how your spouse feels.

Neal Conan: Do you ever wonder that our eyes and ears are constantly assaulted by manipulations of one sort or another, billboard advertisements, television, radio. Can't we just leave the nose alone?

Alan Hirsch: (laughs) Well, you know, the problem is, is that the nose is being assaulted anyhow. You know, when you go into a room there is a smell there, it's a smell of the carpet cleaner—or the smell of the—of the bathroom, uh, deodorizer. So smells are present anyhow. The question is whether we can use those smells to help benefit people and help make their life more comfortable.

Neal Conan: Dr. Alan Hirsch is the neurologic director of the Smell and Taste Treatment and Research Foundation. He spoke with us from our studio in Chicago.

CHAPTER 9: BEING AN IMMIGRANT— CULTURE SHOCK AND ADAPTATION

Listening 1 (4 min.), page 193:
Wasted Food, Discovered Souls

Ray Suarez, Host: This is *All Things Considered.* I'm Ray Suarez.

Robert Siegel, Host: And I'm Robert Siegel.

Americans throw away 96 billion pounds of food each year—about a quarter of the food produced in this country. Those numbers come from an Agriculture Department study released today, and that study says the bulk of the food that's lost simply goes bad in people's refrigerators or is left uneaten on the plate and gets tossed out. Restaurants and grocery stores also throw a lot away.

The amount of waste in this country comes as no surprise to commentator Andrew Lam.

Andrew Lam, Commentator: Last week, I took a cousin newly arrived from Vietnam for a tour of downtown San Francisco, hoping to impress him with America's architectural grandeur. But the tall and shiny high-rises were all too overwhelming for him, and my cousin became very quiet.

Then, as we walked past a large garbage bin filled with papers and boxes, he suddenly stopped and stared. "Brother," he said. "In Vietnam this stuff is all money."

This relative of mine is not an environmentalist. His comment simply reflects his own frugal third-world background. Everything is useful; nothing ever goes to waste.

Back home, he told me, a family could live for a week recycling these papers. "I can't believe they throw all this stuff away," he said, shaking his head. And I felt a slight tug of guilt. My garbage, too, is often full of papers and cans and discarded food.

Yet I am not unfamiliar with his feelings of indignation. I, too, came from that agrarian-based ethos in which land is sacred and everything yielded from the good earth must be treasured. Indeed, what I throw away today would have astounded me years ago.

When my family and I first came to America two decades ago as refugees, my job was to spy on the supermarket across the street from our apartment. When they threw away expired food, my brother and I would spring into action. One night, as we dragged a carton full of outdated frozen pizzas, TV dinners, and cookie dough across the parking lot, we were stopped by a policeman.

Red-faced and stuttering, we offered to return the food to the garbage bin, but the policeman shrugged. "Help yourself, boys," he said, and walked away. But my brother and I never went back. If we were once shocked by America's opulence, we have long since learned to take it for granted that, well, there's plenty more where that came from.

But my cousin got me thinking: perhaps a sure sign of successful assimilation into an overdeveloped society is when an immigrant tosses away his sense of frugality and his deep appreciation for what once sustained him.

At home after our excursion, my cousin helped me prepare dinner. A few pieces of apple and pears accidentally fell from my chopping block onto the floor. Immediately, he stooped to pick them up. "You don't have to do that," I wanted to say, but something in his meticulous gesture stopped me.

Instead, as I watched him, a distant and long-cherished memory emerged. I am five years old standing at the edge of a golden rice field at harvest time in the Mekong Delta where my family came from, and watching farmers stoop to gather rice.

I had wanted to show my cousin America's grandeur, but it was he who showed me something else far lovelier. There, on the shiny tile floor of my kitchen, my cousin, too, was busy gathering bits of our old identities—scattered pieces of our soul.

Siegel: Andrew Lam is an editor at Pacific News Service in San Francisco. He comes to us by way of member station KQED.

Listening 2 (3 min., 30 sec.), page 197:
What's in a Name?

Robert Siegel, Host: There were many things that commentator Andrew Lam had to confront when he came to this country from Vietnam 22 years ago.

He was 11 then. He had to learn a new language and adapt to a startlingly different culture. And there was one question that loomed large for him, the members of his family, and for all his Vietnamese friends: What do we call ourselves in America?

Andrew Lam, Commentator: Wang, Dung, Mai Suan, Noc, Trang, Than, Phat. What are these? Names, Vietnamese names. While in my native tongue they suggest different colors of clouds and precious jade, in English they are twisted into a funny word, a grunt, or even a cough.

Vietnamese names are often turned ugly in America, their magic snuffed out like a birthday candle. My name, Dung, spelled D-U-N-G, which means bravery in Vietnamese, is but animal excrement in English.

Van, Truc, and Trang—meaning cloud, bamboo and elegance—the three pretty girls who walk down the high school hallway, suffered constant pestering from classmates who would yell, "Look out, here comes a van, a truck and a train!"

One summer, Van, Truc, and Trang, after leafing through *Vogue* and *Mademoiselle* magazines, emerged Yvonne, Theresa, and Tanya. They even looked different, wearing more fashionable clothes and makeup.

My sister Noc became Nancy when our landlord, having failed to pronounce her name, threw up his hands and said, "Never mind, let's call you Nancy, as in Nancy Kwan, the actress."

And there's Qua, a friend from college who wanted to finalize his naturalization process with an American name. But which one? He was drinking milk when he was filling out the application, and saw a picture of a lost boy named Kevin on the milk carton. Qua shrugged. Kevin he became the day he swore his allegiance to the United States of America.

Thus, like street urchins, we children of Vietnam gathered our new identities from anything deemed worthy. Then over the seasons, through the years, many of us have learned to embody our new names. For they have given us an assurance of being Americans, part of this country.

Indeed, sometimes I wonder if any of us would have assimilated so well into this country without our new names. After all, it was Hoai who, under the tropical sun, and amid exploding B-52 bombs, mourned for slain relatives. Now, Lucy is busy decorating her beautiful suburban home in the Silicon Valley.

Tao, the jack fruit vendor's daughter who once expected to follow her mother's footsteps, became Christine a decade later, and found herself in a different kind of market instead. Wall Street. Through her computer linkups, Christine, the stockbroker, now negotiates across time zones, oceans, continents.

But what of our old names? Huang, Yung, Mai Sung, Ngop, Jiang, Than, Phat. In our old language, they are kept safe, but more. I should like to think their magic is instilled in us, in us who must adapt and change, but who still cherish the memory of a world full of iridescent clouds and precious jade.

Siegel: Andrew Lam lives in San Francisco, where he's an editor for Pacific News Service.

CHAPTER 10: CHANGES ON EARTH—IT'S NOT WHAT IT USED TO BE

Listening 1 (6 min.), page 212:
Disappearing Languages

Knoy: It's *Living on Earth*. I'm Laura Knoy.

(A man speaks in !Kung)

Knoy: You're listening to the passing of linguistic history. These are two bushmen from the Kalahari Desert in southern Africa speaking a language that is going extinct. It's just one of many languages around the world that will vanish in the not too distant future. There are thousands of languages spoken today, but lingua diversity is in steep decline. The 10 most common languages are spoken by 48% of the world's population. More than half the world's languages are spoken by fewer than 10,000 people. And more than a quarter are spoken by fewer than 1,000 people. Peter Ladefoged, a linguist at the University of California at Los Angeles, travels the world studying and recording these rare languages. He joins us from the studios of KUSC in Los Angeles. Welcome.

Ladefoged: Very delighted to be here.

Knoy: Tell us about those voices we just heard.

Ladefoged: Well, there were a couple of bushmen. One was just telling the other, "Oh, terrible life. Hunting's terribly bad. We're all going to starve; it will be awful."

Knoy: What's the name of the language that they're speaking?

Ladefoged: That language was called !Kung. It's a language of about 1,000 people in the Kalahari Desert.

Knoy: What's unique about that language?

Ladefoged: (Laughs) What isn't? (Knoy laughs) Well, of course, nearly every language has got something unique to it. Even English. But that particular language has got 83 different ways of beginning a word with a different click sound. And over half the words in that language begin with a click.

Knoy: So the clicking is the most unique part of the language.

Ladefoged: I think so. Although (laughs) you know, you might expect a language like that, which has got all those clicks, to sort of go easy on the vowels or something of that kind. But no, not at all. They've got a very curious set of vowels, so-called strident vowels as well. They've got words like !khaaaaow with a haaaa-type vowel going on at the same time. So they've got odd consonants, odd vowels, just an unusual language from the sound's point of view.

Knoy: Could you give us some examples of other unusual sounds found in other rare languages that you've studied?

Ladefoged: Well, recently I was in the Amazonian rain forest, working with two or three different groups down there. But one of the groups, the Oro Win, had a sound which is made by a kind of T-sound followed by a trilling of the lips, so that the word for a small boy would be something like trrrm. You get totally different sounds from any that occurs except in half a dozen other languages. There are other languages that trill the lips, but actually none of them have that T-sound before it.

Knoy: Do you have other words from that Amazonian language that you could share with us?

Ladefoged: Yes indeed, because interestingly enough, they've used that sound when they have

to coin a new word. Every language develops new words for new things. So the word for a helicopter is known as trrrm trrrm.

Knoy: Now, this has been your life work, preserving rare languages. Why do you think it's so valuable to do this?

Ladefoged: Well, it's largely because I'm just interested from my point of view in the way the human mind works. I want to be able to say all these different sounds could be part of a language, and we've got to have a notion of what is a language and how the human mind creates a language by taking all these different sounds into account.

Knoy: Can you give us a sense of how many languages are in trouble?

Ladefoged: Oh, yes. Mm. Roughly speaking, there are probably about 7,000 languages in the world. It depends on what you mean by a language, of course, but about 7,000. And of those 7,000, probably about half won't last for another century. Maybe that's an exaggeration, because it's very difficult to predict. But in many parts of the world, like the United States or Australia, the number of languages spoken by Native Americans has just gone down, or native Australians has just gone down at an amazing rate. So that we used to have several hundred American Indian languages in the United States. There are probably now about 20 that are really viable and able to last for some time.

Knoy: You have made some predictions about what language diversity will look like in the future.

Ladefoged: Clearly, there will be fewer different languages spoken. And if you don't mind my saying so, it's all the fault of people in your profession, to a great extent. Everybody wants to listen to National Public Radio and other things, and so they all have to learn English to be able to do so.

Knoy: I understand that English is being used as the language of business and a language of journalism and international trade and conventions and so forth. But people can still speak their second language as well.

Ladefoged: Yes, but what happens is that people, for reasons of wanting a better job or whatever it might be, learn English. When they are talking to their children, they start thinking well, maybe I should talk to my children in English for a little bit. Same would apply to other language groups, where the language may be Swahili or something of that kind, the national language of Tanzania. It's the little languages that go because parents, wanting to get a greater advantage for themselves or for their children or both, stop using the language in the household. And as soon as the mothers don't speak to the children in that language, consistently and always in their home language, the language will slowly fade away as people get older and older.

Knoy: How do the people who speak these rare languages feel about that?

Ladefoged: Well, that's a very difficult question. Because there are so many languages and so many different feelings. I know several groups of people who say things like, well, we must have our language because it's the way we keep in touch with our ancestors. It's a part of our whole tribal being to be able to speak this language and to be able to keep our history and to know our beliefs. Whereas other people don't view it that way. In other parts of the world, some people might well say, oh well, I suppose we've got to lose our language if it means that we can lead a more comfortable life, a better life, and my children can go to school. It's progress for some, and perhaps retaining your language and retaining knowledge of your ancestors is something that other people want to do. And to lose it would be a backward progress.

Knoy: Peter Ladefoged is a linguist at the University of California at Los Angeles. He's currently at work on a new book, *Vowels and Consonants*. If you'd like to hear more unusual language, check out our web site at www.livingonearth.org. Professor Ladefoged, thanks a lot for joining us.

Ladefoged: Thank you indeed for asking me.

Listening 2 (2 min., 45 sec.), page 221: Eat Chocolate and Support the Environment!

Knoy: Languages, of course, are not the only things vanishing from the earth. Acre upon acre of the world's rain forest are lost each day, and along with them a certain plant species is disappearing. For years conservationists have searched for an

issue that would motivate all levels of society to protect the rain forest. As commentator Suzanne Elston explains, they just may have found one.

Elston: One of the problems that we've had relating to big environmental issues is, well, they're just too big. Take protecting the rain forest, for example. Everyone knows they're the lungs of the planet and contain more than half the species found on earth. But the impact of their destruction has never hit home for most people. Until now.

It turns out that as we destroy the rain forest, we're also destroying our ability to produce chocolate. The source of chocolate, the cocoa bean, is usually grown on large plantations. Unfortunately, this style of farming leaves the plants vulnerable to pests and disease. When that happens, the farmers just move on. They clear another strip of rain forest and plant new trees.

Now the problem is, we're running out of rain forest. Given the rate of deforestation and the fact that the demand for chocolate is rising steadily, chocolate officials say we're facing a global shortage within 10 to 15 years. Scientists, hoping to head off the potential crisis, discovered that cocoa plants prefer to grow under the canopy of the rain forest. So now, the huge multinational chocolate corporations that have helped to destroy the rain forests are actually working to protect them.

Within the next month or two, a global cooperative funded by chocolate companies will be announced. Development agencies, conservation groups, agricultural experts, and even the United Nations will work alongside local farmers to create a sustainable system of cocoa farming. One of the more interesting projects will involve using cocoa plants as part of a reforestation effort to revitalize war-torn areas of Vietnam.

Now, the cynic in me is disappointed that it takes a chocolate crisis to motivate people into protecting one of our most valuable resources. But if corporate concern about the bottom line actually protects the rain forest, then I'm all for it. Who knows? In our efforts to save the endangered cocoa bean and the rain forest, we might even save the planet in the process.

SKILLS INDEX

WRITING & READING SKILLS

TEXT CREDITS

Page 16: "So What's New With You?" by Adair Lara. *San Francisco Chronicle*, 6/18/98. Reprinted with permission.

Page 26: "It's the Pauses That Refresh" by Adair Lara. *San Francisco Chronicle*, 4/2/98. Reprinted with permission.

Pages 50–52: "Exploring the Land of Mirth and Funny," Steven M. Sultanoff, Ph.D. Originally published in *Laugh It Up*. Publication of the American Association for Therapeutic Humor, July/August 1994, p. 3. Reprinted with permission.

Page 90: Excerpt from "The Internet—A New Research Frontier or an Easy Way to Plagiarize?" by William Stevenson. Published in *Iside English*, May, 1998. Reprinted with permission.

Pages 120–121: "A Seventeen-year Old Girl Visited Her Pediatrician," a case study by Dr. Melvin Levine. Reprinted by permission of Dr. Melvin Levine.

Pages 143–144: "Home Work Time," by Marilyn Snell. *Mother Jones*, May/June 1997 issue. © Foundation for National Progress. Reprinted with permission.

Pages 170–171: "The Smell of Money" Copyright © 1992 by The New York Times Company. Reprinted by permission.

Pages 187–188: Excerpt from "Stressed Out in a Strange Land," by Andrew Lam. *San Francisco Chronicle*, "This World," 3/26/89 Andrew Lam is an associate editor of Pacific News Service. He came to America when he was eleven years old. Reprinted with permission.

Pages 209–210: "What Causes Language Death?" by James Crawford. From "Endangered Native American Languages: What is to Be Done, and Why?" by James Crawford, © 1997. Reprinted with permission.

AUDIO CREDITS

Pages 249–250: From *Say it Right: How to Talk in Any Social Situation* by Dr. Lillian Glass. For more information call 310-274-0528.

Pages 250–251: © Fresh Air with Terry Gross, 1/9/97.

Pages 251–252: © Copyright NPR® 1996. Excerpts and audio are used with the permission of National Public Radio, Inc. Any unauthorized duplication is strictly prohibited.

Pages 252–253: © Copyright NPR® 1998. Excerpts and audio are used with the permission of National Public Radio, Inc. Any unauthorized duplication is strictly prohibited.

Pages 253–256: © Copyright NPR® 1992. Excerpts and audio are used with the permission of National Public Radio, Inc. Any unauthorized duplication is strictly prohibited.

Pages 256–258: © On the Media, 7/12/98.

Pages 260–261: © Copyright NPR® 1992. Excerpts and audio are used with the permission of National Public Radio, Inc. Any unauthorized duplication is strictly prohibited.

Pages 261–263: © Fresh Air with Terry Gross, 5/20/97.

Pages 263–264: Copyright 1993, USA TODAY. Used with permission.

Page 264: © Copyright NPR® 1992. Excerpts and audio are used with the permission of National Public Radio, Inc. Any unauthorized duplication is strictly prohibited.

Pages 265–266: Andrew Lam is an associate editor of Pacific News Service. He came to America when he was eleven years old.

Pages 266–268: © *Living on Earth*, February 12, 1999.

Page 268: © *Living on Earth*, February 12, 1999.

PHOTO CREDITS

p. 5, Courtesy of Dr. Lillian Glass; p. 26, United Features Syndicate, Inc.; p. 31, Brian Leng/Corbis; pp. 32, 48 Photographs by Jonathan Stark for the Heinle & Heinle Image Resource Bank; p. 55, Bettmann/Corbis; p. 72, Arthur Grace/Stock Boston; p. 96, Kevin R. Morris/Corbis; p. 118, Photograph by Jonathan Stark for the Heinle & Heinle Image Resource Bank; p. 143, Sigrid Estrada; p. 147, Laura Dwight/Corbis; p. 160, B Vittoriano Rastelli/Corbis; T Corbis; p. 193, Nathan Benn /Corbis.